Problems of Parents

Problems
of Parents

BY BENJAMIN SPOCK, M.D.

HOUGHTON MIFFLIN COMPANY BOSTON

To My Mother

((◆ ((◆ ((◆ ((◆ ((◆ ((◆ ((

PREFACE

EIGHT YEARS AGO I received a letter from a mother in Texas which made me feel ashamed of myself, and which changed my approach to writing. She said that I showed sympathetic understanding of children and that I refrained from the critical attitude toward parents which some writers take. "But don't you realize," she went on, "that when you always emphasize that a child basically wants to behave well, and *will* behave well if he is handled wisely, you make the parent feel responsible for everything that goes wrong? Perhaps some people wouldn't get that feeling. But I do; and it is more burdensome and discouraging and oppressive than I can ever express. Can't you see that a parent is a human being, too?" A few months later, in a backyard in Philadelphia, a young mother said the same thing to me, only more hesitantly.

I don't think that I was unaware of parents' feelings when I began to write for them twenty years ago. But certainly I was "child centered," like America generally, when I came to put ideas on paper. By the time I began to write for the *Ladies' Home Journal*, and when I revised *Baby and Child Care*, I was thinking a great deal about the parents' tribulations.

In this volume are concentrated a number of topics that involve the feelings of mothers and fathers: their quarrels, guilt about favoritism, resentment at interfering grandparents and difficult neighbors, doubts about comics, movies, and television, the difficulty of talking about death and sex, the frustrations of the housebound mother. But there are discussions of management problems too — manners, duties, traveling, for instance — and about the shaping of personality.

Talking with young adolescents about dating and love is discussed at some length. There is a section on the related subjects of divorce, widowhood, and remarriage which may be informative to even the happiest of couples. The book ends with my serious answer to the question of whether we are rearing our children soundly in view of the world they face.

The chapters of the book are based on articles originally written for the *Ladies' Home Journal* which have been considerably revised, expanded, and consolidated in order to cover subjects more broadly. I thank the editors of the *Journal* for permission to do this. I am grateful to Helen Irwin Thomas for her letter on traveling and to Joyce Hartman for her gracious, expert editing.

BENJAMIN SPOCK, M.D.

CONTENTS

IV
ASPECTS OF PERSONALITY DEVELOPMENT

V
FACING FACTS WITH YOUR CHILD

VI
DIVORCE, WIDOWHOOD, AND REMARRIAGE

Contents

VII
CRITICAL PROBLEMS OF TODAY AND TOMORROW

I

Easing Family Tensions

CAN YOU LOVE ALL YOUR
CHILDREN EQUALLY?

In one sense, "Yes"; in another sense,
"No, not possibly!"

❨ ONE'S FEELINGS FOR EACH CHILD
ARE DIFFERENT

IN DIFFERENT WORDS several mothers have said to me, in effect, "I feel guilty because I don't seem to love one child as much as another." On the other hand, many parents will say firmly, in talking with a doctor or a neighbor, "Of course I love my children equally."

It has seemed to me in working with parents that some of those who confess inequality of love are blaming themselves unnecessarily and that some of those who are trying to show absolute impartiality are trying to achieve what is humanly impossible.

The first thing to realize is that the word "love" in the English language doesn't have one meaning but is used to cover an amazing variety of attitudes and feelings: for instance, a dependent clinging for security, as is typical of a two-year-old child; physical attraction; possessiveness, which occurs to some degree in most close human relationships; religious devotion; adulation for a leader or hero; companionship, as between close friends, based on a pleasurable sharing of interests, thoughts, feelings.

But we are concerned here with those aspects of love that

parents feel for their children. I want to emphasize two of them — devotion and enjoyment — and make a sharp distinction between them, to see if it will shed light on the question of whether parents can or should love children equally.

It seems clear to me that mothers and fathers love their children equally in the sense that they are equally devoted to each one. They try to be fair. They want each to succeed and be happy, and will make any reasonable sacrifice to achieve this for him — and an unreasonable sacrifice, too, if that seems essential. They'd unhesitatingly rush into a fiery building or risk drowning to save his life. While he's a child they'll not want him out of the home or say anything that suggests they do. Even when he's an adult they'll continue to want to help him, no matter what trouble he gets into and no matter how strongly they disapprove of what he has done.

The last example sounds morbid and extreme; but it brings out the difference between the kind of fondness we might feel for anyone's child, which may fade if the child disappoints us seriously enough, and our devotion to our own child, which persists through thick and thin. The child is ours forever.

Insufficient devotion, on the other hand, shows its serious effects in certain cases that come to the attention of child welfare agencies and children's courts. There are the rare parents who don't love their child at all. There are also the foster parents who have taken a child into their home but have not become fond of him. In these situations, if the child becomes too difficult, they want him removed — for good. Any child senses deeply an absence of devotion and reacts to it drastically. He doesn't, like the ordinary naughty child, merely misbehave up to a certain point. He just doesn't care at all how he behaves, or what people think of him, or what will happen to him. The sky's the limit.

I think that devotion is by far the most vital element in parental love.

But when we turn to love in the sense of enjoying the individual qualities in each of our children, it's impossible, it seems to me, for any parent to feel the same toward any two of his children or to treat them the same. In the first place, a boy is appreciated because of his boyish qualities, a girl because she's girlish. One is loved most for his sunniness, another for his earnestness; one for his courage, another for his gentleness; one for his thoughtfulness, another because he's a roughneck. The enjoyment is based on entirely different qualities. There's no scale you can put them on and call them equal — any more than a person can say he loves swimming the same as he loves fine clothes.

It's oversimplifying to emphasize one characteristic. Each child is a complicated collection of traits and it's the collection the parents respond to. Each parent, too, has a complex collection of responses to the characteristics of his children. To take exaggerated examples, think of the parents (perhaps still close to certain European traditions) who almost worship studiousness in a son but are distressed if he gets into ordinary neighborhood scraps or Halloween mischief. Somewhat opposite is the father (an American type) who beams with pride on an athletic son but is disappointed by one who has no such inclination.

It's getting closer to the realities to say that each child is a unique mixture of traits some of which are appealing to a parent, some of which are neutral in effect, some of which are irritating.

Of course all this applies, too, to how *any* two people react to each other. It's probably true that if several qualities in a person are intensely appealing to us, they tend to obscure, keep us from noticing other characteristics which would bother us a lot in another person. And, vice versa, a particularly irritating quality may antagonize us so much that we can't appreciate an attractive one. Finally, none of us stay exactly the same in the way we feel about anybody. If we're frank, most of us will admit that on Tuesday we're irritated by some mannerism of a member of the family which on Monday hardly bothered us at all. I know there are days when it seems to me that most of the people I see, whether I know them or not, appear quite attractive, and other days when they almost all look unappealing. So much depends on our own mood. I've known a number of parents who have been obviously critical of a child for several years — nothing he did was quite right — who have then rather suddenly had some kind of change of feeling, which could only partly be explained by a change in the child, and found him thoroughly enjoyable.

So love in the sense of how much we enjoy a child's appealing qualities, balanced against how much we are irritated by his faults, is a highly individualized matter and quite variable from time to time.

What are some of the roots of our positive and negative feelings? Generally speaking, we are pleased to find in our child the qualities which our parents wanted to inculcate in us and which we proudly succeeded in acquiring to some degree. Each family puts particular emphasis on certain ones. But in addition, every individual in growing up develops his own very personal ideals based on qualities in those members of his family whom he loved especially. If these reappear in his children, he will be particularly delighted.

Contrariwise, every family's disapproval of certain undesirable characteristics tends to be passed on from generation to generation. In addition, each one of us in growing up must also become particularly irritated by certain traits in brothers and sisters and parents which made life hard for us. Most of all, we are apt to be upset by finding in our children disapproved qualities or habits which we ourselves had when we were growing up.

It is no wonder that every individual parent feels strongly and somewhat differently — either positively or negatively — about the various characteristics that appear in his child, who on the one hand is so close to him as to be almost a part of him, and who is also likely — in appearance or manner — to remind him of other members of the family. This is the system — the parents' feelings of approval or disapproval — that nature and society have always counted on to foster the desirable traits and suppress the undesirable ones.

Perhaps by now you've become impatient with me, feeling that I've oversimplified the distinction between devotion and enjoyment, and that I've only stated the obvious in pointing out that every parent's feelings toward each child are some special mixture of enjoyment and irritation. If that's the way you feel, you're exactly right to feel that way, and you are one of the parents who have no particular confusion about this subject.

I'm only trying to find a sensible way to look at the question for those who worry about it. I think there are many, many conscientious parents who believe that they *somehow* ought to be able to even out their feelings, think just as fondly and as often about each child, give equal attention, manage to show equal patience and equal disapproval. Realizing that they don't, they feel unworthy. They feel particularly guilty about inequalities of impatience and irritability, assuming that this surely indicates some fundamental deficiency in their love. This, I think, is an incorrect oversimplification; it only further complicates their relationships with their children.

Having concluded that a parent can't and shouldn't try to feel the same toward each child, I'd like to turn the discussion around briefly and ask what a child would like.

I don't believe that a child really *wants* his parents to feel (or pretend to feel) the same toward him as they feel toward another, or expects only the same amount of disapproval or irritation. What each of us wants most, whether child or adult, is to be enjoyed for himself alone. In the long run we prefer not to be compared with anyone else or lumped with anyone else, in the feelings of a person who's important to us.

Each of us wants a niche of his own in another person's heart. Some examples from everyday adult life may be easier to visualize than family situations. If you have a boss who tells you that you and B are the two most promising people in the office, your pleasure may be diminished a lot by realizing what a rival you have in B. It would have been better if he'd said, "I want to let you know how well I think you're doing your job." If your friend whose good opinion you value says she considers you as well dressed as her other friend, M (whom you don't like as well as she does), this may be quite a letdown. She should just have said, "My, but you look glamorous in that suit!" If an acquaintance whose taste in decorating you look up to is raving to you about the attractiveness of T's house and then adds suddenly, out of politeness, "But of course your house is very attractive, too," the forced compliment doesn't really please you at all. In fact, it's irritating.

In a similar way a child doesn't enjoy for long being compared with, being put in the same category with, a brother, or being officially treated just like him. Least satisfying are similar favors which he senses are forced in his case. Such procedures put him in uneasy competition. They whet his appetite for advantage and sharpen his eye for any disadvantage. (The mother of fiercely rivalrous boys who tries to appease them by always buying identical toys complains that they have eagle eyes for minute differences and always reproach her in the end.)

As for disapproval and impatience, I don't think a child expects or wants only the same amount as his brothers and sisters either. He, like each of us, knows that he has traits or habits that are unappealing or irritating and knows when he's acting badly. He is trying to some degree to overcome them and underneath he wants the parents' help in overcoming them. If disapproval or punishment is fairly due him, according to family rules, he will feel better inside after getting it.

I think we parents can do our best by our children by comfortably admitting that we are only human, with all the strong feelings — irrational as well as rational — that are the essence of our species. Our real devotion to each child, our frank enjoyment of what is enjoyable in him and our efforts to curb his unattractive traits are the main things we have to offer him. In most cases, this combination does the job well and suits him best. If we are always questioning our feelings or trying too hard to make them come out even, we lose some of the natural heartiness with which we could respond to each individual. And hearty appreciation is what each wants most.

Though this summary may be true enough, it of course leaves many questions still unanswered. I'd now like to carry the discussion one step farther and try to explain a few of the theoretical reasons why we may find ourselves constantly and intensely impatient with one particular child when we can't explain it on any rational basis.

❨ CHRONIC IMPATIENCE WITH ONE CHILD

A mother (I'll call her Mrs. V.) once wrote me, in part:

To ease my own mind — that we are not unnatural parents — I have made a tactful effort to discover if our problem exists in other large families, and have found it does. Other parents, too, have shamefacedly confessed that there was one child — often it was the third or fourth, rarely the first — who always seemed to rub them the wrong way, toward whom they did not feel the spontaneous flow of affection they felt for the others. They all, like us, wanted large families, so it is not a case of an unwanted child.

We have six children, all attractive and healthy. There are times and stages when any child is taxing, but we feel vexed or hostile toward our second child all the time — from age one to date. There are times when everything he says or does provokes us. He does not have the sense of security that the others do. We know that this is wrong. We do our intelligent best to make it otherwise.

In none of the families I've consulted has there been anything to throw any light on why either or both parents should feel as they do, no rhyme, no reason. You would be doing a kindness for many larger families just by bringing this painful subject out in the light.

Mrs. V. expresses well the bewilderment and guilt that parents feel when they find themselves in this situation. The only details in which I would disagree with her would be in her impression that irritation is less frequent toward a first child and in her assumption that such feelings crop up mainly in large families. I have no statistics, but my own impression is that they occur commonly in families of all sizes and can be felt toward a child in any position in the family.

I first have to admit that I know of no easy ways to overcome such feelings. I can only point out in a theoretical way a few of the explanations that have been discovered, mainly in child-guidance work. They are samples that cover only some of the cases, not all.

A mother, for instance, may get along quite enjoyably with one son who reminds her of a beloved older brother. But she is easily irritated by another son who looks and behaves much like her younger brother whose birth, when she was two, made her insecure and jealous for quite a while. If she recognizes these connections and doesn't feel too guilty about them, they won't cause too much trouble in her relationships with him.

But when irritable feelings in childhood toward brother or sister or father or mother were more intense, were longer lasting and were more deeply repressed, they may carry over into adulthood and cause considerable tension between parent and child.

Suppose this mother in her early childhood had been made to feel excessively ashamed about her antagonism toward her younger brother, partly because her parents showed strong moral disapproval of any jealousy whatsoever, partly because she loved him as well as resented him. In such a case a child may become so guilty that she succeeds in hiding her resentful feelings altogether — even from herself — and before they've had a chance to wear off. If she later has a son who reminds her of this brother, consciously or unconsciously, the old insecurity and crossness may get stirred up again underneath; and with it, all the old guiltiness.

This idea — that a mother may be made to feel uncomfortable by her own small child as if she were still two years old and as if he were her brother — may sound too farfetched to be plausible to some of you. I can only say that I've been convinced, as have others in this field, many times. Fathers just as often as mothers experience these baffling tensions. In fact, most of us feel them to at least a mild degree. The parent usually doesn't have any idea where the irritation is coming from. He (or she) only knows that he feels tense much of the time he is taking care of this child and that he keeps correcting him, scolding him for very minor misbehavior or for nothing at all. The parent is very conscious of the guiltiness, though, and it further complicates his management of the child.

(Incidentally, it is such cases that make us feel that it is better not to make a small child feel too deeply ashamed of his jealousy of a baby. This doesn't mean allowing him to be mean to the baby — that would load him down with guilt, too, aside from being unfair to the baby. He has to be stopped from putting his feelings into action. But if his parents at the same time can let him realize that they understand how he feels: "I know how cross the baby makes you feel sometimes," or "I know that sometimes you wish the baby would go away again," it helps him to get over his fears, fears that his parents will stop loving him and that the baby is a love thief, fear that he himself is an unnatural villain.)

Chronic impatience with some characteristic in a child can also be traced occasionally to a similar characteristic in the parent himself, and to all the trouble the parent had with it. A fairly common example is the father who in his own childhood was timid. Though he has outgrown most of the outward manifestations of this, he still remembers keenly all the shame and misery of having been a sissy. A father who has had such experiences may be understandably intolerant of timidity in his son. It's as if the distressing problem which he thought he'd finally solved were coming back to haunt him again.

One might think that a problem or trait which a parent had

largely overcome in himself could be easily coped with in his child. Sometimes. But often the parent finds he can't help or cure the child at all. In fact, he may without realizing it be contributing to the difficulty despite his efforts. In the first place, he's likely to react so impatiently to the signs in his child that he arouses antagonism instead of cooperation. In the second place, there may still be traces of the parent's old trouble, not entirely eradicated, which in a subtle unconscious manner influences the child. The father who overcame timidity in childhood may still have a cautious kind of personality. Since a son models himself in part on his father and in other indirect ways is molded by him, the son may very easily end up with the very trait that his father would least like to see in him. In similar ways a parent who in childhood had a long struggle with selfishness or aggressiveness or untruthfulness or procrastination has a chance of finding the same problem in one of his children, of being irritated by it, but ineffective in solving it.

When the trait is one that the parent was quite conscious of in his own childhood and recognizes again in his child, there can be tension enough. It's apt to be worse when the parent's difficulty was so painful or shameful that he has largely erased his memory of it. Then he may not recognize just what the vague quality is that he's objecting to in his child or why he's so critical. But the less he can explain his irritation, the more unworthy he feels.

I want now to refer briefly to several other kinds of factors that may interfere with the enjoyment of a child or create impatience that's hard to understand. Mrs. V. speaks of the fact that she and her husband and the other parents she's talked with all wanted large families. And so, she says, none of these children could have been unwanted. But this assumes that anything we want in life we want without reservation.

Actually there are only a few things we desire so one-sidedly, such as health and happiness. In most of our choices we give up the lesser good for the greater, and then from time to time we feel regret or resentment. So I'd agree that of course these parents Mrs. V. speaks of wanted large families. And if they ever had a chance, by magic, to lead their lives over again they'd probably make the same choice a second time. But that certainly doesn't mean that there won't be moments of regret, especially for the mother who bears the brunt of the nine months of pregnancy, the labor, the years of care of the child. And more especially still if the child proves disappointing in some respect or if family life becomes difficult for any reason.

Most every family has a year or two when things go wrong. If there are great tensions from any source — the father's work, illness and death of a close member of the mother's or father's family, disharmony between the parents — then the joyfulness of the anticipation of a baby may be lessened.

We all know that we can't order our heart's desire: boy or girl, beauty, athlete, scholar, charmer, hero. But the fact is that each of us has at least a secret picture of what he'd prefer and, no matter how rational he tries to be, an expectation — to some degree — that his wish will be granted.

Babies when they first arrive are often homely, and a lot of them make themselves and the family miserable for a while with frequent demands, fretfulness or colic. These troubles subside in time. But by a year of age some babies can be exasperatingly independent, uncooperative and obstinate. (I'm reminded that Mrs. V. says her child has been provocative "from age one.") If all your children prove equally easy or difficult, you adjust to this level. But if one child stands out like a sore thumb because of his crochetiness, you can't help feeling put off by him.

Most of these false starts straighten themselves out in a short time because most parents learn to enjoy the stranger who took them by surprise. But some simply can't make the extreme adaptation that's called for, despite mighty efforts. Others learn eventually to cope with the child who is more difficult, but, if they are very conscientious people, they continue to blame themselves for their original intolerance.

I have listed a few of the reasons why the very best of parents may be unable to enjoy one child as much as another. Whatever the reason is, they react with feelings of guiltiness to some extent (and this is where, I suspect, Mrs. V's problem became complicated). The commonest way parents show their guilt is by allowing the child to get away with behavior they'd never permit otherwise: uncooperativeness, demandingness, rudeness, sometimes even abusiveness. There are at least two reasons for this. The parents feel that the child is entitled to punish them a little. And unconsciously they almost welcome definite misbehavior because then at last they know what they are cross about and feel more justified. But it's now the child's turn, having got away with murder, to feel guilty. Deep inside he wants to be stopped and perhaps to be punished. If this isn't forthcoming, his instinct is to behave worse — to draw the punishment. We realize today that this is often the explanation when a child goes on, hour after hour, provoking his too-permissive parents. It's as if he were saying, desperately, "How bad do I have to act before you'll make me behave?" Of course the parent has to explode with anger eventually, which may clear the air temporarily.

When a parent who is confident about his love for a child occasionally punishes in righteous indignation, he and the child feel all right about it afterward, because both know that the child "had it coming to him." The child's behavior stays good for quite a long time.

But if the parent feels chronically unworthy, his guilt sweeps back over him in a heightened wave soon after his outburst of anger. It can show itself in a variety of ways. Perhaps he too readily permits the child to be abusive in words or action during the punishment itself. Or soon afterward he withdraws the penalty or pretends not to notice when the child begins acting up again. One guilty parent keeps reminding the child in an unconvincing tone how much the child deserved the punishment. Another parent may merely stay grumpy for several hours (slightly ashamed of himself). Or he may without realizing it — just like a guilty child — actually needle and provoke the child to retaliate.

Anyway, the child gets the message — that the parent is ashamed of himself again. Now he has several inviting reasons for resuming his disagreeableness.

And so it goes, round and round in an endless whirlpool. It isn't just a few parents who get caught. All of us get spun around at times, after we think we've been unfairly cross with a child. But most of us, fortunately, can come back to equilibrium before too long.

We don't know what got Mr. and Mrs. V. off on the wrong foot. I sense from the letter that they are unusually devoted to all their children. I don't think it was any lack of love that upset the second child. For some good reason the parents found him more difficult to enjoy at an early age — and being people of high standards, they reproached themselves too severely. That's where I suspect the real trouble began. What makes me feel fairly confident that they're caught in the whirlpool is Mrs. V.'s statement that "there are times when everything he says or does provokes us." A child can't become that obnoxious all by himself. He must have learned just what irritates his parents most; but he's also learned that they don't feel free to stop him.

At first glance it may seem to the parents, who suddenly realize that they have been permitting a child to be constantly provocative, that the answer is to become constantly harsh with him, or at least constantly disapproving. But both these stages mean that the parents are still letting him go too far and then can't help feeling resentful. In theory, at least, the aim is for the parents to become confident enough so that they can insist on good behavior in the first place, in a friendly but firm manner — to stay in control of the situation — so that there is no reason to become exasperated. In actual practice this is very difficult to do, as every parent knows, especially when there has been a long history of tension. In reality, when parents resolve to insist on cooperativeness and agreeableness, there are bound to be clashes at first. If the parents can be firm for a week, they're usually delighted to see how much happier the child has become. This relieves them of some more of their guiltiness, convinces them that they are on the right track and makes it easier for them to make further progress. The downward whirlpool is turned into an upward spiral. However, most parents who are caught in the situation Mrs. V. describes will do a lot better, faster, if they can get some outside assistance. This is what child-guidance clinics, psychiatrists and family social agencies are for.

GETTING ALONG WITH
GRANDMOTHERS

Most of them are a great comfort.
A few have to be controlled.

SOME TIME ago, I received this unhappy letter:

I gather, since you commented once that young mothers have a tendency to flaunt your book at grandmothers, that you feel that grandmothers are more put upon than offending, where conflict exists. Believe me, the grandmother is often the offender.

The first seeds of resentment were sown in me during my pregnancy when my mother-in-law kept saying, "I only hope the baby will have my son's features" or "I hope he'll be smart like his daddy."

Since the baby's arrival I have been subjected to constant disapproval, especially in regard to toilet training (which my mother-in-law feels should be imposed early with a strong moral emphasis), in regard to my refusal to force feedings, and in regard to my easygoing caution which permits my child to explore by himself, even if it may result in a bump, a mistake or a mess. My mother-in-law assures me that because of her experience and age she inevitably knows best and that we are wrong not to accept her judgment. Frequently, I must confess, I reject a good suggestion because of the dictatorial manner in which it is made. She regards my refusal to accept some of her ideas as a personal rejection or an affront.

She disapproves heartily of my outside interests (which do not interfere with my duties), calling them frivolous, and she makes us feel very guilty when we call on her two or three times a year for big occasions. Yet when I hint that I might get a baby sitter she is highly insulted.

Occasionally I want to leave the baby with my mother. But my mother-in-law masks her selfishness in the guise of generosity and won't hear of it.

The faults of this grandmother are so apparent that perhaps you may not think it worth while to discuss them. But an exaggerated situation makes it easier to see factors that might not be obvious at all in a more ordinary situation. One thing that seems quite plain is that this grandmother is not just "selfish" and "dictatorial" — she's very jealous.

Before we go any further we should admit that we've heard only one side of this case. I continue to be amazed how different a domestic conflict sounds after you hear the story from the party of the second part. In this particular case, though, I doubt whether the grandmother's story would make us change our minds very much. But if we could see the two women in action together I imagine we should see that the young mother is unwittingly playing some part in making this conflict possible. It takes two to make a quarrel, even when one is clearly the aggressor.

I don't want to pretend to know for sure what is going on between this mother and grandmother, because I, like you, have only the letter to go by. But I've worked with a number of young mothers whose main problem was their inability to stand up to an interfering grandmother, and most such cases have features in common. Perhaps you don't think it's fair for me to assume that the letter writer surrenders too easily. She implies that she does hold her ground in some respects — toilet training, feeding, avoiding overprotection — and that's all to the good. But she apparently gives in on the sitter situation. The most important evidence, to me, that the mother is surrendering too much is her tone of reproach and hurt feelings. Whether she wins or loses each argument, she seems to end up feeling the victim. This is not wholesome.

I think the basic problem is that such a mother is afraid
to hurt the feelings of the grandmother or afraid she will make
her angry. There are several factors at work here. The mother
is still young and inexperienced. The chances are good that
when she's had another baby or two she won't be so timid. But
this bashfulness of the beginner is only partly a matter of inexperience. We learn from psychiatric work that a girl in the
adolescent period is apt to be quite rivalrous with her mother
in her unconscious feelings. She feels that it's her own turn now
to be the glamorous one, to lead the romantic life and to have the
babies. She feels that it's time for her mother to take a back
seat. These rivalrous feelings may be expressed by a bold young
person in open defiance — that's one reason why delinquency,
among both girls and boys, begins to be a common problem in
adolescence. But the girl or young woman who has been brought
up very strictly may react to her rivalry with her mother (or
mother-in-law) in a guilty manner. Even when she knows she
is technically in the right, she finds herself giving in, to a greater
or lesser degree. Then, too, there is a special rivalry between
daughter-in-law and mother-in-law. In the unconscious sense the
daughter-in-law has succeeded in stealing the precious son of the
mother-in-law. The self-assured young woman may enjoy this
triumph. The overly considerate daughter-in-law is more apt to
feel guilty about what she has got away with, especially if she
is up against a possessive and disapproving mother-in-law.

The most obvious factor of all will be the character of the
baby's grandmother — not only how opinionated and bossy and
jealous she is, but how sharp she is in taking advantage of the
young mother's sensitivity. This is what I meant by saying it
takes two to make a quarrel. I didn't mean that the kind of
mother who wrote the letter is quarrelsome in the aggressive
sense. I meant that the mother who doesn't have enough confidence in her own convictions or who gets her feelings easily
hurt or who is afraid of making the grandmother angry is the
perfect victim for a grandmother who is overbearing and who

knows how to make people feel guilty. There is a neat dovetailing between the two personalities. In fact, they are apt to accentuate progressively the defects in each other. Any tendency of the mother to submit to the grandmother's insistence encourages the grandmother to be still more dominating. And the mother's fear of hurting the grandmother's feelings makes the grandmother shrewdly threaten to have hurt feelings on every occasion. The grandmother in the letter "won't hear" of the mother's getting a sitter and she takes differences of opinion "as a personal affront." The angrier the mother becomes over the little insults and the domination, the more frightened she becomes that she will show it. She doesn't know how to get out of the painful situation. Like a car stuck in the sand, she digs in deeper and deeper. As the months go by she learns to do what all of us do when pain seems inevitable — we begin to get some perverse satisfaction out of it. One way is to feel sorry for ourselves, to dwell on the outrages we suffer and enjoy our own indignation. Another is to tell of our torture to others and enjoy their sympathy. These painful satisfactions tend to sap our determination to find a real solution. They become permanent substitutes for real happiness.

How can the young mother who has been submitting to a dominating grandmother extricate herself? It's not easy at first, but it *can* be done gradually, with practice. She should remind herself often that she and her husband are responsible for this baby — legally and morally and practically — so they have to make the decisions. If the grandmother has raised doubts in her mind, she can go back to her doctor for clarification. (Doctors will back up mothers who are doing right because they've all been irritated at least a few times by having certain bossy grandmothers contradict their medical advice!) A father should show clearly that he believes his wife and he are the ones to make the decisions, and that he doesn't like interference any more than she does. Certainly he should never side with the grandmother against his wife in an open argument between the three of them. If he thinks the grandmother is right about some point, he should loyally wait to discuss it when he is alone with his wife.

The most important step for an intimidated mother is to realize clearly that it's her own guiltiness and fear of angering the grandmother which make her a target for bullying, to realize that she has nothing to be ashamed of or afraid of, and to develop gradually a thicker skin so that she can go her own way without feeling uneasy.

Does the mother have to blow up at the grandmother to gain her own independence? Perhaps she may have to, once or twice. Most people who get imposed upon too easily have trouble learning to take a firm stand unless and until they feel thoroughly outraged — only then can they let loose with justifiable anger. The trouble with this system is that a dominating grandmother senses that the mother's unnatural patience *and* her final explosion are *both* signs that she is too timid. Both these signs encourage the grandmother to resume her bossing and needling again. In the long run the mother will be able to hold her ground and keep the grandmother at bay when she has learned how to speak up for herself right away, in a matter-of-fact, confident tone, before she gets angry. ("This is the way that works best for me and the baby" . . . "The doctor recommends this method . . .") The calm, assured tone is usually the most effective way to convince the grandmother that the mother has the courage of her convictions.

In regard to the specific problems that the mother writes about, I think she should use her own mother and a professional sitter as often as seems appropriate, without mentioning it to her mother-in-law. If her mother-in-law finds out about it and raises a fuss, the mother should try not to seem guilty or to get mad but act as if it was the most natural thing in the world. She should try to avoid as many discussions about child care as possible. When the grandmother insists on arguing, she should try to act only mildly interested, refuse to argue, and change the subject as soon as politeness will permit. When the grandmother expresses the hope that the next baby will be smart and handsome like her side of the family, the mother can kid her about it, if she can learn to do it without showing hurt feelings. What all these steps add up to are: refusing to be put on the defensive, refusing to let her feelings be hurt, refusing to get excited. After a mother has learned the fundamentals of defending herself, she can go a step farther by learning not to run away from the grandmother and not to be afraid to hear her out, because both these attitudes reveal, in a way, that she feels too weak to stand up to her.

I have been concentrating so far on the basic attitudes of the mother and grandmother and I have ignored the specific differences of opinion between the two women about such matters as the urging of food, the method and spirit of toilet training, the question of how much to try to protect a small child from minor accidents and how much to let him learn his own caution. Of course the first thing that can be said is that when there is a clash of personalities, the opportunities for differences of opinion are endless. In fact, two women who in actual practice would handle a child just about the same could still argue till kingdom come about theory, because there are two sides to any theory about child rearing — the only real question is where you decide to strike a balance. But when you are mad at somebody it's part of the fun to exaggerate the differences between your viewpoint and his and to battle on. If you detect an area of possible agreement, you shy away from it.

Now we ought to stop and admit that there have been violent changes in child-care teaching in the past twenty years. It requires extraordinary flexibility on the part of a grandmother to be able to accept them, to be able to stifle her anxiety about them. The grandmother was probably taught, when she was raising her children, that to feed a baby off schedule caused indigestion, diarrhea and spoiling, that regularity of the bowels was a cornerstone of health and that early rigorous toilet training would foster this. But now the grandmother is suddenly expected to believe that flexibility in feeding schedule is not only permissible but desirable, that there is no virtue in regularity of bowels, that toilet training should not be imposed against the child's will. It's hard to make these changes sound drastic to a young mother of today who is so familiar with them. To be able to sympathize with the alarm of a grandmother she would have to imagine some fantastic new advice such as to feed her newborn baby fried pork or to bathe him in cold water!

When a girl has been brought up with considerable disapproval — chafing against it and yearning to prove her competence — it's natural that as she first becomes a mother she will be touchy about advice from either grandmother, even if it is sensible, even if it is given tactfully. As a matter of fact, practically all new mothers are still close enough to adolescence and need so much to prove themselves that they show at least mild sensitivity about unsolicited advice. Most grandmothers, being sympathetic and tactful, realize this and try to keep their suggestions to a minimum.

But the young mother who, from her upbringing, has a bit of a chip on her shoulder is apt to carry the battle (about controversial methods) to the grandmother, without waiting for signs of disapproval from her. I've seen situations in which I was pretty sure that the mother was going to great lengths in self-demand scheduling or in delaying toilet training or in allowing the child to make a terrible mess at meals or in permitting him to be dramatically rude, not because she herself really believed in such extremes but because she sensed unconsciously how much the grandmother would be upset. Here was a chance for the mother to kill several birds with one stone: to tease the grandmother endlessly, to get back at her for all her past disapproval of the mother, to prove how old-fashioned and ignorant and wrong the grandmother was in her methods, to prove how enlightened the mother is. Of course most of us as parents and grandparents use arguments about modern or old-fashioned principles of child rearing as weapons in our family squabbles. Usually no great damage is done and there is even some enjoyment in it. The harm comes in carrying on a major war over a period of years.

Before ending this discussion I want to remind you that I took a letter about an unusually tense situation in order to bring out some of the underlying factors that make for tension. Such cases are few. At the opposite end of the scale are the fortunate families in which all is harmony between the generations. In a majority of families we have mild to moderate disagreements, particularly in regard to the first child. I think it is admirable that we can usually get along as well as we do, considering the recent changes in philosophy which act as a constant temptation to argument.

In some respects it's too bad that we in America have such a strong belief that it's better for a young couple to set up housekeeping in a separate home, preferably removed at some distance from the grandparents, and that the grandmother should be very careful not to offer advice. Instead, the inexperienced mother gets her instruction from doctors and public-health nurses and other counselors. To be sure, there are lots of advantages in such a separation of households, especially during a period of transition.

But throughout the greater part of the world the young parents live with or near the grandparents, without ever stopping to think of this as a hardship. They take it for granted that the grandmother is the expert in child care and that she will devote a lot of time to teaching and helping the mother. This can be an enormous comfort to the inexperienced mother, especially at those times of stress such as the newborn period and during illnesses. The young mother then acquires knowledge and assurance and independence by easy, natural steps.

In America, too, the mother who lives close to the grandmother and who gets along with her should be able to gain a great deal of help and support from her, even though there are doctors and nurses to advise on medical matters. There are literally hundreds of questions the first few weeks at home and every time there is a new development or a new illness. It's the mother who is most mature and most secure who can ask for advice with the greatest ease, because she has no fear of being dominated. If she decides that what she hears doesn't suit her or her baby, she can tactfully turn it down without making a fuss about it, since she doesn't have pent-up feelings of resentment or guilt. The grandmother, on her part, is pleased to be asked advice. She doesn't accumulate anxieties about how the baby is being managed because she knows she'll have a chance to express her opinion from time to time. Though she's careful not to do it too often, she isn't afraid to offer an unsolicited suggestion occasionally, since she knows that the mother will not be upset by this and will feel free to turn it down if it doesn't suit her.

Perhaps I make this sound too ideal for real life, but in general outline I think it is correct. Anyway, I want to make it clear that it's a sign of maturity and self-assurance to be able to ask for advice and help. I want to encourage mothers and grandmothers to find ways of getting along easily because of the profound benefit and enjoyment that not only both of them but the children, too, will receive from such a relationship.

PARENTS' QUARRELS

*The ease with which they resolve them
is more important than the number.*

ABOUT PARENTAL QUARRELS I suppose there is one thing that can
be said right at the start: It might be better if there were none.
But there almost always are. Of course there are great variations
in the amounts and in the expression of disharmony between
different couples. There are some husbands and wives who are
so self-disciplined that they never shout or hiss or mutter or even
glare. In fact, there are a few individuals who don't even tighten
their lips — they become apologetic if they find that their
spouses disagree with them. They have such a fear of angriness
that it's transformed immediately into submissiveness. But all
these are forms of quarreling in the sense that there is disagreement which involves at least a slight degree of angriness. I'm
not discussing differences of opinion that generate no heat at all.

We might admit that in one sense it would theoretically be
better for a child to grow up with parents who were entirely
harmonious in their feelings. But in another sense this would
be an incomplete preparation for life. Sooner or later a child has
to realize that other children, other adults and he himself have
angry feelings at times, that they usually get expressed in a relatively harmless way and that they pass. To be sure, it's better
for a child to learn about really violent anger and ugly moods
from someone other than his parents, because he senses that his
basic security depends on the solidarity of the relationship between his parents.

Many of us who have been brought up very "properly," whose parents have carefully controlled their own anger, so that it has shown up only in a strained manner, are apt to think that the way parental anger is expressed — or suppressed — is the most important factor in how it affects children. But psychiatric work reveals clearly what all of us really know underneath: that children immediately detect their parents' off moods. They are apt to be more bothered by a strained silence that lasts all day than by a hot argument that's over in a few minutes.

That doesn't necessarily mean that if a mother feels like hurling a plate or the father feels like slapping her face, it's better to let go. Perhaps a blow would be preferable to a cruel insult or threat which left a permanent hurt in the other parent and a long-lasting fear in the child. Hurts hurt, whether they are physical or mental. They usually leave resentment in one person and guilt in the other, both of which linger on. Another reason for moderate self-control is that parents who have been brought up to feel that blows or even shouts are shameful are apt to feel particularly unworthy for a long while if they have used such weapons.

What about postponing a quarrel, if a child is present when the occasion arises, or blunders in on it in the middle? Certainly it's wise for the parents to sidestep what looks like an inevitable argument until they are alone, if they can behave cheerfully in the meantime. (They may even forget the quarrel.) But if they are going to glower and mutter at each other for an hour while they are with the child, the gain is doubtful. It's sensible, too, to stop temporarily a quarrel that's interrupted by a child, but it's important to be casual and frank about this. If a child has heard angry sounds through the door and then finds two strained, guilty-looking parents, who either remain strangely silent or crossly order him out of the room, he'll imagine something much worse than the reality. Better to summon a bit of *savoir-faire* and explain, "We were having a cross argument, but let's all do something else now."

Perhaps it seems to you that I have just been going around in circles, saying that quarrels are inevitable and that they can be upsetting to children in any form. Can't we be a little more constructive?

What counts most, I think, is not so much the manner of the parents' quarrels, or even the number of them, but the basic relationship between the parents, and what they are expressing in their quarrels. If they fundamentally love and respect each other, if they basically agree with each other about their aims in life and what they want to inculcate in their children, if they quarrel mainly about secondary matters such as money, relatives, card games, personal appearance, if they try to get their quarrels over as soon as possible, then their children will not be too upset by them.

But we can be a little more specific than this about how to take some of the curse off quarrels that do occur, and even get a little educational value out of them. One of the principal reasons that young children worry about their parents' anger (and their own) is that their own anger is more violently, more barbarically felt than is the adult's. The young child senses that when he is angry at his parent he wants, momentarily, to do away with him or her. But realizing that he is utterly dependent on the parent — and loves him too — he is filled with anxiety and guilt. He has no confidence yet in his ability to control his anger. He hasn't been around long enough to know that there are 10,000,000 fights for every one that is lethal. He assumes his quarreling parents not only have murderous feelings but might carry them out.

A psychiatrist, working with a certain type of child who is unusually anxious and guilty, is apt to spend a great deal of time reassuring him that it's natural to have angry feelings at times, that angry feelings don't harm the other person, that it's all right to admit angry feelings and talk about them. This usually brings great relief to the child, and improvement in some of his symptoms.

So when a young child sees parents in a quarrel, it's good to let him know what it is and what it isn't, so that he will not be unnecessarily upset by it. The mother or father can say something to the effect that: We are having an argument about whether to get a new car, just the way you and Tommy have fights about your toys. Don't worry. All mommies and daddies get cross at each other once in a while. Pretty soon the argument will be over and we'll all be cheerful again.

I don't mean that the parents should use just these words, or that they have to say them every time there's the slightest disagreement — that would be an awful bore for everybody. A lot depends on how many and how intense the quarrels are and how much the child seems to be upset by them.

We ought to get back to the question of what the parents' quarrels are about, not so much the official topics but the underlying attitudes. Even very mature couples who respect each other deeply will find, from time to time, that they disagree vigorously about such matters as the desirability of certain expenditures, choice of friends, behavior in company, plans for the children, disciplining of the children. When I said that parents "find" that they disagree, I meant that they discover these differences of opinion unexpectedly, especially in the early years of marriage. Right from the beginning of a wholesome marriage, the husband and wife are both finding out, during each argument and during a cooler discussion that may follow, exactly where they differ and why they differ. They learn about each other and they often learn things about themselves that they didn't know before. Misunderstandings are lessened. The partner who sees for the first time that he has had some irritating quality or irrational opinion either confesses or (more typically) decides silently to mend his ways a bit. When differences of opinion still persist at the end of a discussion, the couple come to some kind of spoken or unspoken compromise, based on each one's estimation of how important the issue is to the other person and to himself. In other words, a wife may finally agree that her husband should buy the new car, even though she still secretly thinks it's a crazy idea, because she sees that it's so important to him and because she loves him and respects him so much in other matters. He may promise not to fly in planes, in spite of not agreeing with any of her reasons.

In good marriages, quarrels tend to be resolved because of love. In troubled marriages, they don't. If there is a preponderance of antagonism between the partners, then at least one spouse is actually looking for excuses to tangle with the other. Goodness knows there are literally hundreds of little issues lying around any home, on any day, to blow up into big issues if the disposition exists.

I've been talking as though there were only ideal marriages and shaky ones, whereas most of them are in between. The harmony varies from week to week and year to year, depending on multiple factors inside and outside the family. Some of the factors are obvious. More of them are hidden, even from the couple themselves. For example, some people have grown up in a family atmosphere which was a continuous succession of fights and love feasts. This may cause them to seek and enjoy frequent battling in their own marriages, though they never would admit it to others or to themselves. They don't feel really loving until they've been through a fight. The neighbors, listening to the uproar, swear the marriage is breaking up, but it goes on and on. It may produce children who will follow the same pattern. Another factor which, in an occasional family, makes for frequent irrational quarrels is one parent's too close identification with a child who doesn't get along too well with the other parent. Every time, for instance, when the mother scolds or deprives the child, the father feels it more than the child does and protests loudly. If the mother is lined up with another child in the family, she may be accusing the father of being unfair to that one. The children play up to and play into the parents' antagonism and the quarrels multiply.

Fortunately, a lot more is known now than used to be about the common factors that make for marital tensions, and there are professional people in several fields ready to help couples to understand and overcome their difficulties. There are marriage counselors, there are social workers in family agencies, there are psychiatrists in guidance clinics and in private practice. Some ministers are naturally good in helping couples to see where the trouble lies, and some have taken special courses in counseling.

Of course it's best, in terms of practicality and favorableness of attitude, if husband and wife are both willing to consult the professional. More often it's the wife who sees the need of consultation, and it's the husband who is reluctant or adamant. But a great deal of clarification and improvement can usually be gained even when only one partner seeks help, and even though that partner is playing the lesser role in the quarrels. Whether the bull charges or not depends a great deal on whether the bullfighter is waving a red flag.

MOTHERS NEED A BREAK, TOO

The sense of confinement and isolation
can frustrate even the most devoted of mothers.

WOMEN confess that one of the toughest aspects of becoming a mother is the sense of loss of freedom. I wonder if this is more accentuated in America than anywhere else in the world. Our adolescent girls are allowed to roam with their group or go on dates in a way that is quite startling to many Europeans. By the time they are finishing high school they make important decisions on their own. Many choose to go to college, but this means independence and meeting the world as much as it means studying. After school or college they have, in theory, a wide-open choice between career and marriage, or some combination of both. Perhaps this gives them an illusion of freedom which is not conceivable to their brothers, for whom a lifelong job is inevitable, or to women in many parts of the world for whom one role is more or less decreed. When American women do go to work, they don't have to think of this as a commitment for life, as long as they envisage the possibility of marriage. The job itself seems like a means to freedom because the wages provide independence from parents' authority and perhaps a place to live away from home. A job after marriage retains an element of free choice in it.

In all these stages there's always an escape hatch in the mind's eye.

When the first baby comes, the escape hatch seems to bang shut for an indefinite period. In motherhood there is no quitting. Vacations are not usually vacations at all. There is no salary. There are no promotions. The mothers with the most children have, on the average, the least time off, the fewest luxuries, the rarest distractions.

Of course American women aren't forced or abducted into marriage and child rearing. In fact, most of the unmarried girls spend a good deal of time dreaming about how to be rid of their freedom. And this isn't because grass always looks greener in the other pasture. Most basically it's because each of us who has grown up as a child, loved by a good mother and father, wants to become a loving mother or father more than anything else in the world. It's the desire to be like her mother that makes a baby girl want to learn to play pat-a-cake before a year, say words and eat with a spoon before she's two, play house and play with dolls every day until she's six or eight, then be a student for twelve or more years. It's the same almost irresistible force that leads her into the right marriage and the planning for children of her own. Otherwise there would be no real marriages and there would be no wish for children. What I mean is that there are no practical or selfish reasons for having a spouse or a child, as any confirmed bachelor or spinster can prove in five minutes.

But the fact that most of us would rather be married and have children than anything else in the world doesn't alter the fact that many women feel moments of panic and regret when the first child is on the way, and often again when each additional child comes.

From what I've read and seen in pictures about civilizations that are simpler than ours — in the South Seas or in Africa, for instance — the transition to motherhood does not seem to involve the renunciation that's involved in ours. In the first place, child care often begins at four or five years of age when a girl has a younger brother or sister entrusted to her care. She continues to be chiefly a mother's helper through the rest of childhood — caring for children, preparing food, making clothing, if any. There is no school or college to distract her from life as it is lived, or to offer tantalizing choices. (Similarly, boys and men stick to the same job — usually procuring food — from child-hood to old age.) This may sound a bit monotonous to us. But I doubt that learning to do things the adults do — which takes years in any civilization — is ever unexciting to children.

So the woman in a simple society does not have to change her activities or give up any cherished dreams when she marries and has a child. She does the same work that she did before, but in a much more satisfying way because it is her own baby she's taking care of, rather than her relatives', her own husband and children she's cooking and making clothing for.

Another aspect of the deprivation that many American women feel with the coming of children is the relative isolation from other adults for so many hours of the day. I remember the re-mark of a very busy young mother who said that she actually looked forward to a trip to market as if it were a gay social event.

This sense of isolation varies a great deal in individuals. Mothers who are able to identify with their young children, and see life through their eyes, find it fascinating even for long pe-riods. Women who have worked for a number of years and loved not only the job but the companionship of it often find children quite limited as company.

In the kinds of communities and in the climates most of us live in, a mother has to stay in her house a major part of the day because of the endless jobs she has to do there. And unless there is also a safe and satisfying back yard which she can survey while she works, she may feel that it's better to keep the young children indoors.

The woman who chafes at the monotony of child rearing (and I'm assuming that most mothers do at times) is really beset from two directions: the separation from adult companions, and being bottled up with the continual demands of the children. I don't think Nature ever intended the association to be quite so exclusive. During the evolution of our species I suspect that woman was designed with the expectation that she would have the company of adults as well as of children for most of the day.

In many simple societies the huts are not far apart or self-contained. They are huddled together and they are mainly for sleeping and storage. The walls and doorways are easy to talk through. Often the cooking is done outdoors, and the washing and weaving too. Pictures of villages show many women doing their job together in a central clearing, surrounded by swarms of children. Obviously in such an existence having children doesn't cut you off from social life, it makes you a full-fledged member of it.

When I listen to women who, despite genuine love for their children, confess a constant gnawing frustration in motherhood, I keep thinking of the ways in which some mothers do manage to find relief from these feelings of confinement and isolation.

Nursery school comes to mind first of all, but there are several limitations. There aren't enough good ones. They don't exist at all in many communities. They are too expensive for many parents. These obstacles have been lessened in some parts of the country by the development of cooperative nursery schools in which the mothers take turns assisting a trained teacher.

We should admit immediately that the pioneering nursery educators didn't conceive of these schools as a means of relieving oppressed mothers. They wanted to provide young children with ideal surroundings — that would make up for any limitations of space, equipment and companionship that they might have at home — so that they could mature optimally. They wanted to be able to help parents see the potentialities in children so that parents could do a good job at home. Nursery educators have hotly denied the criticism that nursery schools encourage mothers to shed responsibility. I agree with the teachers. The mothers I've known in good nursery schools were obviously making a sacrifice for their children's benefit and learning a lot themselves. There are probably a few mothers who think of a nursery school or a day nursery only as a place to drop a child off while they themselves do something more enjoyable, but they were that way before — they were never made that way by a good school. Besides, it's not a bad idea for a neglected child to be well cared for a few hours a day.

I think it's fine when a devoted yet frustrated mother enters her child in nursery school, not only for his sake, but also because she senses that she will be able to be a better mother to him if for a couple of hours each day he isn't under her heels.

When we lived in New York and our children were young, my wife, Jane, took them to Central Park every morning and afternoon, and so did thousands of other mothers, including those who consulted me as a pediatrician. They chose their apartments with the park in mind and walked half a mile if necessary. They combined fresh air and companionship for their children and social life for themselves. The idea was to find a spot where the children were the right age and the mothers were enjoyable, and there were plenty of spots to pick from. When we went to live in other places we realized how few good parks there were and how few mothers used them. Perhaps it's only apartment dwellers who appreciate a park. Perhaps householders who can see grass out their windows are satisfied to stay indoors.

When we lived in Rochester, Minnesota, after the war, many of the fellowship men in training at the Mayo Clinic, having been in the armed services, were already married and had children or were having them. Most of them lived in a temporary housing development known as the Prefabs. And though the young mothers complained of the cramped and inelegant quarters and the long hours their husbands had to work and study, I had the impression that the majority were able to make the best of the confinement of child care and their low budgets because everyone was in the same boat. They were all close neighbors, there was lots of visiting around and there was sharing of everything. Similar housing developments for young married students were put up in many universities, and I think that most couples who were part of them look back on this as a hectic but very satisfying time of their lives. They were like South Sea Island communities in several ways. The huts were packed in close. There was so little room inside it was natural to go out on every occasion. The earth between the huts was worn down by flocks of children. Often the laundry was done in one public place.

There must be better ways, though, to make it easy for mothers to get together, without having to leave their children behind and without neglecting their other chores. I keep wondering why none of the giant shopping centers that have mushroomed everywhere has included a large and glamorous Mothers and Children Club. There would be playgrounds outside and a number of playrooms inside for children of various ages and interests. There would be rooms or alcoves for block building and toy cars, for doll play, for coloring. When activities such as these are separated, children become more absorbed and quieter. There would be comfortable chairs for the mothers to sit in while they talked with one another and kept an eye on their children.

There would also be a room in charge of a nursery-school teacher where children who had learned to trust her could be left for an hour while mothers shopped, had beauty treatments or took part in organized activities of their own. For mothers who were interested there could be art classes, sewing classes, fashion shows. There could be special clubs which met weekly for the discussion of books or current events or child care. The possibilities are endless. The essentials are that mothers have a place to gather and enjoy one another frequently where their children would be welcome too. I picture certain activities occurring each week on the same schedule and each woman making it a habit to come on those hours of those days when she could expect to do the same thing with the same acquaintances. Then her children would see their same friends too.

I don't know whether the lack of such a club means that no

man who has developed a shopping center has thought of it, or whether he'd doubt that the increased popularity of the center would pay for these facilities. Maybe the mothers would pay dues or fees.

I think all churches should be interested in providing meeting places for mothers and children, from Monday to Saturday. There could be swings and slides and sandboxes in the yard, with chairs for the mothers. In the church house or church basement could be rooms or alcoves for children's play. If there were enough funds or interest to engage a nursery-school teacher, she and a few of the mothers in rotation could supervise the play while the rest of the mothers carried on recreational or cultural or religious activities in scheduled groups. I realize that some churches have organized regular nursery schools, and these are fine for the parents who can afford to pay for everyday nursery-school care. But I am thinking now of a system which could provide supervision for many children and sociable activities for many mothers.

I don't know what would be the best answer. There are probably a number of solutions. Anyway, I refuse to believe that we can't find ways to give mothers the companionship and fun and stimulation which women in more primitive societies get without the asking.

II
Everyday Management

❦❦❦❦❦❦❦

GOOD MANNERS

Parents shouldn't be afraid to teach them.

A WOMAN who had apparently been reading the first edition of *Baby and Child Care* once wrote me as follows:

Why do you belittle good manners? I couldn't disagree with you more. All around I see children who can only be described as rude brats. Their parents don't seem to mind being insulted and abused. I think it's unfair to children to bring them up without a sense of consideration for others and a knowledge of what's considered polite behavior.

The letter writer didn't identify herself or the children. I pictured her as a grandmother chronically irritated by her grandchildren. I could imagine that every time she made the slightest complaint to the mother, the latter would quote my book at her. I guiltily looked up the section on manners and saw that it began with the sentence, "Teaching a child to say 'How d'do' or 'Thank you' is really the least important step." And the conclusion read, "It isn't wrong to tell a child how to be polite. I only mean that friendly feelings come first, that good manners then come naturally, and that pushing party politeness too early and too hard works in the wrong direction."

I agree that those sentences sound pretty negative (even though there are a couple of positive paragraphs in between), especially to a person who is indignant and looking for the culprit.

Actually I feel the same way as the letter writer about most of the points she made. I can hardly bear to be around rude children. I have the impulse to spank them, and to give a lecture to their parents. I think their parents are doing them a disservice. Considerate individuals get farther in the world — in making friends, in winning husbands and wives, in finding and holding jobs. They make life pleasant for everyone around them, and they bring out the pleasantness in others. And each individual has to learn most of his manners from his parents.

I'm sure that practically all of you would agree to these points too. But all this agreement is too easy to be worth much. We'll all differ when it comes to the questions: What kind of good manners? How far carried? At what ages? By what methods?

Styles in manners are so very different at different periods. In the Victorian age, well brought-up children at the family dinner table were expected to be seen but not often heard. I wouldn't have argued with the Victorians if that's what they thought best, and I doubt if that kind of silence, in a family that was basically kind, would have hurt the child. Nowadays most of us parents *want* to hear our children's conversation when it's agreeable and as long as there's enough chance for us to speak too. Much of the conversation of friendly children is fresher and more colorful than adult conversation, which sometimes has a tendency to run to complaints, weather and clichés.

When I was in college in my own home town and my friends and I brought girls to our house at prom time and football games, my mother was disappointed by the way we called each other by first names right after introduction. She said that in her day young men and women called each other Mister and Miss until they had known each other for a long time. She said it was a big moment and a romantic milestone, which we were all missing, when a man said earnestly to a girl, "Miss Jenkins, may I call you Marian?" I could see the point, but I couldn't follow the example.

A couple of generations back it was not permissible for women to work on their make-up in public, but they have broken through that barrier all right.

Manners are quite different, not only in different parts of the world but even in different parts of our own country. Many properly brought up Europeans are shocked at the informality, breeziness, forwardness of American children, even the ones that you and I would consider well behaved. (Americans, in turn, complain of the table manners of some well-bred Europeans: noisy eating, for instance, or stacking food high on the back of the fork by means of the knife.) In some elegant circles in eastern American cities little girls are taught to curtsy when in troduced to their parents' friends. This is considered desirable, as a matter of course, by everybody concerned, and I'm sure it doesn't upset the girls. But it would look mighty strange to most people from other parts of the country. In some places and groups it's perfectly all right for a young man to comb his hair or use a nail file in public, but in others such behavior would be considered as shocking as an illegal act. And think of the different attitudes about toothpicks.

Sometimes when we are complaining of the manners of another adult or child we really mean we just don't like that person. We pick on a manner of his which wouldn't bother us at all in someone we enjoyed. I know that when I feel antagonistic toward someone I'm apt to be particularly irritated by any mouth noises he makes while eating. So I doubt whether anyone can make a catalogue of good manners which would exactly suit many other people. I think we have to come back to the spirit behind a child's manners and the relationship between him and other people.

I sometimes think that human beings at three months of age are the friendliest they will ever be. They smile delightedly in response to a greeting from any other human being, whether he is young or old, irritating or charming, parent or stranger, ugly or handsome. In fact, Dr. René Spitz, a psychiatrist who studied smiling in infants, found that they grinned at him and squirmed with pleasure even when he was wearing a horrible Halloween mask. To me this is one of the clear indications that people are born with a preference to love rather than to hate — they have to be taught to hate.

At five or six months some babies become uneasy when strangers come too close. Most one-year-olds will instantly turn crying to their mothers if an outsider (such as a doctor) tries to touch them, and they'll back away from any unfamiliar adult who tries to start a conversation too quickly. Much of this timidity and bashfulness continues past two years of age, and some of it past three. But underneath there is still the basic human friendliness. The one-year-old who has yelled bloody murder during his physical examination may, ten minutes later, come over and put his hand on the doctor's knee, or sweetly hand him a toy and then take it back. This latter trick may look like Indian giving, but it's really an expression of generous companionableness at this age. Two-year-olds show their friendliness sooner than one-year-olds, and three-year-olds quicker still. Some four-year-olds are bolder than grownups.

When I suggest that parents not push party manners at two and three it's only because I think you make a small child self-conscious and leery of strangers by forcing him to say "How d'do" or give his name and age, right after being introduced. You're reducing instead of developing his enjoyment of people. This is the age to let him take time to get acquainted in his own way.

At three and four and five years, children from reasonably happy families are almost as outgoing and affectionate as three-month-olds. They love children and adults who give them half a chance. They make friends quickly. More important still is their intense imitativeness of anyone they admire. They strive mightily to acquire the same table manners, tone of voice, vocabulary, hobbies as their parents and other grownups of whom they're fond. Even more fundamentally, each one is forming attitudes that will, to some extent, persist for the rest of his life. The tenderness he will feel for those of the opposite sex, the proportions of enjoyment and rivalry he will feel about those of his own sex, his basic feelings about himself and his place in the world, are mainly based on the parents' example. In such respects these are the most formative years of all. And manners are definitely included — surface manners in the sense of how the parents handle the silverware and the English language, basic manners in the sense of how the parents feel toward each other, toward outsiders and toward the child.

In this sense, the parents are teaching their young children manners all day long without necessarily mentioning them or even noticing them. And in this sense they can't really teach their children anything that they themselves aren't feeling.

So far I've been stressing these points about the child's readiness and the parents' example so earnestly that I make it sound as if there were no place for the explicit teaching of good manners. This I don't mean. It's only that first things have to come first.

Children *do* need to be guided and reminded and corrected — no matter how well disposed they are — and that's the parents' job too.

In the first place, young children have to be gently reminded that they themselves are part of a social situation. Most of them are completely absorbed in the impressions they are taking in and quite oblivious that they themselves are making any impression at all, good or bad. A couple of strange two-year-olds will stand one foot apart just gazing at each other intently, silently, with no social (or antisocial) expression at all. They gradually become more self-conscious. But at four, six, even at eight, they'll sometimes gawk with slightly open mouth at someone the mother is greeting, until she nudges and reminds them of their greeting too. How soon the teaching is to begin depends on how early the child gets over his shyness — which varies a lot.

How much to teach depends, of course, on how formal the parents are, and want their child to be. A casual parent may be satisfied if the child will grin agreeably. A more particular one wants some conventional words of greeting and a handshake.

I think this is the parents' right. A parent has to be satisfied with his child's behavior or he will take it out on the child in some other way which might be worse.

But even if the parent is quite particular, I think he should still be tactful and avoid shaming the child in the presence of the stranger. For a parent who is socially self-conscious, this is difficult to do. The immediate impulse when embarrassed by a child's discourtesy is to hiss at him fiercely right on the spot — to show the stranger that at least the parent knows better — which doesn't improve the child's feelings about politeness.

Another effort worth making is to avoid, if possible, interrupting or reproving a young child who, from a genuine feeling of friendliness, is spilling the beans, for instance, about some private family business. For a child to want to share interesting matters with others is the soul of good manners, and it shouldn't be turned into embarrassment unless the consequences would be really serious.

So far we have been pretending that the woman who wrote the letter was merely pressing me about whether I believed in manners, and I have been protesting that I do. But suppose that she has been infuriated by some really rude children and that the mother has defended the children and herself by saying that it's no longer considered necessary or wise to insist on politeness.

Though a majority of the children I see have manners that are plenty good enough for me, I'll admit that there are some obnoxious ones around — they usually seem more numerous than they are — and that some of them belong not to neglectful, rude parents but to devoted, well-bred parents. I am thinking (in the milder categories) of children who come late to meals and leave early without permission or apology, who mess up their food at the table on purpose, who regularly interrupt the parents' conversations and ignore their requests, who brush by visitors as if they didn't exist, who make demands in imperious tones.

In the more serious categories are children who regularly talk back to their parents and others, call them names like "dope" and "stupid," or defy them.

When the parents are unloving, rude, hostile people, the explanation for the children's behavior is obvious. When the parents are devoted to their children and considerate of other people, you have to search harder for reasons. Certainly one factor is the exaggerated "self-expression, no repression" idea which has been bobbing around for half a century now. I don't think that any well-trained, experienced professional leader in any of the children's fields has ever advocated full self-expression or total lack of repression. However, many new concepts of child rearing have been propounded in the twentieth century and they have certainly mixed up some parents. They are discussed more fully on pages 282–291 ("Overpermissiveness — An American Phenomenon").

A basic mistake is confusing harshness with firm guidance. It is true that chronic parental antagonism is hard on children and makes them, when they grow up, either harsh with their own children or excessively permissive. But firm guidance that springs from devotion is not only good for children, they love it.

All children are uneasy about their own lawless impulses (the rude child is always an anxious, unhappy child) and it comforts them when they know they have parents who will help them keep these under control.

I have been trying to explain that though all children need parental teaching about manners, this goes fairly easily in families where the parents are reasonably happy, agreeable people (no parents are happy or agreeable all the time) because then the children feel friendly toward people, too, and want to be like their parents. In those families where the parents are polite and the children are rude, it's not so much the lack of teaching but the fact that the parents' own feelings are out of kilter — they are, without realizing it, inviting their children to be rude.

But in the end we must admit again that style is playing its part. We have been going through a half century in which the trend has been progressively to throw off stiff forms and rely on the good intentions underneath. In writing that section of *Baby and Child Care* in the mid-1940's, I was conforming to that trend. My own hunch is that after having pushed casualness as far as we can we are due for a reaction — as happens so regularly in human affairs — and that good manners will come to be almost universally admired and taught again. I do hope so.

HELPFULNESS AND
HOUSEHOLD DUTIES

*It isn't the number of jobs but the sense of
obligation that's important.*

THERE ARE lots of differences of opinion about family chores —
between parents and their children and also between different
parents. A great majority believe in the principle that children
should have duties. But some of these parents find that they can
do the jobs so much more efficiently themselves or that they become so irritated in trying to make their children perform them
that they give up the attempt. A few parents say, "I don't want
my children to have to work all the time as I did," or, "They're
only young once. Let 'em have a good time while they can."
Then there are the questions of what jobs are appropriate, at what
ages, and whether or not they should be paid for, by allowance
or other methods.

I disagree with the parents who believe, as a matter of principle, that children should be spared all duties at home, especially if they are the kind who don't ask their children for
considerateness or politeness either. This parental attitude tends,
to a greater or lesser degree, to create children who are unattractive, self-centered, demanding — in the neighborhood and in
school as well as in the family. It develops adults who in their
jobs and in their marriages expect to be pleased and favored.
They have little awareness of what needs doing, whether on a
picnic or in the office. When their marriages begin to come
apart at the seams they only see the faults of their spouses.
When they lose their jobs they blame the boss.

I think it's almost as much a mistake to excuse children from work because the parents can do it more quickly or expertly by themselves. Every teacher in nursery school and elementary school has learned that children will develop an increasing sense of responsibility from helping her and the class; and they won't if they don't. So she asks for this assistance even if it slows other work down. Parents should be just as concerned about character building — really more so.

But I don't want to make it sound as though a child has to perform any certain number of hours of work to have a good character. What counts, of course, is the spirit in which the parent asks for his cooperation and the feeling of the child as he does his share. When parents love a child in a balanced wholesome way they not only enjoy him and want him to have the good things of life, they know that he won't be happy in the long run unless he learns to serve others. They won't feel that they have done right by him or the world unless they have taught him a sense of obligation.

What are considered appropriate obligations for children to assume will vary enormously depending on family circumstances and traditions. In a well-to-do family with high academic standards and with a servant who takes care of most of the housework, an adolescent daughter who has a great deal of homework may be doing her part if she gets school grades in accord with her ability and keeps her room in order. But in a family in which there is little or no outside help a girl of the same age might be expected to share some of the dishwashing, cleaning, bedmaking with her mother, especially on weekends. A teen-age boy should take over at least half of the car washing, yard and cellar work from his father. Even at six or eight he should be expected to help a little. In one family it's considered quite proper for the boys to make their own beds and to do their share of the dishes. In another family it would give everyone goose flesh, including the females, if the boys were to do "women's work," but there would be plenty of masculine chores to go around.

You can get a pretty good idea of what jobs a child can do at different ages by just watching thoughtfully. Even a three-year-old can put the napkins on the table for meals. He can bring a diaper to his mother when she is changing the baby. It's good for him to help his mother put away his toys at the end of the day. But it's unrealistic to expect a three- or four-year old to be able to pick up a whole afternoon's mess all by himself. He probably doesn't have that much sense of order. He certainly doesn't have enough persistence. A ten- or twelve-year-old boy should be able to do an hour's mowing or leaf raking or snow shoveling all by himself. It would be overoptimistic in most cases, though, to expect him to remember the job regularly each week without a tactful reminder.

If you are in doubt about the wisdom of insisting on a certain job, either because you haven't had enough children to be sure or are too irritated, by a child's failure, to trust your own judgment, it's a good idea to sound out the teacher or some neighbors on their experiences with children this age. If it seems that you're all wrong in your expectations, it's better to know it. If they agree that you're right, it's a great comfort and gives you a conviction that will help to get the job done.

Should all duties be paid for, by allowance or other fees? I think different families vary a lot in how much they link money to jobs. It depends partly on such things as how much the parents can afford, customs in the neighborhood, whether the parents want to encourage the children to earn extra money, and whether the chores get done without any inducement.

There's no doubt that the knowledge that you won't get paid unless a job has been done is an efficient regulator for adults as well as children. It avoids a lot of prodding and argument. I think almost everyone will agree that a child shouldn't be allowed to demand payment for *everything* he does. If you ask your son to pick up the used tissues and other trash that motorists have thrown onto your lawn (they do it to my lawn almost every day and it always makes me mad) and he, in a money-making mood, says "How much do I get?", I think you're entitled to answer that all of us do some things for the family that we don't get paid for. I feel that all children should have duties and that all children need a little spending money but that it's not an important issue whether these two matters are linked together.

The real meat of this discussion is: What makes children unwilling or willing to be helpful around the house? The largest factor in a child's balkiness is his feeling that the job is basically unpleasant and oppressive. This feeling usually does not come from the nature of the chore itself, since under different circumstances he may be positively enthusiastic about doing the same thing (when visiting another family, for instance!).

In most cases the cause is the tone of voice of the parent when assigning the job or giving a reminder. Goodness knows there will be plenty of reasons why a mother will be irritable when asking her daughter to stop her play and clean up. There's the mess and perhaps some damage. There may have been a lot of squabbling between the kids all afternoon, or there's too little time before supper, or it may be simply that the car or the television set has broken down again. But most often it seems that we parents easily fall into a kill-joy tone when assigning a duty. If I'm right about this, I think it's an attitude left over from our own childhoods. One of the commonest and most frustrating aspects of human nature is that what our parents did to us in childhood that made us cross we have a way of doing to our own children in turn — even though we disapprove of it. If we resented the way our chores were assigned us in childhood, that irritable feeling is apt to creep into our directions to our children.

But there are more cheerful aspects to all of this. The first is, though it's hard to remember, that children want — more than anything else — to be grown up and do the grown-up thing, especially the things that their parents do. They not only want to do the glamorous things like drive cars and have babies, they want to do housework and mend the plumbing. You can hardly keep a two-year-old from sweeping, or a three-year-old from making a cake when you do. A father has to push his young son away from the workbench when it's necessary for safety or efficiency.

Furthermore, children positively *love* to be helpful if their efforts have generally been appreciated. They feel particularly proud of themselves when they take the initiative in doing a job. Another favorable factor is that children, like adults, get tremendous satisfaction from bringing the job itself to completion — the joy of workmanship.

One problem we have to keep in mind is the discrepancy between the motives of a parent and of a child in regard to household jobs. Having the lawn look good, the house clean, the dishes promptly washed and put away are distinctly adult concerns, because adults like orderliness, want to make a respectable impression on neighbors and visitors and have pride in their home. None of these means a thing to children. They like to set tables, do dishes, wash cars because they want to be like and want to help their parents. (By ten or twelve the need of money becomes powerful too.)

Therefore, to keep them at such duties parents not only have to be reasonably agreeable about them, but should try to continue to perform them *alongside* their children as much as possible. You may be able to turn such duties over to children as they get older and more responsible, but if you try it too soon most of the enthusiasm goes out of the occupation. Of course even for grownups such chores will be not only less boring but positively enjoyable when done in company. Even a two- or three-year-old will have fun putting toys away if the mother is doing it too, and making a game of it. And dishwashing in some families is the most harmonious time of the day.

What this all adds up to is that children contain within themselves the seeds of all the motives that are needed for cooperativeness. The seeds are sprouting well by two and three years.

The hard job for the parents is to cultivate them patiently for the following fifteen years. This is mainly accomplished by setting an example, by asking confidently for the kinds and amounts of helpfulness that are within the child's growing capacity, by showing appreciation as one would to an adult. But positive programs break down at times in the best of families. Then parents have to fall back on firmness — not cross reproaches that the job has not been done but calm insistence that it be done.

PLAYTHINGS

The best are the ones he can make
himself or use in his own way.

THE MOST IMPORTANT general truth about toys is that children love to use them creatively. They aren't satisfied for long merely to obey directions and to use them as the inventor and the manufacturer intended. They want to follow their own personal interests, express their own feelings, create their own dramatic situations, make their own inventions. The more a toy is limited by its nature to one particular activity, the sooner it palls. The less specific it is, the more it stimulates a child's imagination. This is why I feel that, for most young boys and for some young girls, blocks are the most absorbing and stimulating plaything of all. My sons had a large chestful of them which they began using at the age of one and played with frequently until twelve or so. They made Empire State Buildings, garages and ramps for cars, bridges and tunnels for trains, corrals for farm animals, forts for soldiers, whole cities for pretend people. All nursery schools have hundreds of blocks and consider them basic equipment.

The most satisfactory blocks are the relatively large wooden ones which come in a set in a variety of related shapes. The shape which has most uses for building is 5½ x 2¾ x 1⅜ inches, but there are others which are only half as wide (for pillars), or half as long (squares), or twice as long (for planks), or cut diagonally (for ramps), and so on. The original cost may seem high, especially for hardwood blocks that do not splinter. But blocks never break or wear out or disappear or lose their fascination. So the ultimate expense is small. A handy father may be able to save some of the cost by sawing and sanding the blocks himself.

For boys of all ages, cars and trucks and buses and trains have a fundamental and lasting appeal, partly because they are symbols of masculinity, and also because of the variety of ways and levels in which they can be used. Two-year-olds push them clumsily along the floor. Six-year-olds build road and track systems. Twelve-year-olds create elaborate, realistic layouts. Sixteen-year-olds build their own railway cars and model automobiles.

When I was a boy, toy trains were large and expensive and I was never lucky enough to own any. But whenever I had the invitation, I helped a friend play with his. As soon as I had a son out of diapers, I began buying trains for him — first the wind-up kind, later beautiful replicas of real locomotives, freight cars and passenger cars, in HO gauge. In my enthusiasm, I was always years ahead of him, suggesting arrangements that were too complicated, interfering, taking over. Needless to say, he got little pleasure from them and no benefit. I saw eventually that I had gone at it all wrong, but this realization didn't keep me from making exactly the same mistakes with my second son. A child, in order to enjoy play and to mature from it, must be permitted to take the initiative himself and to follow his own imagination. It's all right for parents to be assistants when asked. But it's almost impossible for some of us to accept this subordinate role, at least in certain activities.

After the age of eight or ten, some boys — not all — become fascinated with building model cars, planes, trains, boats. This kind of activity develops not only manual skill, interest in mechanics, sense of history, but also basic creativity. I always loved model building and so did my sons. It's a great temptation to make a gift of a model kit to a boy who is known to be an enthusiast, and the kits are relatively inexpensive compared to the beauty of the finished product. But I've noticed that the kits given as presents are much less likely to be completed than those which the boy has chosen and bought himself. So I'd give money to buy kits, not give kits.

Woodworking tools appropriate to a child's skill and discretion make wonderful presents but are too seldom thought of by adults. The cheap, flimsy hammer and saw sets sold for small children are a fraud because even a skilled adult can't accomplish anything with them. A hammer has got to have enough weight to drive a nail, and a saw has to be sharp and of moderately good size to cut wood. So buy adult tools. Lots of mothers worry that all tools are too dangerous for young children. Some tools are, including power tools. But hammers and saws cause only minor injuries when used with a little supervision, and I've seen four- and five-year-olds building happily and productively in nursery school. At a slightly older age children can make use of a screwdriver, a plane, a square to mark a right angle, clamps to hold glued work together until dry. Mothers and unhandy fathers need to be reminded that sawing and many other woodworking operations can only be carried out when the wood is held in a good-sized vise, attached to a workbench that is solidly built so that it doesn't move or sway. Workbenches can be bought or built.

Building sets made of wood consisting of round sticks (like lollipop sticks) that plug into the rims or centers of wheel-shaped pieces will keep children between three and eight busy for hours creating carts, windmills and endless other structures. For boys six and older there are absorbing construction sets consisting of metal girders to be bolted together, axles, wheels, pulleys.

In fairness, I ought to turn for a while to girls' playthings. The overwhelming favorites throughout the world are dolls, dolls' clothes and equipment, housekeeping equipment. Baby dolls nowadays not only close their eyes and cry but drink and wet. (I've even been consulted by an inventor about the idea of a mother doll who would give birth to a baby doll and then nurse it!) Modern girls become inflamed with the desire to own the latest type, in order to be in the swim, but these fancy attributes are not what give long-range satisfaction. That comes from the infinite variety of imaginative care-taking activities which are possible: dressing and undressing, changing diapers, bathing, grooming, perambulating, feeding, putting to bed. With dolls of older years, the child can play out a thousand dramas of parent-child relationships, friendships, school life, adventure, romance, domestic existence. Since dressing and undressing are so appealing, I applaud the manufacturers who have put out a wide variety of modish costumes of standard size to fit a standard doll. Then there are dolls' cribs, buggies, bureaus, china and cutlery. Child-sized stoves, refrigerators, dining tables, laundry equipment are exciting to own; but a child can get nearly as much long-term joy from cardboard cartons serving as imitations of these.

Needlework sets, hand looms, bead-stringing sets are splendid for girls who have shown enthusiasm for such work. They are entirely uninteresting to others.

All children of both sexes crave a tricycle or bicycle. This is as basic as the car for adults. Almost as important are an express wagon and roller skates.

About table games I have contradictory impressions. There are certain old standbys like checkers and Parchesi and Monopoly which begin to challenge competitive children by the age of eight or ten, at least on rainy days, especially if there are older brothers and sisters or parents who enjoy a contest. On the other hand, every year there appear on the market at Christmas time elaborate new scoring games which are based on football or war or geography or history. They are equipped with dice or spinning dials or flashing lights or buzzers. They look exciting in the store. But as far as my own family's experience goes, they get played with once for fifteen minutes and then are put away on the closet shelf forever. What's the matter with them? One trouble often is that the rules are too complex and time-consuming to learn, except for game fiends. Perhaps another handicap is the demand, which such a narrowly specific game makes, that everyone must immerse himself completely in the atmosphere of football or history whether it is appealing to him or not.

I have a similar skepticism about newly invented indoor games of skill — target games, for instance. They soon go to the closet. The exceptions I've seen have been darts and ping-pong. These games have proved and built their popularity over the years. So there is a chance that older members of the family will want to participate, and this is what stirs and holds the competitive interest of the younger members.

While I'm in a critical mood, I'll mention all the tricky toys that will do one remarkable thing, such as a propeller wheel that spins high in the air or a plane that flies or a rocket that shoots. They are thrilling for an hour or two. Then they usually get lost or broken. If not, they soon lose their appeal for the same reason that certain other toys pall: there's only one thing you can do with them. This is entirely different from the situation of the dexterous adolescent who spends dozens and dozens of hours making a plane which will fly with an elastic or gasoline engine. If it fails to function or breaks, he spends dozens of more hours remaking it. The apparent climax of all the activity is the actual flying. But the true satisfaction is in the construction. This would be demonstrated if the same boy were given a factory-made plane ready for flying. It would soon become boring unless he could invent new ways to fly it or decided to try to make improvements in its design.

I have one strong indignation to express. It is against television and radio hucksters who have recently been taking advantage of the trusting nature of children by misrepresenting toys and describing them in such glowing terms that children are in a frenzy to own them. The most effective way for a parent to prevent a repetition of such a fraud is to write an indignant note to the local station itself, with copies to the Better Business Bureau in town and the Federal Communications Commission in

Washington. It doesn't take many complaints to impress a responsible station official.

How do you deal with a child who insists on a toy which you feel is beyond your means or which you believe the child will find disappointing? I don't think a parent should ever let himself be bullied or nagged into giving a present which is unreasonable. All he has to do is say firmly that it is too expensive and quietly stick to his guns. (To vacillate is to surrender; and to become cross at the child is to betray uncertainty about whether one is entitled to deny the present.) But if my child or adolescent wanted to buy with his own money a possession which I felt was likely to prove unsatisfactory, I'd be inclined, after advising him, to let him go ahead, as long as it was not a dangerous possession. The only way he will learn to balance craving with caution is by a few bitter experiences at his own expense.

What about toys of mock violence — pistols and machine guns and daggers? In earlier years, when I had learned how natural and wholesome it is for even the best of boys to express their aggressiveness in play form — as soldiers and cowboys and robbers — I used to emphasize only this side of the picture to idealistic parents who were inclined to forbid such possessions and games. More recently, bothered by the extremes of violence to which television, movies and comics have gone, made uneasy by certain parents who have interpreted modern concepts of child psychology to mean that almost no limits should be set on children's expression of aggression, I've tried to present both sides of the issue. I believe that children, especially young children, should be surrounded by predominantly constructive, civilizing, loving, respect-creating influences. Parents should set an example, correct and guide their children's behavior in no uncertain terms, select stories, programs and playthings that conform to the parents' ideals. Naturally these will be different in every family. I myself would allow a small son to have a toy pistol or two, and to play cowboy or soldier or robber. But I would worry if he wanted to play nothing else, and I would certainly interfere if I saw him threatening to hurt another child or being mean in any way.

Back-yard play equipment is not only good for children's bodies and souls but fosters neighborhood sociability and aids a mother's supervision. For young children there is the old-fashioned platform swing with two seats facing each other, the jungle gym which will keep a crowd imaginatively and acrobatically busy for hours, the sandbox which is as endlessly fascinating as blocks, the rope swing. (A swing for small children can sometimes be hung indoors, too, in a doorway, for instance.) For older boys add a basketball basket at the correct height above the driveway. Badminton makes a fairly successful activity for both sexes and is relatively inexpensive.

I've neglected babies and one- to two-year-olds. The biggest development in playthings for infants, before they can sit up, has been the use of bright-colored birds and other mobiles that dangle and sometimes jingle. Babies watch them with delight for hours. There are also rings and bars which can be progressively watched, reached for, batted at and finally handled at will. Then there are the old favorites: rattles, teething objects, strings of giant beads, woolly animals. Floating toys are important at bath time.

With the age of walking come the push-and-pull toys (cartons are as satisfying as the store-bought types), xylophones, hammer-and-peg sets, rings that go on a peg, cloth or cardboard picture books. This is the age when the most fun is putting one thing in another, so kitchen utensils and cardboard cartons are as fascinating as the most expensive toy. The first two or three years are the age of rhythm. A jouncing chair is very satisfying from the age of six months, and a jouncing horse from one year on. My daughter-in-law took advantage of the one-year-old joy of climbing by building a small platform, with steps and railing, just the right height for a mother to change a climber's clothes without breaking her back.

I'll never be able to complete this list of playthings. But I do want at least to mention a few other activities that have long proved their popularity and creative potential. Collections of stamps, of rocks, of butterflies are engrossing to many children after the age of seven or eight. I've observed in a number of families, though, that the idea must start in the child's own head. And most of the building of the collection must be by the child's own efforts. Nothing kills the collecting craze faster than for a child to be given a large collection already made by somebody else.

There have been painting and crayoning sets since the time of the cavemen. Poster paints in jars (and large sheets of paper on an easel) have been found, in nursery schools, to be much more inviting for young children than the hard little pellets of paint that give up their colors so reluctantly. A stack of sheets of paper of many different colors, a pair of scissors and a pot of rubber cement open up endless possibilities for designs, pictures, greeting cards, chains, paper dolls, houses, farms, theatrical scenery. I wish I were a child again.

TRAVELING WITH SMALL CHILDREN

Foresight saves pain and trouble.

IN AN EARLIER volume (*Dr. Spock Talks with Mothers*), I quoted a letter by Helen Thomas Irwin which was full of ingenious suggestions for handling a convalescent child. This imaginative mother also has good advice on the subject of traveling with a small child. You'll enjoy reading her letter to me as she wrote it:

My husband is a musician. I am, too, but retired from "active duty" to work at being a mother. We have traveled with our boy since he was seven weeks old until now, when we are temporarily settled in Chicago and he is five and a half years old.

We were nervous parents, the baby having arrived late in our lives, and we being used to *quite* another type of life and hours. I had a choice to make. I could remain in New York with the baby and let my husband travel alone, or I could gather up my wee son and go too. I chose the latter. Naturally, as a woman musician, I had traveled a great deal, and I knew how to do it and how to stay well and happy in the process. But, you know, traveling with a harp is one thing. It is *quite* another with a child. I had much to learn "the hard way," of course, but so far we have succeeded and are all intact, very adaptable people, and all well.

So many people now travel with children. Any airport, any train station is full of mothers and wee ones who would not have dared risk it a few years ago. On many trips I have seen fantastic things happen which could have been prevented with a little advice. For instance, mothers making a forty-eight-hour trip with two bottles in their kit. Both get broken — and the baby has to starve. This has happened so often! I know a dining-car steward who could not stand any more babies crying with hunger and frantic mothers trying to push scrambled eggs down children who had never had solid food. He now carries a nipple which will fit over a pop bottle and he can have the chef make that sterile.

No matter how hot it is when you board a train or plane, a sweater and a pair of long pants will be handy. It can get cold as ice in the air conditioning. You carry drinking water, which is bottled spring water, available at any drugstore (almost), and in each city you buy that same water. A child cannot adjust to constantly changing water. Loose bowels and illness result. (Even "old troupers" of adults buy bottled water and don't keep changing.) You carry enough nursing bottles that if an accident happens, you have a spare or two. You also carry a small jar of prune juice, or prune mash; travel often brings constipation to the child who has never been away. Prunes will produce a normal movement. Laxatives won't.

You also always carry food. Fruit, crackers, sandwiches or something that you could feed a child if the diner is full, or if you are on a plane that doesn't serve lunch, even though it is lunchtime for the children. (Planes don't figure the time it takes to get to the airport, and how hungry a little child can get.) A vacuum bottle of milk, hard-boiled eggs, bananas and cheese (if the child does not have a tendency to constipation) are easy to carry, and often make the difference between a good trip and a miserable one. Very often, planes do not have any milk on board, but they do not object to your carrying a bag of food.

On a long trip, a new little toy, hidden away, can be a wonderful surprise when the child begins to get tired and restless. Or a new storybook. (Better, really, to have a picture book, since it is often hard to read to a child on a plane because of noise.) A new pencil and a tiny pad of paper will keep a little child of under five happy quite a long time.

The most important thing to carry is a box of salted crackers. They can do wonders for a stomach that is beginning to get airsick or trainsick. It is an old remedy for pregnant women, and it certainly works for children. Ah, the salted crackers that I've passed around in these five years. Take a large box of cleansing tissues, too.

One of the greatest boons to the traveling mother is the plastic tablecloth, large size, purchased at any dime store. You buy the thin, transparent kind, which takes little space. It is best to have two. One goes over the mattress of the hotel bed (or the bed of the relatives you are visiting) in the case of the child still small enough to wet the bed. This piece of plastic can also be handed to the Pullman porter to protect the mattress on the berth of the train. (He doesn't care for wet mattresses, either, and *there* is a man to have on "your side" and *keep* on your side throughout any trip.) The thin, plastic tablecloth is much easier to carry than the old rubber pad.

The other tablecloth is laid over the carpet whenever the child plays in the living room (or any other room, for that matter). It is especially valuable in the case of water colors or crayon work, or clay. It keeps him clean (from what may well be a filthy carpet) and keeps the carpet from spots which may anger a hotel manager. It is cheap to buy — priceless as a "nerve-rester" for mothers.

We always go to apartment hotels, and I suppose most people traveling with children do that too. It is better to clean a kitchen or kitchenette than have your child get sick in a strange restaurant or refuse to eat in the midst of such excitement. In these apartment hotels, for a secret reason known *only* to managers of hotels, the space underneath the table and chairs for eating purposes is *carpeted*. That's where you use the second piece of plastic tablecloth *again*. You put it under his chair. Thus any spilled egg is neatly disposed of by merely washing off the plastic.

A lot of hotel managers are allergic to small children. I don't know that I can blame them. Therefore, when a mother makes a hotel reservation, she must state that she is bringing a child or children. It is better to be refused admittance beforehand than to reach your destination in the middle of the night, only to be presented with a small sign saying "No dogs or children allowed."

As for the "food sack" which simply *must* be carried these days on any kind of trip (I take an inexpensive bag used by many people for carrying bowling balls), I forgot to tell you that I also add a small supply of lollipops. I am *not* a believer in candy for children, but on trips I always have a supply of lollipops. They take a long time to eat . . . and are frequently "just the thing" not only for *your* child, but for the children of fellow passengers. Naturally you ask a mother's permission. Heaven knows, it is a terrible experience to make a long trip with somebody's child crying most of the way.

The last thing I have to suggest applies only to mothers who must do extensive traveling with children. I bought a very small suitcase for Dean to carry himself. There are round cardboard ones in the dime store which cost a dollar, and better ones, the size of a small lunch box, in drugstores. This suitcase he packed himself before every trip. The contents changed as he grew older. When we began, at the age of two and one-half, with the suitcase, it was full of animal crackers, a package of raisins, "fuff-fuffs" (bits of yarn he held while sucking his thumb and going to sleep) and a lollipop. As he has grown older, he fills the case with small cars, strings of beads, old keys, small containers of pennies, small memo pads, pencils and crayons. He packs this bag (it measures about 8" x 6") himself, and he is in charge of it. It is placed under his seat, and when he gets tired of looking out the window, he can open his "private suitcase" and play with the things. This is a good idea for mothers who have a lot of trips to make. The child, beginning at about two and one-half, knows better than you do what he'd like to play with on the trip. Only the suitcase has to be kept small enough that he can carry it.

Oh — one more *important* thing! When you get to a new place, hotel or otherwise, even if it is late, let the child explore it completely. They are like cats in this respect! If you put them right to bed before they get a chance to look the place over, they wake up in the night and decide to see it. We learned *this* the hard way! Sometimes we thought Dean was too tired to be allowed to explore the new apartment hotel. He went right to sleep, and we did, too, since my husband faced the training of a whole new orchestra the following day. But those times that we did not allow Dean to explore the new place, he woke up at about 1.30 A.M. and decided to see where he was. Nothing could get him to sleep again until he had seen every inch of it. We *learned* to let him do the exploring before we put him to bed.

This letter covers so much of the ground about traveling with a small child that I need only to fill in with a few points about babies and the special problems of automobile travel.

With infants, the biggest problem is formula. If you'll be traveling only one day you can prepare the bottles as usual, chill them in the refrigerator, then put them in the sterilizing pail and pack it full of chunks and pieces of ice. Wrap the sides and bottom of the pail and line the inside of the cover with ten layers of newspaper, which is a good insulator. If you have a picnic icebox or ice bucket, you can pack the bottles in ice in that.

If you are going on a train that has a diner and don't want to carry a large iced pail, put the sterilized formula into a sterilized quart bottle and ask the porter to put it in the refrigerator in the diner. At each feeding pour the required amount into the nursing bottle. Afterward, wash the bottle and nipple thoroughly with hot water, soap and bottle brush and it will be reasonably clean for the next feeding.

For a trip of only a few hours, one or two nursing bottles of formula, well chilled, can be wrapped individually in ten layers of newspaper, without ice.

For a trip of more than one day I think it is easiest, for a baby on an evaporated-milk formula, to make up each bottle separately just before feeding. You carry as many small five-ounce cans of evaporated milk as there will be feedings, and water for mixing. At any drugstore you can buy 2-quart bottles of distilled, sterile water, with screw-on caps. (Or you can bring boiled tap water from home.) You'll need a funnel and a couple of nursing bottles, preferably plastic. Neither the cans of milk nor the bottles of water have to be kept cold.

At each feeding pour the proper amount of water into the nursing bottle, add the sugar and dissolve, then add the evaporated milk from a freshly opened can. Your doctor can tell you the proportions for each bottle. For instance, if the usual total formula is evaporated milk, 13 ounces; water, 17 ounces; and corn sirup, 3 tablespoonfuls, divided into five bottles, then each bottle would be made with water, 3½ ounces; corn sirup, 2 teaspoonfuls; evaporated milk, 2½ ounces (throw away the rest of the can of milk). After the feeding, wash the bottle and nipple thoroughly with water, soap and brush, and it can be used again.

If the baby is on solid foods, bring the baby-size cans of the ones he likes best and don't try to duplicate everything that he regularly gets at home. Traveling reduces the appetites of many babies. Don't urge.

If you can afford it on a train get a compartment. It's a great help when a baby becomes fretful.

Disposable diapers are most practical.

Avoid buying for children, when traveling, such foods as custards, milk puddings, cakes and pastries with soft fillings, creamy salad dressings on salads and sandwiches, cold meats, cold fish, cold eggs and egg salad. (Hard-boiled eggs are safe in the shell.) These are the foods which most often cause food-poisoning when improperly refrigerated or handled. Better stick to freshly cooked foods, milk in individual containers, bread with butter, peanut butter or jelly, crackers and cookies.

Automobile travel brings up special difficulties and special opportunities. In most families the biggest problem is the restlessness of young children. Another problem for some children is less-than-normal appetite at mealtime, partly caused by the distractions of strange eating places and sometimes also by a slight degree of carsickness. Usually the best answer is fairly frequent stops — for a little exercise and play, for toileting and for a snack of food. The snack doesn't have to be at a restaurant or drink stand — it can come from the trunk compartment of the car: a few crackers or a simple sandwich, a drink of milk or fruit juice from a vacuum bottle or a picnic icebox, perhaps a piece of fruit.

The most important quality in the stopping place is that it have some place where the children can run around without having to be warned every minute: a field or grove away from the road a bit; a park with children's play equipment in a town; a filling station in the country. To put the last point the other way: stopping at a filling station where there is no space for children to run is time and opportunity lost.

For a small child, who likes things always to be the same, it may be worthwhile to carry along his own toilet seat or potty.

Arranging the passengers in the car can be important. Most parents prefer to be together in the front seat and let the small fry have the back. However, persistent squabbling between the kids can often be stopped only by separating them, which separates the parents. Wherever the small fry are, they usually can't abide sitting for long and they must have some space to move around in. To be sure, there is more danger of their being hurt if they are standing up, but if you watch families in cars you'll see that nine out of ten parents have given in to letting them stand. If you do let them stand up, you ought to insist that they stand on the floor. Standing on seats is the most dangerous position, not only in case of a crash, but in all sudden stops.

The floor space of the rear seat of a sedan is fairly safe for standing; the seat then becomes a play table. A crawling baby or small child can be free to roam or fall asleep if the leg space in back can be built up level with the rear seat by means of baggage or boxes, and padding.

The rear space of a station wagon may be ideal for young children to play and sleep in, provided the luggage can be arranged or secured so that it will not slam into them in case of a sudden stop.

A four-door car can be equipped with an accessory that allows the rear door to be unlocked only with a key.

A special car seat will keep a sitting baby happy for a while. A car bed is fine for a small infant.

The hardest but often the most important rule of all, on a long trip, is to stop for the night by 4 P.M. — when it is still fairly easy to find a motel or hotel room, before the children are frantic with restlessness and fatigue, and while there is still time for them to play around and get used to the place before supper. You can save some of the time that would be lost, by early starts in the morning.

The reason, of course, that such a stop-for-the-night rule is hard for adults is that they (especially men) take pride in covering distance and they can suppress their hunger and fatigue for long periods. It's often impossible for a mother to get a father who has the bit in his teeth to stop by arguing on the road. The stopping-hour rule had better be settled by mutual agreement and solemn promise before the trip is ever begun. Men can be relatively reasonable in a theoretical discussion, but they hate to be curbed in the middle of an ambitious project.

THE NEIGHBORS AND
THEIR CHILDREN

The adults and the children will impose on
you less — and like you more — if you
can stand up for your rights.

I want to bring up some common difficulties parents have with
neighborhood children and adults. One mother asks, "What's
the best treatment for the neighbor child who flatly disobeys a
rule such as 'No playing with the power mower'? Do we scold
or send him home or speak to mamma? What about the gang
of ten-year-olds who stay around for half an hour's sport, leaving
wrecked trikes and wagons in their wake? Do we stand guard or
use a club? What about house rules such as 'No building sets
in the living room'? We can't keep on sending children home.
Or can we?"

Another writes:

What on earth do you do about other people's children? I don't
know where my duty lies. I attended a teachers' college and took a
lot of psychology and I love children. They always love me, too, no
matter how I treat them, because I am fair. But when my three
(ages six, four and one) are quietly sleeping or playing elsewhere,
I hate answering the door time after time — or worse, having everybody walk in on me without knocking. I just wish I could, in some
way, have other children for one or two hours at a time. We have
lived in a half-dozen communities in our eight years of marriage and
have had the same trouble in all of them. Parents do not know

where their children are or what they do because they do not watch them. It seems they just don't want to be bothered with them.

Last year in another city, two little girls came before my children got up and stayed till we sent them home at night. Apparently their mother served no lunch at their house. I did not feed them, though they always asked me to. I had tried that before and ended up feeding certain children five times a week. I cannot manage or teach my children when there are others around all the time.

If our garage is not locked, they help themselves. Then we can't find anything when we want it — toys, fishing equipment, lawn tools.

I have been out four times this morning to tell a little neighbor boy to stop throwing rocks (from his yard, and both his parents home) at my daughter who is minding her own business in our yard.

Today I missed my fountain pen. I have to lock all doors whenever I go out to hang clothes or weed the garden. I have to watch the children when they are inside. This is the third pen taken in this manner. Then I went outside and the spokes of two tricycles had been broken badly. Since my son is away today, the gang wants to borrow his new skates. I told them they could today, but never again. I can't know who destroys things when so many use them. We can't afford to buy toys for the whole neighborhood. Surely that should be understood by parents who can't replace the things their children have broken.

I can tell how harassed this mother feels by the way she jumps from subject to subject.

There is no doubt that many children are not very welcome in their own homes. A mother who feels kindly toward children finds a lot of waifs on her hands. And one who gives them a good time draws them like a Pied Piper. Parents who keep their children well supplied with equipment — bikes, wagons, swings, sandbox — find they have created a crowded amusement park in their own back yard. (It was that way in our yard on Cold Spring Street in New Haven when I was growing up.)

It's not all disadvantage in running a popular home. It helps to teach your own child, particularly if he's an only one, how to get along with all kinds — not just how to put up with them, but how to enjoy them. Some of your own popularity and the popularity of the equipment rubs off on your child. In the long run he can't get very far in the world with reflected popularity, but still it may send him off to a good start and make it easier for him to build his own popularity.

A great advantage of having the children come to your house is that you can keep better track of who your own are playing with and what's happening. If I had to choose between having my child always elsewhere or having the whole mob in my yard, I'd much prefer the latter. (Perhaps that's partly because I'm not a mother and wouldn't have to take the consequences.)

There are simple rules which, if the parent sticks to them consistently, should avoid some of the problems raised by the mothers I quoted. Of course they would differ in different families. I myself would make it plain, for instance, that my children don't come out to play until 9 A.M. when chores are finished, and that visitors don't come in before that. I'd also have a rule that my young children come in for supper at 5:30, and that the others are expected to go home at that time.

For families which are extremely popular or in which the children are always asking the mother if a visitor can come to supper, right in front of the visitor, a simple rule is: No guests to be invited unless mother and child agree to it in private, before anything is said to the guest. At all other times, the would-be guest can be told cheerfully, "We'd love to have you for supper, dear, but it will have to be another time."

If bold neighbor children were making nuisances of themselves in the garage, I'd close the doors, have a very firm rule that nobody is to go in, and make a big issue of it the few times the law is disobeyed. There's not only a lot of damageable stuff in most garages — there are usually several poisonous substances, too, nowadays.

I think a mother is entitled to be very definite about when she wants neighbor children inside her house, in which rooms, doing what. When young neighbors try to get in at unwanted times, there are a half-dozen good excuses the lady of the house can give, like, "Helen is busy right now" or "Helen will be out in a little while."

The question of whether neighborhood children should be allowed to use the family's playthings, with the greater likelihood of damage, would be answered in the affirmative by most parents. They want their own children to share and to share graciously. And most playthings are subject to damage when used continually. But this answer doesn't cover the situation, for instance, when a group of older boys appear on the scene in a troublemaking mood and start deliberately to abuse the equipment. Then the parent has to come out and firmly interfere.

When other children come asking to play with the possessions of a child who is not at home and who therefore can't protect his things against misuse, it seems fair all around for the parent to say, "I'm sorry, but Jackie isn't here. Why don't you come back tomorrow morning?"

As far as general principles are concerned, I think the most obvious one is that a mother is entitled to lay down the rules for all the children playing on her premises and that she doesn't need to be deterred by a visitor who says, "At home I don't have to do that." What do you do if a visitor deliberately disobeys a rule? I think that calling his mother is, for general use, an inferior method, because it implies that you aren't capable of managing him yourself — you're just a tattletale. In the long run he'll respect you much more and behave better if you show him that you feel quite confident in managing him. Of course there are exceptions, when the misbehavior is very serious and something that his own parents would definitely want to know about. Sending a visitor home is often a logical and effective punishment, but I think it is best saved as a last resort, for occasional use. It, too, implies that you've given up trying to control him, at least for today, and this weakens your own discipline. In theory, the most effective method — just as in the case of your own child — is to show by your assured and firm approach that you *can* make him behave and can even make him like it. But of course in actuality this is the hardest to accomplish.

How firm or how disagreeable is the parent entitled to become in making neighbor children behave? All of us can remember in our own childhoods certain adult neighbors who were particularly unpleasant. We hated them and were prejudiced against their children. Or we remember adults who were easily provoked, and, although we were generally law-abiding, we never lost an opportunity to tease them or make trouble for them. On the other hand, we can usually remember people who were strict but whose strictness we respected, especially if they showed that they liked us. There isn't too much connection between strictness and unpopularity. In fact, the too lenient, the timid neighbor will often be scorned or taken advantage of. The crux of the matter is the spirit with which the adult operates. If he is basically friendly and self-assured, he can get away with reasonably firm rules and have them obeyed. But if he acts as if he is expecting to have trouble, if he has a chip on his shoulder, if he's cross to begin with, he'll either be resented or persecuted or scorned, and his children will bear some of the brunt of these feelings.

The principles are the same that apply in the parent's management of his own children or in the officer's control over his men or in the executive's relationships with his subordinates. The leader who is agreeable but who isn't sure of what he wants or is afraid to ask for it runs a confused, inefficient outfit. The individuals under him are uneasy and demanding. The leader who is harsh, unfriendly, yet capable, keeps things in order, but he is heartily disliked. The leader who is unsure of himself and expresses it in an irritable, mistrustful attitude toward his charges usually has the worst organization of all. His subordinates take delight in living up to his worst expectations. They don't want to get along with him. They want to tease and provoke him. When he becomes punitive, it doesn't chasten them. They feel unfairly treated and react with more hostility.

So good leadership, I think, always has to combine the ele-

ment of confidence in one's right to lead, a genuine liking for
those being led, and definite ideas of what to expect from them.
Then subordinates not only respect the leader and do their
best, but they enjoy it too.

This brings us back to the second mother who sounded so
frantic. She isn't having trouble with other people's children
simply because she can't think up some sensible rules herself or
because she hasn't read the right articles. The problem must
lie in her own feelings. Something is making it impossible for
her to protect herself from being imposed upon. Before we try
to guess what her trouble is, we'll have to admit that there are
always plenty of adults and children in every community who
are ready to impose. Some of them are bold and completely insensitive. It seems as if you have to fend them off with a club.
At least you have to speak very frankly and with a loud voice
to be understood. Other people impose in a more sensitive
manner. Unconsciously they are watching to be sure they don't
go far enough to make you really angry. But they keep inching
up when they sense they can get away with it (something like
"Still pond, no more moving"). I guess it's more honest to say
that almost all of us will take advantage of a too-willing victim.
If he will *always* cheerfully run an errand for us or loan us his
clothes and money or take care of our child, we will have to be
extraordinarily scrupulous to resist the temptation to impose.
Some people never get imposed on, some people get imposed
on all the time, and the rest of us know how to protect ourselves
most of the time but get imposed on occasionally when we are
caught off guard.

A very few individuals enjoy being willing slaves. It gives
them a feeling of being appreciated which they can achieve in
no other way. Most people who get imposed on, though, resent
it, but they are afraid to resist.

The person easily imposed on is usually a sensitive individual
who has been brought up close to his parents but in excessive

awe of their disapproval. They, in training him, have relied heavily on the threat of not loving him. Instead of simply saying, "You mustn't be impolite or selfish," they have implied, "We won't love you any more (or nobody will love you) if you are impolite or selfish." I don't mean that the parents have necessarily used these words. They may have given him the feeling of being rejected merely by their look of severe disapproval. (They aren't just disliking the behavior, they are disliking the child.) This is a frightening feeling to a child who is close to his parents, especially in early childhood, because he senses that his entire security depends on their continued love. He gets mad at his parents occasionally, as any child does, perhaps more so, but any anger expressed toward them brings a shocked condemnation which is particularly disturbing. So the child grows up with an exaggerated fear of disapproval or anger, an excessive need to please, and an inability to stand up for his own rights. As an adult he or she accepts inferior merchandise without outward protest, lets himself in for tough assignments in the office or on a committee, is easily pressured by door-to-door salesmen, and by relatives and neighbors wanting loans of money or equipment or food. He fumes and kicks himself afterward, but the next time he finds himself saying, "Of course, I'd be glad to," all over again. The mother in the letter says she loaned the skates to the gang that morning, but she must have realized that it was the wrong thing to do, because she told them, "This is the last time."

I think that the mother who finds herself being imposed on by neighborhood children and their mothers can help herself to some degree by recognizing the fact that it is her own fear of not being liked which is creating the difficulty and realizing that the neighbors, young and old, will actually like her better if she can stand up for her rights and keep them from taking advantage of her. She can also be more on guard against her weakness if she will draw up some rigid rules and will deliberately practice making some stock excuses, whether they are truthful or not. When she finds that they work and that the neighbors like her just as well, she will be emboldened by success.

Another kind of neighbor problem is brought up in a recent letter from a mother who complains that the other women on her street are always questioning her child-care methods. She sounds like a highly conscientious person who puts a lot of thought and time and effort into caring for her children. The neighbors, all of whom seem to be much more casual than she, keep asking her rather critically why she takes such precautions when a child has a cold, why she watches her younger children so carefully when they are out playing, why she bothers with naps for the three- and five-year-olds, why she reasons so much and spanks so little.

Of course every parent differs from every other in his methods, to one degree or another, but this rarely presents difficulties with the neighbors. When there is a lot of argument, one generally suspects that special factors are operating. Perhaps the criticized parent is way out of line in leniency or severity or fussiness and the neighbors can't help being bothered by what they see.

Another more likely possibility is that the mother who feels criticized is, without intending to and without realizing it, frequently calling attention to her own methods and implying that they are superior. In this way she puts her neighbors on the defensive. She makes them feel a little bit guilty and they try to defend themselves by arguing back. Now one person doesn't go out of his way to criticize another when he is really sure he is right. He is only trying to convince the other person and himself that he is right. When a human being is truly self-confident, he has a serenity about his own beliefs and is quite willing to let other people have theirs. If somebody else criticizes his point of view, he can let it pass. In other words, it's really true that it takes two to make an argument and that each of the two has to be slightly unsure of himself.

So it's possible that the scrupulous mother who feels that she is being criticized all the time is less convinced about her methods than she thinks; or perhaps she is insecure in general and is trying to boost her self-confidence by being critical of others. They sense her attitude and they counterattack.

I certainly don't want to suggest that it is a mistake for parents to get into discussions of child care. All parents feel the need to compare notes. They need sympathy from one another for the difficulties they are having at times. They need the comfort of hearing that others have got into the same jams. They know that they can get valuable tips and new outlooks from one another. People in all lines of work — farmers, mechanics, lawyers, beauticians — have always enjoyed talking over their occupational trials and triumphs. But if discussions between two people about children usually lead to tense feelings, it's a sign that there's too much sensitiveness on one or both sides and that it's better to avoid these discussions.

How do you stop someone who insists on arguing? The answer is simple but difficult: don't argue back. You can change the subject or you can act politely bored or you can just keep listening and nodding your head. The head nodding doesn't have to signify that you've suddenly changed your ideas or that you've become completely insincere. It only says, "I see what you mean." The argumentative person is always compelled by his inner doubts to try to provoke arguments with others. But it's a great relief to him to find occasionally someone who is so secure that he can't be provoked and so understanding that he can listen sympathetically.

THE QUESTION OF OFFICE
VISITS FOR ILLNESS

They have advantages — for patient and
doctor — as well as disadvantages.

EVERY ONCE in a while there comes a letter from a mother who's unhappy and indignant because her doctor — whether he's a pediatrician or a general practitioner — will not make house visits for ordinary illnesses in children. He asks her to wrap the child in a blanket and bring him to the office. This seems unkind and risky to the mother.

When I was a child in New Haven, Connecticut, our pediatrician, Dr. Harry Steele, was always ready to make a house visit whenever any one of the six of us was sick enough so that my mother worried. I was impressed with his kindliness and the fact that his clothes smelled of cigarette smoke, an aroma I was not used to. In those days there were no specific drugs that cured infections such as tonsillitis and pneumonia, so throat cultures were not often important. The doctor had only general measures to recommend, like bed rest and fluids. If you had a sore throat, you gargled with hot salt water. If you had a bad cough there was only codeine, to make it less frequent. Most doctors then felt that a sick person couldn't begin to get well until his bowels were cleaned out. Dr. Steele would prescribe castor oil and I, no matter how hard I tried to keep it down, would vomit it promptly. If he had asked my mother to bring me to the office when I was very young she would have had to order a horse-drawn cab from the livery stable. If I had been a farmer's son, my father would have had to drive me in an open carriage. When family automobiles became more common they were mostly open touring cars until about 1930.

When I began to practice pediatrics in New York City in 1933 (with an old open car inherited from my mother-in-law) I assumed, like every other pediatrician I knew, that any parent was entitled to ask for a house visit — and to get it — whether I thought it was necessary from a strictly medical point of view or not. Partly this was because none of us had ever questioned the tradition of house visits. Partly it was a matter of economics and of the doctors' having the time. Up to the past fifteen years there was a much smaller proportion of the population who felt they could afford to pay for private care, especially house visits, unless the patient was seriously ill. (There were few private rooms in the average hospital because most people went into wards; now in some university hospitals it is hard to teach physical diagnosis to medical students because so many of the patients are private.) In the depression years even the most distinguished doctors had time on their hands. A beginner like myself was willing not only to range the length of Manhattan but even to cross the bridges into Queens, the Bronx and Brooklyn to make a call.

With so many doctors in the armed services during the war, house visits became an obvious impossibility in many parts of the country, except in real emergencies. And after the war the rapid increase in prosperity and the continuing high birth rate meant that young doctors sometimes became too busy within a year of starting practice.

So it was pressure of work that broke the tradition. But that was only half the story. Conscientious and well-trained doctors who found themselves simply unable to make house calls also came to realize that this caused no harm to the sick child, and often enabled their medical care to be more thorough. The child could be wrapped in a blanket and transported to the doctor's office in a closed car, with heat if necessary, in a relatively few minutes in most cases. There was no problem of chilling or exhaustion.

On the positive side, an office visit for illness often has very real advantages. An important question nowadays, when a child has a sore or red throat, is to determine whether it is due to the streptococcus that sometimes causes ear and gland infections, nephritis and rheumatic fever. It's usually *much* simpler to get a throat culture started in a doctor's office than to do the swabbing in the home and bring it back to the laboratory some time later. Likewise the securing and testing of a urine specimen, the performing of a blood count when called for, are quite easy in the office. It takes longer to secure such specimens at home, and then the doctor has to return to his office later to examine them or to bring them to a laboratory. The same applies to other laboratory procedures that are occasionally required. Consultants are nearer at hand. What this all means is that in those border-lines cases in which further investigation would be helpful, though not absolutely necessary, it is more likely to be carried out during an office visit. When, once in a great while, examination reveals a situation which needs prompt treatment, in office or hospital, it obviously is achieved earlier through an office visit than if the condition had to wait to be discovered until the doctor could make a house visit.

What about the danger of a sick child giving his infection to other children if he has to remain with them in the waiting room? I don't think we know enough to answer this question definitely. The contagiousness of each disease would be different and the risk would depend on such factors as the size of the room, the circulation of air, the length of time the sick child was there. But the chance of contagion is much less than people ordinarily think. A school physician knows that sometimes a child who is coming down with a highly contagious disease like measles or chicken pox will sit throughout the entire school day in a roomful of susceptible pupils, and yet usually only a small percentage will catch the disease. Whenever I myself had a cold during the years I was in private practice, I would continue to examine dozens of healthy infants and children, including plenty whose mothers were inexperienced enough so that they would call if the baby developed the sniffles. But I don't remember ever being called about a cold which developed soon after such an office visit. (I used to keep track because I felt guilty.) In other words it usually seems to require a fairly prolonged and intimate exposure, such as occurs in family living, to pass along an infection. Doctors who see sick children in the office try, on principle, to examine them as soon as possible and to keep them as far away from other children as space permits.

I think there are two things that can be said against office visits for illness. One is the real inconvenience when a mother has other children to care for. She has no idea, when she is trying to find someone to take care of them, how long she will be gone, and they will be no help at the office or laboratory or hospital. The other trouble — and I think this is what bothers the mother who feels indignant — is that if she has grown up assuming that any sick person is entitled to be in bed at home, and fully deserves the attention of a doctor there, it naturally makes her feel, way down inside, that she and her child are being neglected when the doctor declines to come. I confess that I myself, even though I know all the reasons in favor of office care for illness, would feel slightly hurt if I had a sick child and the pediatrician declined to visit. So it's mostly an emotional problem. Perhaps we'll all stop expecting house calls for children's ordinary infections eventually, but it will take some of us another ten or twenty years to outgrow the habit.

I want to make it quite clear that I am not trying to decide — for parents or doctors — whether office visits or house visits are generally preferable, or for what illnesses. This is something that each doctor will decide, depending on the facilities and the kind of practice he has. Probably he will vary his procedure depending on the particular illness. I have a much more limited purpose. I'm only pointing out to those parents who are unhappy or uneasy about office visits that there are real advantages in certain cases, and very little risk.

III

Anxieties and Overprotection

WHEN YOUR CHILD GETS
ANGRY WITH YOU

*You can admit to him that such feelings
are natural, but don't allow him to be
abusive or rude.*

WHEN I WAS a child I never told my father and mother I was
angry with them. I wouldn't have dared. Nor would other children of that period, either, except a few who were quite out of
control. As for telling my parents I hated them, the idea would
have been too awful to have entered my mind. Of course I
would feel angry with them occasionally when I thought they
had punished me unfairly or favored one of my sisters or refused
what seemed a reasonable request. But I showed my resentment
only by sulking.

When child-guidance work began, it was realized that one of
the problems of an excessively worrisome child may be that he
feels too guilty about his hostile feeling toward other members
of the family. He acts as if he believes that his mean wishes
toward them would actually do them harm. Or he fears that if
his parents ever discovered just how angry with them he sometimes feels, they would punish him horribly; or they might turn
against him for good and throw him out. In fact, a child may be
so afraid of his resentful feelings that he completely represses
any awareness of them, deep into his unconscious mind. Buried
there, they may play a part in creating a neurotic symptom such

as a phobia or compulsion, or a psychosomatic symptom such as a chronic skin rash.

So the child-guidance-clinic worker, in his efforts to cure the neurosis, tries to reassure the guilty child that angry thoughts in themselves don't hurt people; that everybody has them at times, even toward people whom they love; that the child's parents wouldn't do anything terrible to him if they knew how he felt.

Hardest of all is to demonstrate to the timid child that he actually does have hostile thoughts, since he is an old expert at hiding them even from himself. So the child psychiatrist is on the lookout for little signs of irritation to which he can call attention. If the psychiatrist is late for an appointment, and at the next appointment the child is late for the first time since he has been coming for treatment, the psychiatrist may say, "I guess you were cross at me for being late last time." The child protests, "Honestly, I wasn't cross. I know how busy you are." Perhaps the child is making up a play, using miniature dolls representing adults and children. He has a boy doll punch a doctor doll in the nose. The psychiatrist says, "I guess you sometimes would like to do that to me." "Oh, no," replies the child. "I like you because you are trying to get me well." In another play the child makes a boy doll say "I hate you" to the mother doll because the mother doll compelled him to eat a vegetable he didn't like. "Probably you feel like saying that to your own mother when she makes you eat something," says the psychiatrist. "Oh, no!" says the child. "I don't get angry, because my mother is only doing it to make me get strong and healthy." Another time, the boy is playing a kind of cops-and-robbers game with the doctor and tells the doctor to put him in jail for robbing a bank. When the doctor pretends to do so, the child gets excited in trying to escape, and really conks the doctor with the butt of a toy pistol. The doctor says, "You feel like hurting me when you are afraid I'm going to punish you." And so on and so forth. It is amazing how persistently a neurotic child can deny feelings that are so obvious to everyone else.

In the early days of child-guidance work it was believed that if a child who repressed his anger would really cut loose in a number of sessions with his doctor, and thoroughly vent his feelings, it would bring about improvement, even though he did not understand the basic causes of his angriness or what his fears were really about. But experience proved that the improvement from a blowup was only temporary. The symptoms would keep returning until, with the help of the psychiatrist, the child understood the deep roots of his tensions.

Another mistake that was sometimes made, when child psychiatry was in its infancy, was to let the child, when he finally showed his anger, take it out by breaking playthings or damaging the room, or hitting the doctor. Time showed that whenever a child was allowed to become destructive or assaultive — even for therapeutic purposes — there was an unfavorable reaction. In the first place, it is disturbing to any human being, whether child or adult, whether good citizen or delinquent, to get out of control. The worst harm it does is to make him mistrust himself. (Occasionally a very severe delinquent or criminal will leave a message at the scene of a brutal crime: "Somebody please stop me.") For the child under treatment, getting out of control also causes mistrust of the psychiatrist who permits it. And it adds to his load of guilt which was already too great.

So it came to be realized that it was unwise and also unnecessary to allow a child to act out his hostile feelings. He could more effectively cope with them — and his guilt about them — by learning to talk about them instead. With the help of the psychiatrist he can learn to admit that he is sometimes furious at the psychiatrist or at his parents. The fact that the psychiatrist can listen to these expressions of hostility calmly and without retaliation teaches the child that these feelings are not so dangerous as he had assumed, and that adults are usually reliable people. Then he and the psychiatrist can go on to discover more about where his resentments come from, especially the resentments left over from earlier stages of childhood when he misunderstood many things.

All this leads to an easing of the child's tensions within himself and with his parents, and to improvements of his symptoms.

Up to recent times our morality taught that anger is sinful, particularly between members of the family. Of course earthy people have always taken this prohibition with a grain of salt and been able to joke about household animosities. It has been the individuals with unusually strict consciences, both adults and children, who have tried to deny negative feelings completely, and sometimes developed symptoms as a result.

The past couple of generations have experienced a general relaxation of standards. And the discoveries of psychiatrists about the pervasiveness of aggressive and sexual impulses have been interpreted by people as justifying the relaxation. Parents have learned from lectures and articles and books that it is natural for children, at moments of stress, to feel hostility toward fathers and mothers and brothers and sisters, and that too severe a repression of this can cause neurosis. Those parents who take human nature for granted — in themselves and in their children — and who have a natural self-assurance have accepted these pronouncements matter-of-factly. In a sense they have always known them. But other parents have been thrown off balance by all the talk about the inevitability of anger and the unwholesomeness of suppressing it. They've allowed their children to express it freely whenever the spirit moved them. In a few cases they've even encouraged them to do so. Sometimes the situation gets completely out of control.

I've received letters from parents who ended up taking verbal abuse from their children all day long and who concluded that they had somehow failed to give their children enough love. This is certainly the wrong interpretation. Unloved children don't bother to berate their parents hour after hour. In most cases these parents are kindly people, devoted to their children, but too ready to blame themselves when anything goes wrong. They assume that their children's occasional hostility toward them is probably justified and believe — mistakenly, I think —

that it should be allowed direct, blunt expression. Eventually a vicious cycle may develop. For if a parent begins, for one reason or another, to play a submissive, apologetic role, it stirs up the child's meanness *and* guiltiness. He can't resist the temptation to be cruel to a person who is, in a sense, asking for it. Yet he knows that this is not the right way to treat a parent. He wants, underneath, to be stopped. So he satisfies both impulses by behaving more and more outrageously, hoping unconsciously that the parent will crack down.

Now I want to tie these ideas together in a more positive way and express my own opinion about how best to apply them. I think today's parents have a real advantage over those of the past in being able to admit that there are many situations in growing up which arouse anger in normal, wholesome children. There are the frustrations and unwelcome requests that a parent must impose; at age one they have to do with avoiding breakable or dangerous household objects and sitting on the potty. At sixteen they concern the borrowing of the family car and the hours for coming home. The arrival of a new baby stirs up resentment toward the parents as well as toward the infant. The possessive romantic attachment that boy makes to mother and girl to father at three and four years causes hostile jealousy which may not show much on the surface but which, we have learned, takes a long time for the child to master constructively. At all stages of growing up children are being occasionally irritated by parental impatience and unreasonableness that come from some other source altogether — such as the father's problems with his boss or the mother's with her husband.

I think it's an advantage for children to grow up with parents who aren't shocked by signs of occasional hostility. Then the children don't have to feel *too* guilty about such feelings. A parent can help to clear the air once in a while after a blowup, especially in the case of a child who is sensitive or overconscientious, by saying in an understanding tone that all children become angry with their parents, even though they love them too; that parents know this and don't think any the less of their children for it. (The parent might even recall how mad he used to get at his father or mother in the olden days.) If a parent thinks he acted somewhat unfairly in a situation which caused the child's resentment, he can admit it frankly without fear of losing face or impairing his discipline.

But none of the foregoing implies, to my way of thinking, that a parent need permit rude exclamations of animosity, name calling, or any other form of impoliteness. A parent owes it to his child as well as to himself to maintain the dignity of his position of leadership in the family. In doing so he is not claiming to be above reproach. He is only teaching that politeness is due to everybody and that a certain respect is owed to any person in a position of authority — whether parent, teacher, minister, judge, employer, lifeguard — even though he may not be filling that position perfectly. If a child cannot respect his parent's position, it will be difficult for him to learn to respect other positions — including his own — later in life. To put it more specifically, if my child were rude to me I wouldn't put up with it, nor yell at him as an equal, nor act as if he had committed an unforgivable sin. I'd just tell him, seriously and as calmly as I could manage, that I don't want him to speak that way to me; it isn't polite; it isn't right.

I want to mention also the child who has learned to say frequently, "I hate you" or "I don't love you" whenever his mother turns down a request or scolds him, because he has discovered that this makes her feel so guilty that she will almost always give in to him. You might imagine that in such cases the mother would be a highly inconsistent or immature person. But almost all those I have known were quite sensible in most respects. Their problem was that for some reason or other they doubted their adequacy as parents, at least in regard to the one child in question. A simple example that's easy to understand is the case of the mother who has adopted a child and can't get over the feeling that she's not really entitled to have him. It's as if she'd done something reproachable, to the natural parents and to the child. Or there's the mother whose child has a handicap and who is convinced, despite what the doctors say, that it must be all her fault. In a majority of cases, however, the reason why the mother gives in to the child so guiltily is not apparent. It may be some inadequacy that would seem insignificant to others but which looms large in the mother's conscience. She may be able to stand up quite sensibly to her other children. You or I would be able to detect immediately that this child was not at all sincere in his declaration to his mother that he hates her, that in fact he was putting on a rather corny piece of acting. Why doesn't the mother notice the false note? It's her own unnaturally severe conscience that is always ready to accuse her anew that she's not worthy of her child's love. The slightest reminder from him, no matter how unjustified, is enough to stir her conscience up again.

Children — even as young as one or two years of age — are surprisingly responsive to their fathers' and mothers' deep feelings of various kinds. It's the smooth working of these feelings that ordinarily does most to keep children reasonably stable and happy. When a child's behavior becomes obnoxious, the cause may lie in his relationship to school work or friends or members of the family. But one question to ask — among many — is whether the parent, without conscious awareness, is accepting the misbehavior too resignedly.

THE CHILD WHO GETS PICKED ON

A timid child can be helped most by parents who are
reassuring rather than overprotective.

I WISH that you would write about how parents can teach their children how to meet the cruel kind of teasing without indulging in it themselves. All the children I have observed engaging in a kind of sadistic teasing have been teased that same way by an older brother, a father, an uncle. (I have never happened to find it a sister, a mother or an aunt. but expect the male sex has no monopoly.)

You might think from my question that in our family we have no sense of humor and do not tease. This is not the case. We distinguish between the kind of teasing which makes us all laugh and the kind whose object is to produce tears, despair or anger.

For examples of the latter type, a playmate locked one of my children in his cellar and left her there for a fair part of the afternoon. My daughter was bothered. Two teen-age boys took a favorite toy from my three-year-old, hid it, and told him it was lost forever. My child was nearly hysterical. How can I help my children not to be too much bothered, without giving them the idea that such treatment amounts to little and that it would be all right for them to treat other children that way?

This mother brings up a major problem. She also throws in a couple of side issues — about the difference between gentle and cruel teasing, and about males being the worse teasers — which I had better try to dispose of first. I'm not sure there is an absolute difference between friendly kidding and the mean kind. Both are meant to hurt, at least a little. A good parent may kid a child who is beginning to make a nuisance or a monkey of himself, as a more playful way of bringing him back into line than scolding him. This parent's intention is good, and he tries not to use an amount of sarcasm that will hurt feelings badly. In the same way an adult may tease a good friend, as an indirect, socially acceptable way of showing that he is irritated with him.

There's a lot of difference — in degree and in intention — when a mean older child shatters the feelings or scares the life out of an inoffensive younger child with cruel stories or pranks, just to see him suffer. This is simply a release of sadistic feelings without any other justification. But even here you can see that the torturer is showing a bit of control in that he's using an indirect, imaginative form of cruelty instead of hitting the child with a stick. (He can't be quite so easily accused of overt wrongdoing, though the effect is just as bad.)

I agree with this mother that men and boys, are, on the average, much worse teases. The possible reasons get us back to the old controversy about whether males are temperamentally different from females and, if so, whether this is inborn or due to upbringing. As I'll be discussing more fully in a later chapter, "Some Differences Between the Sexes," my own opinion is that most boys are born with greater aggressiveness than most girls but that they also, as a safety measure, have more mechanisms for controlling aggression, which parents and other teachers take care to foster. Our society — in the person of fathers and older boys — teaches each generation of younger boys that kidding is one of the acceptable ways, even an admirable way, of expressing irritation or hostility. It is developed to a fine art by the wit. A majority of girls and women don't see the fun in artfully fashioning their hostility into jokes. They are much more apt to express it directly, when they feel justified.

Before we leave the subject of a father's teasing, I want to add that, even if it is well intentioned, it may be too sharp for a young child or a sensitive one. The child hasn't been around long enough to develop a thick skin for such darts or to be able to enjoy a laugh at his own expense. He realizes at a very early age when he is being laughed at, and feels totally ignominious. It will be years before he will be able to fight back with his tongue.

I agree with the mother when she observes that if a child is constantly mean, it is usually apparent that he has been regularly taking meanness from someone else in the family. But I would add that it is not necessarily just teasing, as she suggests, but harshness of any kind from either sex.

What kind of defenses do parents have against teasing or bullying of their children? There is usually no point in moving to a different neighborhood, even if you can afford to. It has been the experience of most parents that there's a mean child in every block. When you move into a new house with a sensitive child, it takes the local bully only an hour or two to show up.

Can the parent physically protect the child who gets picked on? In some ways yes, in more ways no. Preschool children who tease may be stopped as long as a controlling adult stays right on the spot, but the inhibition doesn't usually last very long afterward. A mother who is likable may be able to persuade a neighbor child of school age to be more kind, if he has only a small streak of meanness and has responsible parents who, he thinks, might hear complaints. On the other hand, if the mother flies out like a cross witch, the neighborhood children will consider her an enemy, lump her and her child together as undesirables, and feel quite justified in further persecution. The confirmed bully retreats only temporarily when pounced on, and lies in wait for further opportunities to tease the child, and the mother too. He often has parents who have little control over him and who are either insensitive to neighbors' complaints or rudely refuse to believe them.

I do think that a mother of a sensitive preschool child can accomplish a lot if she is able and willing to devote a part of each day to supervising the outdoor play of her child with others of his age. I don't mean that she should be directing the play all the time and I certainly don't mean that she is there to scold the children who are unkind to her precious one. But a friendly adult, just by her presence, keeps children in line. If she sees tension developing she can distract them into a new activity, and if hostilities break out she can calmly step between the warriors, either as a suggester of compromise or as a stone wall. In the long run a mother's unobtrusive control of a group of moppets helps her timid child to find, gradually, an enjoyable place for himself. Or she can sometimes get her child out of the habit of being a victim by taking him, for a few months, to play with a group farther away which happens to have no meanies in it.

A father who has a knack with boys can, by playing games occasionally with the gang, help his son a bit in gaining acceptance and learning not to be so afraid of teasing.

If we are really going to find the basic answer to teasing, though, we've got to figure out why certain children get teased so easily while others escape almost completely. You might think it was a matter of physical strength and skill in self-defense. That may be a helpful factor but not the main one, for sometimes a husky child is persecuted by one who is much smaller; and you can often see a frail, clumsy child getting along fine in a group that contains mean ones.

There are some children who draw down teasing on themselves the way flowers attract bees. They not only have a fatal attraction for real bullies, they seem to bring out the meanness in average children. Occasionally it is an obvious quality like quick temper. I remember a boy in my childhood who got along with the gang all right most of the time, but if he was needled just right, he'd suddenly explode with temper. He'd race around with a purple face, screaming like a banshee, striking out clumsily at the circle of hooting tormentors. Teasing him was like lighting a rocket, and the temptation to get him going was irresistible.

More often the child who is *very* easily teased is a somewhat sensitive, timid type. He meets other children with a facial expression which is a mixture of distrust and unfriendliness. He does not usually attack, by action or words, but he looks as if he fears that children will attack him and as if he dislikes them all on this account. They detect this instantly. They feel provoked to attack by his expression. Of course his attitude is due, in part, to the accumulation of bad experiences he has had with them, and you can't blame him for that. The question remains, however, of why he started with poor social relationships in the first place. There are various factors in a child's earliest years in the family which might contribute to such a disposition. I think myself that an occasional baby is born more apprehensive than the average; and then the usual run of unfortunate experiences, which hardly make a dent on another child, keep adding to his mistrust. In another case, a mother who is inclined by her own anxiousness to be overprotective may give her child the feeling that he is safe only when he is close to her and that the rest of the population is dangerous. Sometimes the first child of very devoted parents is slow to learn the fun of give-and-take because for his first couple of years he has been the focus of so much gentle or fussy adult attention, and because he may have had little experience with other roughnecks.

To put it the other way around, when parents are fortunate enough to have dispositions composed of reasonable amounts of affectionateness, self-assurance, easygoingness, it is more simple for their children to untie themselves gradually from the apron strings, and to turn to other children with the expectation that they will be as easy to get along with as the parents have been. Children, like adults, find in the world about what they are disposed to find. The neighborhood bully is not tempted to attack the friendly self-confident child nearly so often as he is tempted to attack the fearful, self-conscious one.

All this is not to say that the timid young children who get picked on are doomed. Most of those who are reasonably well adjusted in other respects find comfortable social places for themselves sooner or later. Some of them become unusually successful, having gained strength and understanding from their troubles. It is important to distinguish in early childhood between those who are gaining in assurance and those who are being pushed farther back. The latter can profit from child guidance, or their parents can get help from a family social agency.

But the mother I quoted does not complain of a continuous problem of persecution of one child. She speaks only of occasional teasing of various ones of her children. She asks for advice about how to handle it and whether telling a child to fight back will not make him mean too. I have a couple of suggestions in addition to those I made earlier. I myself would never try to teach a normal child *not* to fight back. Well-adjusted children get into occasional mild fights from the time they begin playing with others (which they should preferably do as soon as they learn to walk). This is one of the ways they learn to respect each other's rights and to stand up for their own. This doesn't make them mean. I would not interfere in ordinary brief scraps as long as the children were fairly evenly matched in spirit, were doing each other no serious physical or emotional harm, and were generally friendly characters. If I had to interfere, I'd do it casually, rather than with shaming. (If my child were more aggressive than the average and fought too much or without provocation, I'd seek professional advice.) In other words, I think it can handicap a child who is a generally friendly person to teach him that it's wrong ever to come to blows. (Incidentally, the parents of a timid child usually find that they can't persuade him to fight back, even when his persecutor is smaller.)

Parents can help a child not to be too upset by teasing, and thereby improve his chances of not being teased so soon again (make him less teasable), by not being too upset themselves. With every new and potentially disturbing experience, whether it is a thunderstorm or a barking dog or an injury, a young child looks to his parents for the cue on how to take it. If a mother, listening to the tale of a weeping or frightened child, becomes visibly agitated and talks indignantly of the tormentor as if he were the devil incarnate, it can magnify the child's sense of the danger he was in, and might be in again. If she rushes out several times a day, obviously to scold the aggressor or to rescue her child, she teaches him that his only defense is his mother. On the other hand, she doesn't need to be hardhearted. She can comfort him for a minute and then cheerfully send him out again, as if she assumes he'll be all right. If he keeps complaining, she might suggest ways in which he could pooh-pooh future threats or fight off the attacks if they come again. It is not that he can surely defend himself the next time with her suggestions, but her assumption that nothing horrible has happened, and her confidence that in the long run he can take care of himself, will make him at least a bit less obviously fearful on the next encounter, and therefore less likely to invite attack. When I point out the consequences if an upset mother constantly flies to the defense of her child, I don't mean that she has to sit paralyzed in her window watching him be bullied. If things look serious she can always saunter out, as if on another errand, and her presence will usually do the trick.

ANXIETIES ABOUT NEWBORN BABIES

They are particularly hard to overcome.

IN THE OLDEN days, when the death rates were high in babies and children as a result of such diseases as pneumonia, whooping cough, scarlet fever, diphtheria and severe diarrhea, the risks of the newborn period did not stand out so prominently. But now that inoculations, antibiotic drugs and pasteurization of milk have controlled so many diseases, the special hazards of the first few days of life are more apparent. This is of course particularly true for infants who are born very prematurely and for those with serious malformations. But a few babies who come into the world full-sized and apparently well formed have their troubles at first. There are the ones who don't start breathing promptly or who breathe weakly and irregularly or who labor too hard to breathe; the ones who remain pale or blue; the ones who are limp and lethargic. It's often a question in such cases of whether the cause is in the heart, the lungs or the brain. Then there are the infants who become more jaundiced than is usual. A very few babies develop convulsions or a paralysis.

Some of these conditions are not as easy to diagnose as parents might assume, despite all our knowledge and tests. X-rays of the heart and lungs are often confusing in a small baby. (He won't hold his breath to make a clear picture.) A spinal tap to detect brain damage may not reveal a hemorrhage of the brain that has actually occurred; or it may show blood which, it turns out, has come not from the brain but as a result of the needle scratching a vein in the spine. There's quite a list of complicated conditions that can cause jaundice, aside from the Rh factor.

When a baby has poor breathing or color or activity during the newborn period, it's natural for the mother to worry whether the trouble might be related to diseases or injuries that she herself may have had during her pregnancy, or to difficulty of labor and delivery. Actually there is not much connection. Bodily injury to a mother has no effect on a baby except that, in rare cases, it starts labor. The only infectious diseases in the mother that may influence the baby, as far as we know, are German measles in the first three months of pregnancy, and untreated syphilis.

It's true that there is a somewhat greater chance of a baby having early disturbances of breathing and color if the labor or delivery have been distinctly abnormal (not just long), or if the mother has had the serious complication called toxemia at the end of pregnancy. More often, however, there is no such connection. In most of the cases in which the baby has trouble, labor and delivery were considered normal; and in most of the cases in which labor and delivery were long or difficult, the baby does well from the start. So there is no scientific justification for jumping to conclusions, for assuming in an individual case that difficulty during labor or delivery is the cause of trouble in the first few days of life.

It's even more important to realize that of those babies who *do* have, in the first week of life, poor breathing and color or moderately severe jaundice, a great majority recover soon and show no physical aftereffects.

But the distress of parents, when a doctor has to tell them that their new baby is having trouble, is intense underneath. However, like human beings in other alarming situations, they instinctively tend to protect themselves against the suddenness of the blow. They may not seem to hear what he is telling them. Or they may listen to his words and then casually brush aside his warning, as if they themselves are absolutely sure there is no danger in their particular case. They may direct all their concern toward some other minor problems in the baby, such as a rash or a slight difficulty in feeding. It's often only months later, when the danger is long past, that parents can look the crisis in the eye and discuss it freely.

The doctor too is in a difficult situation. He knows that in a great majority of cases everything will turn out all right. And he would naturally like to be as optimistic as possible. Nevertheless, a small percentage of the babies who are in marked distress at first will not survive the first week, or will not develop ideally. A doctor feels it is his obligation to explain the danger, so that the parents will be prepared and so that, if the worst happens, he will not be reproached for having failed to recognize the seriousness of the condition. He is often on the spot too because it may take a number of days of observation and tests before the diagnosis is clear. And the outcome in terms of eventual development may not be certain for several months.

Statistics collected by Dr. Stuart Stevenson showed that when there are serious difficulties in the newborn period, there will be a somewhat increased likelihood of behavior problems in the following years. There are several possible theoretical explanations for this. My own belief is that parents are in a particularly sensitive and impressionable state at this time; and if they acquire deep fears about the baby, it is hard for them to shake these off later, even after the fears have proved to have been groundless. Their overprotectiveness may lead to feeding problems, sleep problems, dependency, spoiling.

This continuing anxiety is especially evident in some mothers of premature babies. If a premature infant is not extremely small to start with and if he does well in the early weeks, his chances in the future of withstanding infections and of developing in a healthy way are essentially the same as those of full-term babies. Yet this is almost impossible for some mothers to believe. Even though their baby at six months or a year is now obviously robust, they continue to talk about him as if he were frail and weak. They ask when he will catch up to "normal" children. They ascribe his ordinary infections to his prematurity.

Of course the parents of a premature baby are subjected to worrisome influences not just for a few days but often for several weeks. Though the doctors say he is largely out of danger after a week, he continues to live in an incubator. He is taken care of by nurses with gowns and masks. The parents aren't allowed in the nursery, at least until he is almost ready to go home. Through the window, he looks pathetically small and weak. It's no wonder that the parents get the feeling he belongs to the hospital and the nurses, not to them, and that he's entirely different from ordinary babies. It's also no wonder that when finally they are allowed to take him home they sometimes act quite frightened. They can't believe he is ready to live with ordinary people. They may try to ward off taking the awful responsibility by protesting that they haven't bought all the equipment yet or that home is unsafe because someone has the sniffles there.

I suspect that the explanation for the great anxiety in the newborn period is simply that Nature intends that all parents should be particularly concerned about the helplessness and the smallness of new babies. When I say "Nature" I mean that in the long process of evolution through the ages — not just of the human race but of all the other mammals who care for their young — those creatures who didn't have the disposition to fret and hover, during the period when their young were helpless, sometimes allowed them to die of neglect. It was the offspring of worriers who most regularly survived and who passed this trait along.

To get back to the present — how can doctor and parents best handle a crisis in the newborn period? How much should the doctor say? Some people would express the opinion that a modern doctor, when dealing with educated parents, should explain fully the possible causes, the risks, the steps in diagnosis, the appropriate treatments. If I had not been a doctor and if I had known no parents who had been through such an experience, I think that this philosophy of full disclosure would have appealed to me. But from what I've seen, I don't believe that this course is fair to the parents or the future of the child, and most of the doctors I've known feel somewhat the same way. I agree that if a baby's condition is not good, the doctor should tell the parents that he is concerned and that he is watching carefully. But since a great majority of the babies with most of these conditions recover and develop well, he is being not only kind but correct in being as optimistic as is warranted. If the diagnosis is definite, the parents should know it too. But if, as is true in so many cases of poor color or unsatisfactory breathing or serious jaundice, the cause is not yet clear, I think it is unwise for the doctor to run through a list of all the possibilities. At best this will be only partially understandable to the distraught parents. And experience shows that such a wide-ranging discussion will raise dozens of mistaken and morbid ideas in the parents' minds, which are worse than any reality. After all, the baby has only one disease, not a dozen, even though it's not yet diagnosed. When tests are to be performed, it usually does not prove helpful for the doctor to try explaining the complexities of their purpose; but it is wise for him to mention the tests in advance so that the parents will not be surprised when they find out by chance that some procedure is being done. Everyone would agree that when the parents ask explicit questions the doctor should answer them honestly.

For the past several years a dozen of us in the Department of Pediatrics and Psychiatry at Western Reserve University have been engaged, with a small group of cooperating families, in studying closely how professional people such as pediatricians and general practitioners and public health nurses can be most helpful to parents in the rearing of their children. (The study has been made possible by generous financial support from the

Grant Foundation, established by William T. Grant.) Several of the babies had temporary medical difficulties in the first few days after birth. A year later, we asked the mothers and fathers how they thought such crises should be handled by doctors, and the gist of their remarks was: "Of course we wouldn't want to be deceived. But don't tell us anything more complicated or threatening than we need to know." They agreed, too, that it's a great help when the parents have had an opportunity to become acquainted with the doctor who will be caring for the baby, before the latter is born. In ordinary practice this opportunity is not taken very often, but we all agreed that it ought to be — in all cases.

I'll broaden the topic a bit and offer these suggestions to parents who have a child of *any* age who develops a serious illness in which the diagnosis or the future course remain in doubt. Ask the doctor anything you really want to know. In fact, you'd better make a list, because the anxiety aroused by discussing the disease usually drives half the questions out of your mind while you are with him. But if you see that he can't be definite beyond a point, it will probably work out better for you in the long run if you don't ask him to speculate — unless there's a specific worry behind your question. If you can't feel satisfied with his explanation or management, it's your privilege to ask, as a matter of course, for a consultation with a doctor of your choice or his. This usually eases the tensions all around.

ILLNESS AND INJURY

A child's attitude reflects his parents'.

IN THE EARLY years of our marriage my wife Jane and I found
that the most difficult adjustment we had to make was to our
different attitudes toward illness. When she was sick occasionally with acute sinusitis, she admitted she was sick and stayed
home from work. If she had fever, she went to bed and expected to have a doctor take care of her. She wanted the appropriate medicine or other treatment. When I had an illness, I
ignored it unless the symptoms were truly alarming. I kept on
working, though this was a disservice to my patients and col-
leagues as well as to myself. I would take medicine if ordered to
by a doctor, but if he gave me a choice I would brush it aside.
I'd rather take the pain of tooth filling than take Novocaine.

But it wasn't just that I reacted in this way to my own illness.
It made me uncomfortable to see Jane doing what I called "giving
in" to her symptoms. I ostentatiously ignored them and I made
it clear that I thought she should change her attitude and ignore
them too. Needless to say, she felt that I was an inconsiderate
husband — in this respect, anyway — and I was. To make matters worse, I was spending all my working hours taking care of
other people's diseases.

Differences like these are, of course, built up during childhood
by family attitudes. But even in the same family the influences
on a boy are apt to be different from those on a girl. Boys are
usually taught not to cry, not to run to their mother when hurt
(or insulted), to work things out for themselves — taught not
only by words but by their father's example. Most girls are per-

mitted to have feelings and to show them, to admit the need for help, to put themselves in the care of another person when the occasion demands it.

Dr. Sybille Escalona in a study of young mothers found that the ones who took naturally to a woman's role in other respects were more often able to relax and enjoy being waited on in the obstetrical hospital, in contrast to others who felt, as soon as the baby was born, that they ought to be giving themselves their sponge baths, hopping out of bed to go to the bathroom.

It's believed that an important emotional characteristic of the men who get ulcers of the stomach and duodenum is a particularly strong denial of the normal human need to be cared for at times. It's interesting, too, that though four out of five ulcers used to occur in men, the proportion in women has been steadily rising in recent decades, presumably because of woman's changing role.

In different parts of the world there are widely varying traditions about the acceptance of suffering. In some northern American Indian tribes boys used to practice torturing themselves in order to learn to endure pain without a trace of emotion. I remember when I was first an intern and had on my ward a patient from another country who was moderately sick. He was taking it well. But in the visitors' room there were ten or fifteen of his relatives, most of whom were weeping or wailing. One woman threw herself on the floor with a shriek. I was bewildered and embarrassed. The way I'd been brought up, the more strongly you felt about a situation the stiffer you kept your upper lip and the lower you kept your voice. It took me a long time to realize that this stern self-control is a peculiarity of only certain groups, and that the dramatic show of feeling in the family in the visitors' room was only their way of showing a proper sympathy with the patient.

What's the application of this to child rearing? We can see that parents who make a great fuss about illness will, in general, bring up children who act the same way. And stoical parents will raise little stoics. It seems to me sensible to avoid either extreme.

The child who grows up too easily alarmed about bodily ailments is apt to be generally worrisome. He'll always be a hindrance in emergencies. Furthermore, his friends and associates, in the American scene, will consider his anxiety undignified and boring. And the person who has to ignore any infirmity in himself constantly jeopardizes his own and other people's health. Because he also can't stand having his family admit their diseases, he creates tensions in all of them.

The issue is first apt to present itself dramatically in the three- and four-year-old period. This is the age when children are unusually sensitive to ideas of injury, illness and death. They also readily become worried about the physical differences between boys and girls. Partly this is because they are intensely curious, and interested in cause and effect. Partly it's because they identify with other people and can imagine what it would feel like to have the afflictions they see. So they are easily frightened by pains, cuts, blood. (The reassuring concept of making things get well has great appeal, too; at times they search their bodies for scratches to cover with bandages.) So they have to depend on their parents for their cues about how to take injuries and illness. Only the parents have the experience, the knowledge, the stability to set the tone realistically. If a mother goes all to pieces over a small accident, the young child has to assume that he is in desperate danger. If the father sternly insists that a hurt doesn't hurt, the child has to learn to deny his feelings in order to keep his father's respect and his own.

Though it's good for children when parents can avoid overanxiety, there is no need for them to be hardhearted. To put it positively, they can aim to be realistic. Then they teach their children the real significance of different injuries and diseases, and how to care for them. They should feel free to be sympathetic to the degree warranted, because everyone who's miserable needs comforting. If a mother then sees that her child is making too much fuss about a small injury, she reassures him in a matter-of-fact tone, tapers off on her sympathy, changes the subject.

Occasionally there is the problem of the young child who persists in being excessively apprehensive about injuries and diseases despite a levelheaded mother. Then the question should be considered of whether he is unduly troubled in the unconscious levels of his mind. It may be sensible to get help from a child-guidance clinic or a family social agency.

Sometimes the explanation, when a child keeps running to his mother or the school nurse begging for sympathy and bandages for imaginary scratches, is that the mother without realizing it is stern and critical most of the time and melts into sympathetic kindliness only when he is suffering physically.

I've often been consulted the first thing in the morning by a mother who suspects that her child is using a physical complaint to avoid going to school. As she says, she would feel guilty if she hardheartedly sent him off and it turned out that he was developing a real disease. On the other hand, there is something in his tone of voice that makes her suspicious. She doesn't want to have the wool pulled over her eyes and she realizes that in the long run it wouldn't be good for the child to get away with this. I myself would lean in the direction of taking the child's word for it the first time. One day lost out of a school year is not that serious. I'd put him to bed, take his temperature morning and afternoon, keep an eye on his behavior. If he was full of beans all day and developed no further signs of illness, I wouldn't reproach him, but I'd be quite firm about packing him off to school the next morning. It's fairly common for children to form a mild aversion to school after being reprimanded by a teacher or having a fight with another child. Adults sometimes yield to the impulse to avoid going to work or to a certain social function on a similar basis. However, if the dread of going to school is intense and persistent, the problem is potentially more serious. On the one hand, the parent should promptly get in touch with a child psychiatrist or guidance clinic. (Clinics are apt to accept school phobias on an emergency basis.) Meanwhile, it is usually considered best to insist that the child continue to go to school because the longer he stays away, the harder it will be for him to return.

There is considerable variation throughout the world in beliefs about what causes illness and injuries. In the uneducated regions they are most often considered the work of displeased gods or mischievous demons or malevolent neighbors. But right in our own country there is a wide range too. There are people who always see a significant connection between their disease and one that occurred long ago in a relative, no matter how dissimilar these may be from a medical point of view. There are millions of Americans who hold superstitious beliefs about certain ills; for example, that the umbilical cord becomes wrapped around the unborn baby's neck when the pregnant woman reaches for an object on a high shelf. Others tie every symptom to some indiscretion in diet. There are people who assume that all their afflictions are intended by God as just punishment.

These attitudes of adults are not essentially different from those that small children develop. This first became apparent in child-guidance work. When a child visits a psychiatrist regularly over a long period of time, he learns gradually that the therapist will not criticize him for "bad" thoughts, and feels free to express his ideas in the stories he makes up, the pictures he draws, the dramas he creates with dolls. Almost invariably he will ascribe his own sickness or accidents (or those of his parents and brothers and sisters) to naughty things he has done or to evil wishes he has had. Partly this is due to parental teaching. "You caught a cold because you didn't wear your rubbers." "You fell off your tricycle because you were riding too fast." "You've given mother a headache because you were quarreling all day." "You got a stomachache because you ate too much candy." "You might put his eye out with that stick." Parents, trying to teach healthy habits and good behavior, have the natural impulse to make use of all the misfortunes that come to hand. But even when mothers don't use this approach, I think their children often come to the same conclusions. They are normal human beings, so they disobey occasionally and they have guilty feelings. Then anything that happens to make them feel sick or uncomfortable automatically hooks up with the guilt. And because they all have mean wishes at times toward other members of the family (and don't know yet that thoughts don't cause bodily harm), they assume that these actually cause the hurts and illnesses that afflict others.

Since it's preferable to keep children from becoming excessively guilty people, and from being guilty about the wrong things, I think it's preferable not to accuse them of having harmed themselves and, particularly, of having harmed others, when there is no proof of bad intention. Even when a child has hurt another deliberately or in anger, but is a generally considerate character, it may be wise to reassure him that he didn't mean to hurt him that badly. If a child is definitely mean, he (and his parents) needs professional help rather than more and more reproaches that are doing no good.

When a member of the family has a serious disease, it's good to remember that a child may well be harboring a completely unrealistic conviction that he's partly to blame. A parent should at least explain in simple terms the cause of ill health in a close relative and then listen to a child's questions and comments, to see how he understands it or misunderstands it. If the parent gets a hint that the child feels guilt, it's wise to get it out in the open so that he can be reassured. "Maybe you think you made Susie sick because you were mean to her that day. But that didn't make her sick. It was a germ she caught."

IV
Aspects of Personality
Development

❮◦❮◦❮◦❮◦❮◦❮◦

HOW EARLY IS
PERSONALITY FORMED?

*It takes shape surprisingly young, but continues
to be influenced all through life.*

IN WORRIED TONES a parent will ask a doctor or a lecturer, "Do you really believe that a child's personality is largely formed by three years of age?" The question comes up most commonly in regard to the first child when he has reached about that age. Raising him, the mother confesses, has been no cinch. There have been some tensions, especially in the second year. They may have arisen around feeding or around toilet training, or around management in general. Some young warriors fight their mothers in all these areas at once. The child may be showing the wounds of battle in the form of exaggerated balkiness or frequent temper tantrums or apprehensiveness.

The mother feels somewhat the worse for wear herself. Though she has been an unusually devoted parent, and knows it, she feels guilty about the tensions. She's really asking whether she has warped her child for good and all.

A great many people are incredulous or indignant when they hear any statement about personality being formed carly. I can still remember the time when I first knew my future wife Jane (who had taken several psychology courses in college and had been a volunteer worker in a child-guidance clinic), and she explained this theory to me. I, who hadn't even taken one course and who certainly didn't know beans about it one way or the other, immediately declared with great scorn, "That's ridiculous!"

For one thing, most of us don't like the idea of somebody else deciding our fate, or our children's fate, for us — whether it's a dictator or a psychologist. It threatens to rob us of our free will, which most of us feel is one of our most precious possessions. Also, our common sense reminds us of how much we have been influenced at later stages of our lives by friends, experiences, the career we have chosen.

There's no doubt about it that if you study child development — as a nursery-school teacher or as a psychiatrist or as a parent — you can't escape the conclusion that many of the patterns of personality are quite clear by two or three years of age. One young child is quiet and agreeable and he retains that tendency, more or less, for years. Another is strenuous and independent from first to last. One is cautious. He always has to study a new situation carefully. He doesn't try anything new until he has become sure in his own mind that he can succeed at it. As an adult he's still much the same. Another rushes into everything — the newer the better. One three-year-old is serenely self-confident in any situation, another becomes anxious on slight provocation. One is sociable — he loves people, and the more the merrier. Another shrinks back from crowds and strangers. He likes his companions one at a time. He's comfortable with only certain types and he's quite happy when he's alone. Five years later, ten years later these children may still have the same traits.

The question could be raised right away of whether such characteristics are developed because of experiences a child has had in his first few years or whether he was born with them. This is a question that hasn't been answered yet with any finality or completeness. A few studies have been made which seem to show that certain *general* kinds of temperament — energeticness or quietness, boldness or cautiousness — show up fairly early in infancy and have a tendency to persist throughout childhood. But it's hard to prove whether such characteristics were surely present at birth, because a baby doesn't do many things that show his personality in the early weeks. He sleeps, he cries, he eats, and then he sleeps again. Even a question like whether he cries vigorously or gently depends so much on how hungry he is, how long he has to wait. But the people who see a lot of new-born babies, such as nursery nurses in obstetrical hospitals, are apt to be strong believers in inborn temperament. They are impressed with the variations they see every day. The mothers who are most convinced about differences from the time of birth are those who have had nonidentical twins. They will tell you, "When you have one baby at a time you forget just what each one was like in the first year. With two, you notice right away how differently they react to everything. Pretty soon you find yourself predicting how each will behave in a new situation, and you're usually right."

Though it's a side issue, I should add here that most psychiatrists and psychologists are thoroughly convinced that very *specific social habits* — good or bad — such as truthfulness or dishonesty, dutifulness or irresponsibility, frugality or prodigality, temperance or drunkenness, lawfulness or delinquency, are not inherited at all but are learned as a result of life experiences. These are quite different from general temperament.

But if we admit that the character of many children has taken definite form by two or three, this certainly doesn't mean that it can't or won't change later. In fact, no one — not even an adult — can stay the same from one year to the next. One middle-aged person in a new job rather suddenly develops a self-assurance that he had always lacked before. A still older individual may acquire serenity at sixty or sixty-five after a lifetime of obvious uncertainty. Most of us are aware of going through phases of tension and relaxation, of greater or lesser sociability, of relative optimism or discouragement.

In childhood it's even more clear that no child retains just the same personality for very long. The different stages of development keep stirring him up from within and subjecting him to different conditions from without. As a result, different aspects of his character are being encouraged or discouraged. The striving for some degree of independence in the one-to-three-year-old period accentuates the tendency to balkiness, willfulness in many children. Then much of this will subside again in the next phase. After three, the drive to become just like the parents is particularly strong. So the imprint of father on son and mother on daughter makes for modification of character in all children, great in some, less in others. The years between six and adolescence show a push in the opposite direction. The child now usually resists conforming to his parents' pattern and wants to be as much like his friends as possible. Then a lot depends on what friends are available and how well he's accepted. If he's insufficiently popular to enjoy the gang, he can't so easily fall back on his parents any longer but may find outlets in reading about heroes or in such hobbies as nature or science. These may greatly influence his personality and his career. Sometimes a child who's shy at seven can learn by nine, with the right friends, to be sociable and secure.

Adolescence opens up a maze of new avenues. The sudden intensification of feelings for others embarrasses one child and makes him pull back into himself. Another, who has been a relatively unsociable person before, is swept into intense friendships with a boy or girl who shares the same special interests, or into hero worship of a teacher. A lot depends on whether an appealing companion is available when the adolescent is ready to find himself through friendship. The outcome of bodily changes has a bearing too. Physical awkwardness or prolonged acne is very handicapping to some but not to others. A fat boy who has been poor at sports and something of a joke at parties may turn quite muscular in a hurry and find that he is just what the football team and the girls like.

Many teen-agers, especially boys, go through a very rebellious stage, and some get involved in delinquency. The nonconformity in one individual leads him into a highly productive career in opening up a new field. In a few, it persists only as eccentricities which don't accomplish anything. In most, it disappears, and they settle down as average cooperative citizens. The end result partly depends on the character that existed before adolescence, partly on the opportunities for further education and work.

Marriages are certainly fateful. Each of us is strongly drawn to only certain individuals of the opposite sex in adolescence and adulthood, and the choice eventually narrows down to one. Each spouse of the couple finds in the other what his personality most needs. In this sense marriage is predestined by the two characters which existed before they ever met each other. But then a new process of change sets in as they share a house, an income, children, friends. Though each has sought what he or she most wanted in a mate, he or she also finds other qualities, favorable or unfavorable, that he or she hadn't bargained for. (You notice how impartially I say he or she each time.) A husband can foster the effectiveness, the devotion, the happiness of his wife or he can discourage them. His wife can do the same things for him.

Each of us has some choice in choosing his life's job — more in one case, less in another, depending on circumstances. But then the job turns around and begins remolding the individual. One person blooms at his work, a second has a tendency to dry up. A third becomes bossy with success, a fourth becomes more kindly.

Sure, children's personalities have definite shape by two or three — they'd be quite colorless otherwise. The shape of each personality has a considerable tendency to persist — just as the shape of a house tends to persist even after extensive alterations. But the shape of a child's personality can never stay the same. One changes greatly, another a little. It depends on the thousand influences, favorable and unfavorable, that are brought to bear.

In the following chapters in this section, I'll be discussing three basic factors which play a large part in the shaping of a child's personality — the differences between males and females, the influence of the family, and the learning stages of development.

SOME DIFFERENCES BETWEEN THE SEXES

Are they inborn or taught?

THIS HAS BEEN a highly controversial topic since the beginnings of history. A writer sticks his neck out by expressing his opinions. Certain members of both sexes will want to chop his head off.

The women called feminists, who are resentful of men's advantages, grant that there are certain anatomical differences, but they believe firmly that the supposed differences in temperament and capability are bogus. They think that men have staked out a claim to certain characteristics and privileges by brute strength and bluff, and have simply got away with it.

There is little doubt that men since the beginning of the race have claimed and secured privileges that they had no God-given right to, particularly in regard to property, marriage, occupation. In our own times women have had to fight hard to gain the right to be educated, to vote, to enter many fields of work. It all started back in prehistoric times when mankind lived by hunting and fighting. Men had the strength and fierceness for this work and to lay down the rules at home.

It was only as mankind found more civilized ways to make a living that women got chances — over the centuries — to prove their capabilities in certain fields, and worked on men's consciences to let down the barriers.

Of course throughout these thousands of years smart women haven't been just sitting around waiting for the day of legal equality. As Chaucer's Wife of Bath said in the fourteenth century, what women really want most is control over men, and they have found subtle ways of achieving it while allowing men to keep the illusion that they are still lords and masters.

But we shouldn't be misled, by the obvious fact that women have been unfairly deprived of all kinds of rights, into jumping to the conclusion that therefore women should now be considered the same as men. That's where the feminists have been fuzzy. They have been so jealous of men for their privileges that they have insisted on the very same ones, without stopping to consider whether they were worth very much. They've demanded exactly the same kinds of college educations, exactly the same kinds of jobs. The feminists broke the trail in the nineteenth and early twentieth centuries. American women have followed along the path. They have become more like men in their interests and clothes, in their manner of walking, talking and laughing. The feminists have also been so sure that men had all the advantages that they have failed to notice that there are some men who yearn for a woman's life, though they don't shout it from the housetops.

Of course the argument isn't over yet. There are many shades of opinion and almost no proofs. Those who think woman would be more like man if she had the same upbringing point out, correctly, that a little girl is treated and molded differently from a little boy from the day she is born. It's almost impossible to be sure which characteristics in girls and boys are due to inborn nature and which to rearing.

I have no new proof to offer. I personally think that though there are no absolute differences in temperament, there are quantitative differences right from birth, which then become accentuated, to a greater or lesser degree, by upbringing. I think that there are more baby boys who are restless and insistent and balky from the start, that more girls take life as it comes even in the bassinet. This is the most likely reason why little boys are notoriously more difficult to train to the toilet.

In the one-to-two-year-old period, when children make little distinction between boys' toys and girls' toys, a boy will so often take the ear light away from the doctor and work for many minutes twisting the magnifying glass, attaching and detaching the ear speculum, trying to find and work the switch. This looks like the love of machines and gadgets for their own sake, quite apart from whether they're really useful. I've frequently handed the ear light to a girl of the same age. She smiles sweetly, as if appreciating the friendliness, glances at the light, perhaps tastes it, and then, more likely than not, lays it down without ever trying to twist one of its parts.

I remember years ago a seven-year-old girl who had to be confined to her room in an apartment house in New York for four weeks because that was the rule for scarlet fever in those days. She didn't feel sick for more than a week and she and her mother spent a lot of the time sitting at the window which looked down on a courtyard where some preschool children of the neighborhood played. All day long, they told me, the same little boys were racing back and forth, on foot or on tricycle, pointing pretend pistols at one another and making that fierce *pow! pow!* noise. An equal number of girls were busy riding trikes or wheeling dolls or playing other games. They were often shot at. But not once in that month did one of them rush around with a wild gleam in her eye shouting *pow!*

I'd be the first to admit that there is no such thing as a pre-formed male instinct to point pistols and say *pow*. Little boys learn about pistols from older boys and from radios and movies. I know that a few girls are pistol toters too. But I think that the urge to play at being fierce and intrusive comes more naturally to most boys and that a girl has to be unusually spunky by nature and driven by special rivalry to get the same fun out of it.

Years ago an editor of *The New Yorker* magazine described a scene in a residential area, where he was a guest for the week-end, in which workmen were using dynamite for an excavation. All the boys and men in the neighborhood were there, a huge crowd, from the age of three to the age of ninety, attentive, happy, excited. When the writer and his host got back to their house it shocked them to realize that their wives could have sat there contentedly through all the excitement and weren't even interested in hearing about the violence of the blasting.

In the preschool years, children's primitive feelings — both positive and negative — are close to the surface. Boys have strong romantic attachments to their mothers and at three and four are apt to talk about marrying them someday. Normal girls feel the same way about their fathers. Boys and girls are interested in where babies come from and want to have some of their own. They play house together, the boys wanting to play father, the girls playing mother. It's often not realized that many little boys, when they hear that only girls can grow babies inside their abdomens, become resentful. They obstinately insist that they can do this too. In other words, creativeness — of the most fundamental type — is a strong ambition in young children and boys have it just as much as girls.

After the age of six or seven the child is gradually forced to take a more realistic view of life. The boy denies his romantic feelings about his mother, stops playing at being father, becomes unfriendly toward girls, applies himself to school and to his pals.

What has become of the creative urge in the boy that was so dramatic? It seems to be converted into creativeness of a more general and impersonal sort: the building of model planes and scooters and pushmobiles and tree houses, the laying out of model-train systems, the making of collections, the designing of futuristic automobiles and planes. Girls, on the average, seem to need less of these substitute outlets.

Later in adolescence and early adulthood, artistically gifted individuals write stories and poetry and plays, paint pictures, compose music, produce plays and films. Those with strong drives in other directions make advances in research and invention, establish businesses and industries, design engineering marvels. A much larger number of men reach the top in all these fields. This is most readily explained by the fact that men have to work at these jobs to make the money, and women have to care for home and children. Also, many of these fields have only recently been opened to women. But even when these factors are taken into full account, most experts in the fields in which women *have* had a fairer chance (writing, painting, composing, for instance) believe that a smaller percentage of women achieve the highest levels of creativity. If this is true it can be explained on two bases: (1) women on the average have less aggressiveness (if women went at homemaking and child rearing with the drive of an industrialist or the absorption of an artist, the home would be intolerable to live in); (2) woman's creativeness has a direct, soul-satisfying outlet in the bearing and rearing of children. To put this the other way around, the man (like the four-year-old boy frustrated because he can't bear a baby) is denied the primary creativeness and has to find a substitute.

Another significant development, as the child after six tries to pull back from his intense personal attachment to parents, is an increasing interest in abstract subjects such as arithmetic, algebra, geometry and physics. Both girls and boys experience this shift from the personal to the impersonal, but boys feel it more strongly and on the average take to abstractions with greater enthusiasm. To be sure, a fair number of boys get into trouble with mathematics, because they either are too dull or get mixed up. And a fair number of girls enjoy math for its own sake. (Intelligence tests show that there are just as many bright girls as bright boys.) But what I have been impressed with is how many more girls than boys complain that they hate math, whether they can do it or not. It just seems unappealing, unrewarding, unnatural, obnoxious to them. (Many grown women express the same feelings about balancing their checkbooks.) This is understandable on the basis that girls and women are permitted by nature and by upbringing to retain their natural emotions, to face life realistically as a personal existence. The male, in contrast, is taught to deny his feelings to a greater degree and so he has more energy to divert into the realm of abstract ideas and theory. In this sense pure mathematics (like pure physics) is the perfect escape. It's totally impersonal.

Much the same difference in attitude comes out between grown men and women when they happen to discuss the law, which is a method of establishing logical, impartial rules of behavior. When a man is explaining why the law happens to work out unfairly in a certain case, a woman cries out, "How silly!" Her human sensibleness is outraged. The man is distressed that she can't understand that for general social purposes the law *has* to take this position.

One of the sharpest differences between males and females is in their attitudes toward danger. Most men and boys seem to be courting danger a lot of the time. Girls and women are strictly sensible in this respect — they don't like danger and they keep away from it. It's boys who go out too far on thin ice and climb cliffs and it's men who take risks in boats and cars. What's the matter with them? It's the nature of males to worry — at least a little — about their courage, their ability to compete, their virility. They have to reassure themselves by testing and proving themselves. It isn't just a relief to them to find each time that they can win out — the process of facing danger becomes a positive pleasure. Women are bothered not only by the risks their men take but by the gay spirit in which they do it.

While we're still on the subjects of virility and cars, I want to mention two other aspects of these. For a man, a car is obviously a lot more than a convenience. Most of all it is a symbol of his ambition to be a powerful person: in reaching his goals, in competing with other men, in impressing women. This is why men always have the itch to buy a car at least one notch beyond what they can afford. This is why cars kept getting longer in length and higher in horsepower during the 1950's, when there was no sense to either trend. A man will happily spend hours shining his car and then not want it used for an important family trip because it is raining. By contrast, most women have a very down-to-earth attitude about a car: it's simply a means of transportation. There are two exceptions. Some women are eager to have convertibles despite the expense and impracticality. And some women do stop to admire sports cars, the most impractical kind of all. I suppose these interests are romantic.

Men and boys, in wanting to express their virility through cars, drive on the average faster, more assertively, more dangerously. And that's, of course, why they have more accidents. But man's more aggressive nature seems to carry with it, as a partial corrective, a sharp awareness of the rules and a strong obligation to be cooperative. He feels these even at angry moments when he's refusing to obey them. The average man seems more aware of the drivers alongside him and behind him and takes a certain pride, at least part of the time, in accommodating them. "Typical women drivers" bother men not only because they drive slowly (having no aggressiveness to express on the highway) but also because, when they tie up traffic by being in the wrong lane for a turn, they are blithely unaware of the angry line behind them. When a man ties up traffic, he's apt to be doing it deliberately out of defiance.

I want to mention one other real difference between males and females. Girls and women are willing to admit their dependence on relatives, on professional people, even on passers-by when there is need. Yet this is one of the hardest things in the world for most boys and men. Here is a small example: husband and wife are driving in the country and it has been apparent for some time that they have lost their way. The wife says, "Why don't we stop and ask that man?" The husband answers hurriedly, "I'm pretty sure the highway we're looking for is just ahead." Twenty minutes later they are still as lost as ever and they repeat the same conversation with the same results.

The child psychiatrist often hears the following statement from a mother: "I've been worrying about the child's attitude for months and I've suggested to my husband several times that we seek help. But he has felt that I'm overconcerned, that we should wait a while longer to see if the child won't outgrow the difficulty."

In the first example, the husband knows underneath that he's lost. In the second, the father is just as devoted to his child and just as concerned underneath about the symptoms. Men are usually willing to ask for assistance in a problem that's obviously outside their responsibility and competence. It's agony for most of them to admit they need help in something they feel they should be able to solve themselves. This trait of men may be partly due to their inborn nature, but probably most of it can be blamed on their training — from early childhood — to be independent, to show no "weak" feelings, to ask for no sympathy. (It is suspected by doctors that this denial of the need to lean on others at times of difficulty, when carried to extremes, has a lot to do with the cause of ulcers.)

Of course men aren't indomitable any more than women. They only try to postpone giving in for a longer time. Experienced nurses agree that men in hospitals pretend that they aren't seriously ill when they are and that they don't weep as some women do. But they add that there's no baby like the man who has given up pretending and become frankly worried: he's ringing for the nurse all hours of the day and night, reporting the most insignificant symptoms and asking her to do for him things which he could perfectly well do for himself.

No matter how long they live together, men and women continue to be surprised and baffled by the differences between them. They sometimes make fun of each other and complain of each other. But in the long run it's easier for most people to get along with those who are temperamentally unlike themselves. It's the temperamental differences as much as the physical differences that draw men and women together, and it's a great mistake to try to minimize them in any way. They are there to be enjoyed, not groused about.

CAN WE FOSTER CONFORMITY
OR INDIVIDUALITY?

Efforts to force a child into an
exact mold often backfire.

A NUMBER of books and articles have appeared in recent years
which deplore the increasing pressures which, they say, American
civilization is putting on everyone to conform. This led a parent
to ask me whether I think children should be brought up as
individualists or as conformists.

I was surprised to realize that I'd never worried about this
question before. That is not because I'm not a worrier. I worry,
for instance, about the slowing down of America's industrial
expansion, about the trashiness of some of our ideals, about the
inadequate support we give to education in many parts of the
country, about whether the steady climb in the proportion of
mothers going to work means that child care has lost its appeal.

Perhaps I'd be worried about conformity, too, if I myself saw
dramatic evidence of its increase all around me. The people I
have known best have mainly been students and professional
men and women — a narrow slice of the population. It's true
that in the depression in the 1930's quite a number of students
were stirred up by the desperation of the times, and they ac-
quired boldly radical views in politics, economics, the arts. Nowadays there seem to be few radicals or nonconformists among
university students, and this is disappointing to the philosophers
who say that if an individual doesn't show any protest or origi-
nality in his youth, he never will. But before I get discouraged

about the present, I only have to think back to my student days in the '20's, when athletes got the lion's share of our adulation, "collegiate" dressers set the styles, scholars pretended they didn't study, for fear of being called grinds, and the few individuals who were seriously interested in politics or the world or the arts were considered strange fellows. The most popular occupational choices were banking and stockbrokerage, because they were expected to lead to quick wealth and early retirement. In other words, there was a great deal of conformity, and often in a mold which was self-centered and immature. Most of today's students that I know seem quite thoughtful, sensible, high-principled by comparison. If they are to be called conformists because they don't stress their individuality, at least they don't *stress* their conformity, like a flock of bleating sheep.

It seems a fair statement that America encourages conformity in the sense that teamwork is highly valued and everyone is expected to be a friendly fellow. (I think we carry it too far when our newspapers call our statesmen by nicknames and insist that they grin in all their pictures.) Most American parents (including me) are concerned that their children be socially well adjusted and well liked. But French parents, for instance, have no such aim. It would seem unworthy to them, as if they lacked pride and principles. Their great concern is that the child should conform to his own family's ideals. This relative independence of the opinion of outsiders shows up in the assurance with which the average Frenchman expresses his individual views on any subject. So, different cultures vary in the type of conformity they foster.

But what would make for the difference between conformity and individualism in an American child? Can one or the other be cultivated? Attitudes such as these are mainly created by the interaction between the parents and the child as he grows. But I don't think that it is a simple matter of the parents' deciding which quality they want and then forming it deliberately. To be sure, conforming parents *are* more apt to have conforming children because they teach this by example as well as by word. And children tend — other things being equal — to pattern themselves after their parents. Similarly, parents with very independent views are apt to have a larger proportion of their children end up as individualists.

This general statement still leaves lots of room for variations. Some of the most radical individuals come from conservative families (to the great distress of the latter). A very bohemian couple may find that they have reared a conventional child, much to their surprise. These extreme reversals are apt to be caused by revolt or revulsion of one kind or another. Some of the factors can be seen fairly clearly at certain stages of development.

In the one-to-three-year-old period every child asserts his independence to some degree. He becomes quite choosy about what he will eat. He may want to take over the control of his bowel movements and foil his mother's efforts to train him. He wants to dress himself and decide which direction to go during a walk. If he and his mother are both obstinate people, he may — in the long conflict of wills — become an exceedingly negativistic individual who always does the opposite of what's asked of him, whether he really wants to or not. Some adults are still saying no, automatically, to everything that is suggested.

In the three-to-six-year-old stage boys become rivalrous with their fathers, girls with their mothers. Eventually they decide that this is a hopeless and risky business, because their parents are so much bigger and smarter, so they strive instead to be just like them. ("If you can't beat the opposition, join it.") But a few children can't make the shift with such good grace. A sense of having been defeated by unfair means rankles on in the unconscious mind. This buried seed may blossom, years later, under just the right circumstances (a cruel depression, for example), into an indignant resolve to lead the underdogs against the powers that be.

In adolescence each person goes through a slow, rather painful process of rebirth, of finding his adult identity. He senses that he will soon be big enough, wise enough, self-supporting enough to be on his own. His sexual drives become strong. All this stirs up renewed feelings of rivalry with and rebellion against the parent who has had the upper hand for so long. He sharply questions his parent's rules, ideals, religion, way of life. Yet from earliest childhood he has been molded and has molded himself in his parent's image. He acts as if the conflict were between himself and his present-day parent. He argues and complains and protests against parental authority in all the small issues that seem important at the moment. But this is largely a sham battle. The real conflict is within himself: between the strong pull to become a replica of his parent — in character, in occupation, in outlook — and the urge to rebel, to be different, to excel.

In deciding what kind of person he will be, what kind of career he'll make, he also has to take into account the world around him and the jobs waiting to be done. A boy may go into his father's occupation, whether it's farming or storekeeping or physics. He can carry out the job very much the way his father did. Or he may harp on his determination to use newer methods, or spend all his time trying to make revolutionary discoveries, as if he was mainly concerned with showing up his father's stodginess. Other boys show their rivalry with their fathers — or fear of rivalry — by avoiding the father's occupation like the plague. One will say, in high school or college, "I don't know what I want to be, but I'm sure I'm not going into my father's line of work." Fairly often, such a boy outgrows his fear of competition, in the middle of college or later, and quietly enters his father's field.

Back in the days when few women attended college, a girl's unconscious motive for attending was sometimes a rebellion against her mother's way of life. Nowadays a girl whose mother has a degree may balk at going to college for the same hidden reason. The doctor runs into the young mother who pushes newer concepts of child care to extremes. The explanation becomes apparent when he learns that the grandmother is in a state of constant, agitated alarm about what's being done to the baby; but the more she argues, the more the mother exaggerates the newfangledness of her methods.

Of course this rivalrousness on the part of the younger generation is the mainspring for much of the progress of civilization, so it shouldn't be deplored. The main question that determines the effectiveness of each impatient young person is whether he eventually becomes mature enough to gear his individualistic strivings to the realities of the world he lives in. Are the criticisms he makes of the methods, the attitudes, the institutions which he sees around him well founded, or is he just imagining faults to justify his resentful feelings? And if he has discovered wrongs that truly need righting, will he be able to harness his energy to the job, whether it's a better way to crate eggs, or to teach social studies in the local school, or to bring peace and plenty to the world? Or will he never be able to express his dissatisfactions in any more productive way than to crab, argue, or perhaps grow a beard?

So, to the parent who asked whether children should be brought up as individualists or as conformists, I can't give a very practical answer. Parents really don't have too much choice or control. Whether they are conformists or individualists themselves, they wouldn't want to produce children who were very opposite from themselves, even if somebody told them they ought to, and gave them a magic formula for doing so. They can at least be fairly confident that a majority of their children will suit them in these respects, without their having to make any special effort.

No parents want to create extremes of submissiveness or bullheadedness or eccentricity in their children; and if they see such symptoms developing they'll need professional help to find the causes and correct them.

Certainly it would be foolish and risky for any parent or professional person to think he could deliberately create a certain preconceived type or degree of individuality in a child by applying special pressures. Parents fail often enough when they are merely trying to pass on interests to their children — such as music or athletics or cards or gardening. The child is apt to end up with an aversion instead. To try to manipulate the shape of a child's personality would be a hundred times more complex. It would also imply that the parent was too anxious or too domineering, and these attitudes would have an influence quite different from what the parent was planning.

We can give our children security. We can set reasonable limits on their general behavior in such matters as politeness and dutifulness. We will influence them greatly by our example. But only rarely do we succeed in forcing them into a specific mold. Fortunately, most of us are too busy and too agreeable to try.

LEARNING IS AN ENDLESS
PROCESS IN CHILDHOOD

*And each small skill requires ceaseless striving
and practice for months before it is
finally mastered.*

LEARNING anything new is rarely a simple or brief matter for a
child. It's more like an arduous campaign that lasts for months,
usually with three distinct stages in it. I'd like to take examples
from different periods of childhood which show that the com-
plexity of the process increases with age, but that the three steps
are still visible.

An appealing example from infancy is sitting. The average
baby learns to hold himself erect somewhere around six to seven
months of age. (He has to have help getting into that position
for quite a time before he can do it himself. Even when he
learns to get into a sitting position he's apt to do it at first by
pushing himself up out of a creeping position by means of his
arms.) But long before he can sit steadily — a couple of months
at least — he senses that this exciting development is coming
next. Every time you take hold of his hands while he's lying
on his back he uses your grip to try to haul himself up. He
tenses his neck and shoulders, flexes his arms and gets red in the
face with the effort. How in the world does he know that this
skill is due soon and that it's his job to keep trying? Probably
it's mostly an instinct born in him, just because he's a member
of a sitting species, as a colt struggles to his feet right after be-

ing born because he has the instincts of a horse. But maybe even at this very young age the baby is influenced, too, by what he sees his parents doing and by his desire to be like them. (Blind children have to be encouraged to stand and walk because they haven't been stimulated by the sight of these activities.)

The day comes when he can sit upright for a few seconds before gently toppling over. (It looks so funny to us that he doesn't try to brace himself or even wince as he goes over.)

From this day on, for many months, the mother's problem is how to make him lie down again. He'll lie down to take a bottle and he may lie down when he's dead tired, but all the rest of the time he sits. It isn't just that he prefers to sit. He has a violent opinion about it. He considers it an outrage to be forced to lie down. His mother probably has to push him over forcibly for diapering and then he'll cry indignantly — unless he's distracted with something quite fascinating. No matter how many times a day he has to be pushed down, for no matter how many months, he never seems to learn that it has to be.

It will be *months* before he dimly realizes that sitting is a very practical position when he wants to do certain things, but that there's no obligation to stay in that position just because he knows how.

So the first stage is trying and trying without being able to do it. The second stage — after the skill is achieved — is to keep doing and doing, whether there's any sense to it or not. The third stage is to use the skill when it's necessary but otherwise leave it alone.

You can see the same stages even more touchingly in standing. Weeks before a baby can pull himself to his feet you can see him working on the problem. He moves his hands up the slats of his crib or playpen and then, while he tugs, he tries to arrange his legs so that they'll be in a position to help. His legs *aren't* much help, his arms aren't strong enough to do it all, but he never gets discouraged. The moment finally comes when he succeeds. Then, so often, there follow several days of distress for him and his mother. After an hour of standing he's exhausted. But he doesn't know how to sit down. He begins crying with fatigue. Yet when his mother has mercy on him, unhitches his hands and sits him down, he's instantly indignant about being put into such a babyish position, cries now with anger and — forgetting all about his fatigue — scrambles to his feet again. This time he's tired again in ten minutes, but again he forgets this as soon as he's down. Fortunately, he learns to sit down in a few days — usually by just letting go in desperation and finding that it doesn't hurt, his legs being so short and his behind so well padded. (Think how it would jolt an adult.)

Walking comes next. The baby prepares for it for weeks by "cruising" (Doctor Gesell's graphic word) around his crib or playpen with the help of his hands and occasionally letting go when he needs them to handle something else. After he's once learned to walk alone, the stage of obligatory walking sets in and lasts for months. To be sure, he uses the walking to branch out into other activities — climbing, pulling things, shaking things, feeling things. Yet even when he has nowhere special to go he just keeps going. Later, much later, he gradually realizes that walking and running are good for getting somewhere, but that sitting is more comfortable and practical between times.

If you want a good adjective to apply to these first and second stages of learning, you can use the word "compulsive" — compulsive trying and compulsive practice — because it means having to do something again and again whether there's any sense to it or not. A correct but stuffy adjective for the third stage is "integrated," meaning that the new skill is no longer running the child but that the child has now fitted it in among his other abilities, to use when needed.

A child-development psychologist, Dr. Myrtle McGraw, called attention to these stages of learning in infancy. Dr. Ives Hendrick, a psychoanalyst, noticed the same compulsive elements at the other end of childhood, in some of the activities of adolescents, and used the term "instinct to mastery." Of course this drive to keep trying and then to keep practicing can be seen all through childhood. The two-year-old rocks the pedals of a tricycle up and down for days before he gets the hang of letting the upper pedal come over the top of the circle. Then he pedals with gusto for years without any thought of whether he has anywhere to go.

Perhaps the most important thing that a child keeps practicing in the age period between three and six is being a parent. It's clearest to see in a girl with her baby doll. First come the simple actions — laying the doll in a bed, covering it with a blanket, picking it up again, transferring it to the doll carriage. As the months go by, the play becomes more elaborate and realistic — giving bottles, changing diapers, bathing, dressing and undressing, asking for an ever-more-complete wardrobe. By four or five years of age a girl is talking to her doll (or to a smaller child who has been assigned the role of baby) with the same words and tone of voice that her mother uses in baby care. By keeping at it for three years the child has really mastered the essentials — not just the manual skills but, more importantly, the attitudes — of motherhood. After six, moving into a different stage of childhood, she can gradually put compulsive baby care aside until she really needs to use it at twenty or twenty-five. And if you had been able to make a tape recording of how she talked to her doll at five, you'd be amazed at how closely it would match her talk to her child twenty years later — much the same proportions of affection, bossing, disapproval.

An occupation of the seven-to-nine-year-old period that fascinates me is secret-society formation. A group of boys is suddenly carried away with the idea. The activity is feverish: finding a suitable meeting place, printing the badges, electing officers, voting on the admission or rejection of new members. Is there a realistic purpose to all this effort? It's hard to find. It isn't to make new friendships, because they usually all know one another already. It isn't to guard a secret that exists already — in most cases they have to think hard to cook up a secret. I believe that the underlying purpose, though they wouldn't recognize it, is the compulsion to practice social organization. Deep inside they sense that the day will come when as adults they must be able to take their places in groups set up for honest-to-goodness purposes, whether it's to bargain collectively or combat delinquency or establish a new business. So they feel the urge to go off by themselves where parents and teachers won't bother them, to set standards of behavior for themselves and show disapproval of those who are blackballed, to prove to themselves and others that they can go through the motions of organization and administration just as cooperatively and solemnly as any grownups. As in all compulsive activities, once isn't enough. The club fades out of existence in a few days or weeks because the basic urge behind it has been temporarily satisfied. But months later the itch to practice again has become strong enough to launch a new effort.

Some of you who were on the bashful side in early adolescence and had not yet had any romantic experience can probably remember a long period of preoccupation with the theoretical problems of how to speak to an attractive person of the opposite sex, how to get a date, how to behave on a date. You imagined it a hundred different ways, wanting desperately to be charming, sophisticated, successful. In this daydreaming the mood was one of perplexity more often than pleasure. (At fourteen I had to call on the help of an imaginary disaster during which I would rush to the house of a certain girl — to whom I'd never actually spoken — in a high-powered sports car, the owner of which had luckily been killed. I was always blocked, though, by the realization that I didn't know how to drive.)

Sooner or later the ice is broken and finally there is a real date — or at least an encounter. But getting over this hump rarely leads to a falling-in-love in the grown-up sense. Usually there are several years of what you might call practice romance. The attachments tend to be of short duration, and to follow one another closely. Even when they are very intense they differ from "the real thing" in how absorbed the boy or girl is apt to be in his own feelings and how unrealistic he may be in the choice of the loved one. This is recognized in the remark that's often made about a young adolescent girl, "She's in love with love."

The compulsive quality of the boy's or girl's practicing at romance is shown in another way in his impulse to try to attract a person — or several at the same time — just to see if he can. He or she may not feel particular affection for the member of the opposite sex whom he tries to approach. Or he may consider himself very much in love with one person and still make a strong play for someone else on the spur of the moment. When you think of it, this seems a callous, experimental, promiscuous attitude. But it is probably normal to some degree for both boys and girls in the early teens. Even the ones who are too bashful to try are daydreaming about amorous adventures. To be sure, the egotistical individual will carry this experimental attitude to great lengths. The child who is basically kind is not experimenting because of an unnatural craving for conquest but rather because of uncertainty about his own attractiveness, uncertainty about his ability to play his part in romance.

The road from birth to adulthood is a continuous succession of stages of development. Each one involves the learning of new skills and attitudes. So a child is never free of the compulsion to try, to experiment, to practice, to master. This is often nerve-racking to parents. They have to exert sensible controls — for his sake and for theirs. If they can figure out what he is trying to accomplish (which he often doesn't know himself), they may be less bothered, better able to guide his efforts constructively.

V

Facing Facts with Your Child

❰❁❰❁❰❁❰❁❰❁❰❁

SHOULD A CHILD BELIEVE
IN SANTA CLAUS?

*All young children believe in him — the only
difference is in how the parents present him.*

"I WOULD LIKE to know," a mother wrote me, "if you 'believe in Santa Claus' or in perpetuating the myth of Santa Claus. I actually think it an insult to any normal child's intelligence to expect him to believe the incredible things he is told about Santa Claus' abilities and accomplishments. The shock of discovering Santa Claus does not exist cannot be half as bad as discovering the parents' dishonesty."

I wouldn't dare try to offer advice to experienced parents (those having a child at least three years old) because they have probably settled on their Christmas pattern by now. Every established family has its hallowed ritual that covers all details: the trimming of the tree, the reading of "The Night Before Christmas," the stocking presents, the tree presents, precise foods at dinner, the visits to relatives. And nobody wants his Christmas traditions tampered with, particularly by an outsider.

One year when our children were young, we happened to decorate the mantel with eight fragile plaster reindeer that drew a cardboard sleigh. Each year more antlers and legs broke off and the sleigh became more crumpled. Identical new ones could not be found, so we parents wanted to start over with something different. The suggestion was turned down indignantly by the children. You would have thought we were proposing to do away with Christmas altogether. The crippled reindeer had to be propped up again in ever thicker drifts of cotton snow.

One year a long-leaf pine tree was bought instead of the usual spruce. Its beauty was admired by all grown-up visitors, but the boys couldn't stand it.

However, there may be some young couples just starting out who'd like a discussion of certain Christmas-time issues, before they crystallize their own pattern of celebration. Of course their pattern is in a somewhat fluid state when they are first married because the husband has grown up with different traditions from those of the wife and some kind of compromise has to be made anyway.

Everyone thinks of Santa Claus as being one character with one role to play. Yet, of course, his act is different in every family, and so is his personality. In one case the children are taken to talk to him at the department store by parents who behave as if they really believe that this is the old codger himself. And on Christmas Day a bearded, stuffed relative takes the part and is accepted quite literally, on the say-so of the grownups.

In another family, Santa Claus is never anything more than a vague symbol of the season whom the parents refer to only with a twinkle in the eye, and whom the young children see only in advertisements and books.

Some parents utilize Santa Claus as a major disciplinary weapon from October on, giving him a stern, withholding character. They make it clear that he uses no independent judgment and has little compassion. He takes the parents' word as final and seems more interested in faults than in good intentions.

Some adults, like the letter writer, who incline to maximal truthfulness with their children and who avoid using threats, especially unreal threats which take advantage of children's innocence, worry about all the children in the world who are first led to believe in Santa Claus and then discover that he is something of an impostor and that their parents are deceivers.

I think that such a view is oversimplified. There are a variety of different motives with which different parents encourage their children to "believe" in Santa Claus. I would guess that a majority of American parents foster a literal belief temporarily, but that most of these do so in a loving spirit, with the conviction that belief in Santa Claus is one of the inalienable rights of childhood. I suspect it is only a small proportion of parents who enjoy the deception for the sake of the sense of power it gives them or for the awe or anxiety or obedience which it creates in their young. Even when the motive is ulterior, it's well to remember that this is only one instance of the parents' over-all attitude or philosophy. If parents incline naturally to pulling the wool over their children's eyes, or threatening them with unreal people, it's relatively unimportant whether they happen to do so in regard to Santa Claus or not. When such children learn the truth, it doesn't necessarily lead to a resentful mistrust of their parents (as it might in the case of a child whose parents have taught him to believe them absolutely and then deceive him in one serious respect). They simply learn that their parents often don't mean what they say. So they themselves grow up winking at the truth a bit.

Then there are the parents who want their children to trust their word always. The letter writer is one of them, and I happen to be another. But I don't think such parents have to be on guard to keep their child from believing in Santa Claus. There is no need to worry or get too serious. At two and three and four years, the boundaries between fact and fancy are always blurred and shifting anyway. Young children believe what they want to believe. They are quite capable of believing two contradictory theories at the same time (as in the case of the stork theory and the seed theory in regard to the origin of babies). When they are hearing a story being read, they eagerly swallow it whole, and yet, in another compartment of their minds, they realize, at least dimly, that it's only a tale. They love to pretend that they are somebody or some animal, and play the part without self-consciousness. I think they should hear about Santa

Claus and have the fun of believing in him in the sense that they believe in Donald Duck or Benjamin Bunny. Even the most sincere parent doesn't feel the necessity to interrupt the reading of a fairy story every five minutes to say, "Remember, this is not true — it's just a story."

The parent who is not trying to mislead tells about Santa Claus in a storytelling tone of voice, with a pleasant, day-dreamy expression, which tips the child off that these are not humdrum facts he is listening to. And if, at four or five, a child gets around to asking, "Is Santa Claus really real?" the parent has neither to lie nor spoil the fun. He only has to say, "Well, I suppose he isn't *really* real, but I like to pretend he is anyway."

There are a couple of other aspects of Christmas that I have strong opinions about and I might as well mention them now. One is overstimulation. Christmas at its quietest is still an exciting and exhausting experience for small children. Beforehand there is the buildup of the child's expectations, and of the parents' tensions which the child feels. The day usually begins early. It provides more unusual activities than any other average week, and more new possessions than the child gets otherwise in a year. Parents and other relatives find it hard to refrain from trying to live the children's lives for them all day long, pointing out with exclamations the tree, the lights, the decorations and every present, showing how each new possession works, trying to make the child use it as it was intended to be used. Very young children do not yet have any desire to know the exact purpose that the manufacturer or donor had in mind for a toy. They know right away what they'd like to do with it. But they usually have to wait patiently while perfectionistic grownups demonstrate first.

I remember hearing about a two-and-a-half-year-old girl who ignored all the fine new playthings that surrounded her, and fondly clutched, all day, a cardboard orange which was only meant to be a tree decoration.

So I have several bits of advice for new parents. I'd omit the visit to the department-store Santa Claus. This noisy, intrusive fellow usually frightens the wits out of very young children. Plan Christmas Day to be as near routine as possible without spoiling the fun. Avoid as many visits to or from relatives on that day as can be managed without hurting feelings. Let the children play with their possessions as they wish, as long as they are not destructive, and even hide some of the presents, un opened, until another day, if they are showing signs of imminent nervous breakdown. Perhaps this advice will prove unnecessarily drastic. If so, no harm is done and you can let the bars down next year.

I agree with those who feel that Christmas has been overcommercialized and shorn of much of its spiritual meaning. We spend so much of December (and waste so much money) buying presents for everyone who might give us one, and mailing cards with canned messages to everyone who sent us one last time, it gets more meaningless each year.

Unless parents take a firm hand in setting the tone, children, by the time they are four or five, will approach Christmas in an entirely selfish spirit. "Greedy" is perhaps an even better word. This doesn't prove that anything is fundamentally wrong with them. All children are relatively self-centered and eager for possessions. But they are also capable of thoughtfulness and generosity when properly stimulated. Parents can keep the focus on presents for others. It's good to encourage children to make simple presents, tree decorations and their own Christmas cards. Even three-year-olds can make chains for the tree from strips of colored paper, and can stick gummed holly wreaths on cards to send to their friends.

The explicitly spiritual or religious meaning of Christmas that's imparted to children depends on their ages and on the family's beliefs. But all parents will agree that it's a time to express love and generosity toward others. Three years of age is not too young to begin.

A CHILD'S VIEW OF RELIGION

He comes to it through his relationships
with his parents.

I'D LIKE TO TALK about the phases of emotional development in a child as they affect his attitude toward religion. Then I can mention a few of the problems in religious education that parents have asked me about.

From a psychological point of view I'd say that the foundation for a love of God is the same as for love of parents. A baby is born to be affectionate, as is shown by the fact that he smiles warmly by the time he's a month or two old, long before he can sit, walk, talk or even use his hands. If he is cared for by loving parents, his love for them and his trust in them increase each month. If there is no one to love a baby (as was true in certain cold, understaffed orphanages in the olden days), he grows up with a shallow, irresponsible personality and with little or no capacity to love anybody, including God.

It's particularly in the three-to-six-year-old period that a child comes to realize how much his parents mean to him. He's warmly affectionate toward them. He thinks they are the wisest, the handsomest and the most powerful people in the world. He asks them anything he wants to know and believes what they tell him. All day long he's trying to be more like them, in activities and in character.

If they tell him about God, he accepts their picture, literally. Parents in speaking of God to a child tend to emphasize the attributes which appeal most to them. The stern father will probably speak of a stern God. The gentle father will speak of a gentle God. The parents will show that they look up to God, the way the child looks up to his own father. As a result, the child comes to think of God as being somewhat like his father, only more idealized and on a grander scale. He will have feelings of love, of trust, of awe, of fear in somewhat the same proportions as he has these feelings for his father. If he has a father whom he cannot love at all, I doubt whether he will be able to love God. I remember being told once, by a priest who had studied such cases, that the boy who grows up thinking his father is a hypocrite in his religious practices is the most difficult of all to win to the church.

The child who hears little or nothing of God between three and six will of course form no concept of Him. But the attitudes he is developing toward his father will have a great influence on any religious attitudes he develops later.

After the age of six or seven it is the nature of a child to try to outgrow part of the excessive dependence and closeness he previously felt toward his parents. Though he continues to love them deeply underneath, he's apt to stop copying their diction and their mannerisms. He wants no longer to be considered their good little boy, but rather to be a rough, independent man of the world. He senses that he must get over the idea that his parents are all-wise, so he argues with them about everything and he quotes his teacher as a superior authority. He directs a lot of his emotional energy, that was formerly spent in adoring and copying his parents, into impersonal channels such as learning about the Three R's and science and manufacture. Since he feels the need to be more independent and critical of his father, he won't idealize him to the extent that he used to. Instead he turns to less close, less personal models. He finds the heroes of the comic books and adventure stories more inspiring now, since they are superhuman in their powerfulness, bravery, righteousness. And some of the reverence he previously felt for his father is now more comfortably accorded to God, if he has learned about Him.

But there is another aspect of the change in a child's nature after six which has a bearing on religion. He wants very much to be like the other children he knows — in clothes, in language, in haircut, in the TV programs he watches, in the school he goes to. Other things being equal, he'd like to go to the same Sunday school and church. But this need to turn away from his parent as a model and to pattern himself after his contemporaries is mainly concerned with superficial matters such as personal appearance and manners. Deep underneath he is still loyal to his parents and quite willing to share their beliefs. He is not at all ready yet — as he may be in adolescence — to question their religion or their ethics or their politics. If he finds there's a difference between the beliefs of his family and other families in these respects, he'll feel more secure in lining up with his parents. In a political campaign he wears the same button as his father. He accepts his parents' convictions about what is morally right and wrong, and he will stick to his parents' church if they indicate that they have feelings about it. But at this age his relationship to church and God is a relatively unemotional one — it doesn't involve very intense feelings or very personal feelings.

In adolescence there is a real change. Now the young person's relationships — with parents, with friends, with members of the opposite sex — all acquire considerable intensity. The adolescent who is at all religious is apt to think about God as a real person whom he knows and who knows him. Almost every adolescent becomes at least somewhat introspective and concerned about himself: Am I normal? Am I acceptable? What are my ideals? What do I want to do with my life? He expects to find some guidance from his church and his God. In this sense his religion acquires personal meaning for him, for the first time.

Now let's turn to religious education. It doesn't usually present problems to the mother and father who both belong to the same church and who have a comfortable belief in their church's teaching. When their child in his early years asks questions about God, they find it easy to convey their sense of Him — in a way that is understandable — much as if they were talking about a mortal to whom they are devoted. When he is ready for Sunday school, he usually goes without question, just as he goes to day school without question. The only advice that I would want to give to such parents would be to emphasize the positive teachings of religion, to emphasize the loving aspects of God, and to minimize the punitive aspects, particularly up to the age of six or eight.

A minor problem in religious education occasionally arises in the age period between six and nine years in the case of parents who do not attend church themselves and do not give their child any specific religious training, though they have very definite ethical and spiritual convictions. Let's say, for example, that they are disinclined to believe in the kind of God and heaven spoken of in the Bible or from the pulpit, but that they are more content themselves with the belief that God is the goodness in men's hearts and that heaven is the happiness which a man gives to others and for which he is remembered after he dies. However, they find that their young child picks up the remarks about religion of neighborhood children and brings them home to his parents for clarification. "Do we believe in God and heaven?" "Do people who don't go to church go to hell?"

A conscientious parent of this sort is on a spot. He wants to be honest, he would like to explain his philosophy, yet he realizes that it is too vague for a seven-year-old. Of course he has to translate his beliefs into terms his child can comprehend, just as he has to simplify the facts of life or Santa Claus or the atom bomb. If I were he, I would answer, "Yes, we believe in God and we believe in heaven." I think this is a close enough approximation for a seven-year-old. He isn't interested in the subtleties. He very much wants a definite answer. He really wants to know, "Do we have beliefs, as other people have beliefs? Are we on the same side as the others, or are we different?" It seems wise to me, as a first step anyway, to emphasize the similarities. Otherwise the parents are, in a sense, insisting that the child think of himself as different from his friends just because the parents have a special philosophy. There will be plenty of time for him later to decide whether he wants to come to a regular or an unorthodox religion. If the child asks next, "Do we believe in hell?" the parent might well answer, "No, we don't," because severe punitiveness is not part of the parents' philosophy and perhaps because they sense there is anxiety in the child's question. Then if the child asks, "Why don't we go to church?" the parents could answer, "Some people have a religion that makes them want to go to church and other people have a religion that doesn't make them want to go to church." If the child asks to go to Sunday school, I myself think the parents would be wise to encourage him to do so, on the assumption that it would be beneficial educationally and spiritually. It would help him to some degree in the long run to find his own beliefs.

Next I want to mention the occasional problem in which the two parents have sharp differences in their religious views. More commonly it is the mother who is a strong believer in her own church; and the father is a nominal member of another church, or he is a nonbeliever, and he objects to the child's being indoctrinated in a religion of which he does not approve. Of course most couples who come from different religious backgrounds find, usually before they marry, a compromise that is agreeable to both, because their love for each other makes them want to. One can suspect, when the arguments continue, that it may not be religion which is coming between them, but that for neurotic reasons they have to quarrel and they find religion a very handy weapon.

I think that one parent who is at odds with the other is mistaken if he thinks that he alone can permanently direct a child toward one church or away from another by insisting on attendance or forbidding it. There is no doubt that a child brought up in a united family that adheres to an orthodox religion, in a neighborhood that adheres to that religion, will be strongly influenced for life. But it's very different if the parents are setting an example of unorthodoxy or if the parents are divided in their views, for then the child feels no binding obligation to follow any one creed. He will probably decide for himself in adolescence or adulthood, on the basis of his fundamental attitudes toward life and on his special relationship to each of his parents.

I would guess that the children, or at least the grandchildren, of people who didn't attend church find their way to church, eventually, in much the same proportion as other people do, provided they are reasonably well adjusted. For, though it is impossible to prove the existence of God, at least to a skeptic, it is easy to show that human beings are naturally religious. A majority of those who have grown up with love and respect for their parents have always wanted to express similar feelings of dependence and devotion and obligation toward a Deity.

I would advise parents who have sharp religious differences to make every effort to leave the child out of their arguments, and to come to a compromise which leaves the least tension between themselves. Otherwise the child will only be made miserable. I'd tell a father who was trying to keep his child from adopting a certain religion that he was courting defeat. And if a mother explained that she wanted her child to experience the beauty and the consolation of her religion, but that her husband objected violently to her taking her child to that church, I'd suggest that the inspiration which the mother receives from her church will be felt clearly by the child and will have a potent indirect effect on him in childhood, even if he himself does not attend. This will draw him toward that church later when he can make his own decisions.

There are two reactions to religion in adolescence that sometimes worry parents. An occasional child is so churned up by the changes in his body and feelings that he almost loses the sense of who he is and where he is going. This is a frightening feeling and it may lead him — in his search for security — to an unusually intense, an almost frantic devotion to religion. I wouldn't worry about a levelheaded child who turned more to the church at this age in a serene mood. I would try to get expert guidance for the one who had become anxiously obsessed with religion.

The other adolescent reaction that bothers parents is quite different. It may show itself in objections to the parents' particular church or in resistance to going to any church at all. Of course the adolescent is trying hard to free himself from his childhood dependence on parents and to prove that he can chart his own course through life. But it is impossible for him to admit his doubts about his ability to accomplish these aims. Instead, he automatically pictures his parents as blocking his path. He finds all kinds of faults in them: they are still treating him like a baby or they are hopelessly old-fashioned or their religious beliefs are pathetically conventional. He believes he could formulate, in one evening, a religion that was more inspired and at the same time more in accord with the truth. Another reaction is to feel that religion is just one of those things, like schooling and family rules, that parents impose on their children. I remember in my own college days thinking that a majority of my friends (who came from normally religious families) had turned against religion for good. I was quite surprised a few years later to find that they were all having their babies baptized and that later still some of them were becoming pillars of their churches.

As soon as the adolescent feels convinced deep inside that he is an independent adult — it may come when he joins the service or when he takes a job or when he marries and has a child — then he can stop complaining about his parents and begin, happily, to behave very much like them, in churchgoing as in everything else.

TELLING A CHILD ABOUT DEATH

There is no magical way to prevent all anxiety,
but a serene attitude is
the best reassurance.

MANY PARENTS have asked, "How do you explain death to a young child?" Sometimes the question is brought up by the death of a distant grandparent or an acquaintance of the family. Or it may come up when the child observes a funeral procession or a cemetery, or experiences the death of a pet. I have never heard of an answer myself that could be relied on to prevent all anxiety and misunderstanding.

Many religious parents are inclined to say, "He has gone to heaven," or "God has taken him away." Such answers may be satisfactory to a child of school age, who has heard enough about God and heaven on many occasions to have a fairly pleasant picture in his mind of a Good Man and a Nice Place. And by that age he is likely to have some philosophical acceptance of the inevitability of death and, at the same time, knowledge that it does not often carry away young people like himself.

But the child between two and five has, on the one hand, feelings that are quite easily disturbed and, on the other hand, little grasp of the everyday realities that would reassure the older child. You'll know what I mean if you've ever worried yourself sick in the middle of the night about some sin of your own or some danger to another person. Yet in the light of day you promptly lose 95 per cent of your fear and wonder how you could ever have become so foolishly panicky.

Young children are always in the dark in the sense that their inexperience, ignorance, lack of a sharp sense of what is real, leave them at the mercy of their immediate feelings. Two-year-olds and three-year-olds and four-year-olds are curious, sensitive, imaginative. They feel strongly their dependence on their parents and are easily threatened by any danger of separation from them. The thought of going far away for good, or of being bodily taken away by angels or God — no matter how kindly these people are said to be — can be quite disturbing.

Though I started on the subject of explaining to a small child the death of another person, I've been talking as if the child was worrying about his own death. The point is that a three- or four-year-old is at a stage of emotional development when he applies everything to himself, whether it's pleasant or unpleasant. When he sees a man driving a bus he forgets about the man and immediately imagines how it would feel to drive himself. He begins to act it out. When he sees a cripple he is promptly upset because he automatically identifies himself with the cripple. When he asks what a graveyard is for, and gets his first explanation of death, his next sentence is apt to be the frightened question, "Do I have to die?"

That's why it's so hard to explain to a young child about the death of someone else. As far as he is concerned, it's his death which is being discussed. Since he has a strong desire to remain alive, and to stay near his parents, it is impossible to describe death in such a way as to leave him entirely unperturbed.

Some parents, including myself, have tried to make death seem not threatening by explaining that very old people become so tired that they are glad to lie down and die peacefully, "just like going to sleep." This is partly futile, because a child can't possibly imagine being that tired. And it's a risky analogy because sometimes an anxious type of child will develop a dread of falling asleep, for fear he'll never wake up.

Isn't there any solution? Not, I think, in trying to find some neat or magical combination of words. But this is no cause for dismay in most cases. Everyday experience tells us that a majority of children have learned something about death by the time they are four or five, without appearing to be more than mildly and temporarily upset. They seem to make some kind of adjustment to the idea. This is partly accomplished by the processes of suppression or denial. You can see a child first asking worried questions. Then abruptly he becomes interested in something pleasant and his facial expression cheers up. The rest of the day he may seem unconcerned. Then, perhaps at bedtime, he suddenly declares, "I'm never going to die" — pretending that he can banish the danger with his resolution — or else he comes back to more of the anxious questions. Even in adulthood we try by the same methods to master or stave off what threatens to overwhelm us, though we usually aren't as successful in this as the small child. At any age, when a danger is too great to face, the mind attempts to forget it for a while, but then comes back to it when reminded, and tries to master it, a bit at a time. This may happen during the day, but it's also the explanation of many nightmares.

The child who is intensely disturbed when he first learns about death, and who can't get it out of his mind for long, is the exception. Probably he has been an overly sensitive, overly dependent child from an earlier age. Perhaps he became chronically anxious back at the age of two, when his mother had to leave him suddenly for the first time for a couple of weeks and he despaired of ever seeing her again. Or perhaps his mother has always been a worrier about his safety and he has absorbed some of her anxiety — especially in regard to anything that might separate him from her. The child who does develop a phobia or obsession about death needs professional help, to untangle the background factors that have made him so susceptible to fears. In the course of investigation and treatment it often turns out that one of the main reasons why he worries so about his own safety is that he feels excessively guilty about his occasional angry feelings toward other members of the family and expects awful punishment for this.

The same thing applies to the child who has heard about a disease such as polio and develops a persistent dread of it. It's not that the disease was described to him in a mistaken way, but that he has a store of anxiety and guiltiness in his mind which happens to attach itself to a disease. This child with such a severe dread needs child-guidance help too.

So far I've been making the point that the exact manner in which death is explained is usually less important than the degree of worrisomeness that is already a part of the child's personality when he first hears about death.

Another factor that is highly significant is the parent's basic attitude toward death. The person who dreads it, either openly or secretly, will have a hard time presenting it philosophically to his child. Usually a child's first questions come unexpectedly, giving the parent no time to compose the ideal explanation. The mother who is unworried about anything (who doesn't fear or even think about her own death, and who is not apprehensive about whether she might upset her child) will in general be able to use words and exhibit a manner which imply that death is pretty remote and really not worth bothering about now. The parent who takes death more solemnly, but who has a strong religious faith that to return to God — when the proper time comes — will mean the ultimate happiness, will communicate her serenity to her child, whether or not he catches the exact meaning of her words.

A mother who regards the viewing of the dead at a funeral as a morbid and barbaric custom would naturally not let her child see the body of a deceased relative. And if she saw an accident up the street when she was with her child she'd make every effort to detour around it and distract his attention. She would be very right to protect him so, because he would probably absorb the full impact of her own horror.

Another mother, brought up to consider a wake one of the important ceremonies of human existence, might consider it quite proper to let her child see the body of a relative. And her feeling of familiarity with death would make the experience for the child quite different from what it would otherwise be. I am not trying to judge whether one or the other of these opposite parental attitudes is the more wholesome. In either case the specific impact on the child will depend largely on his parent's attitude, and also on his individual personality make-up. But this doesn't mean that the form of the explanation is of no consequence.

Needless to say, in a religious discussion of death with a young child I would avoid any reference to hellfire, or to the possibility that, if he was not a good boy, he might not please God or reach heaven eventually. But knowing that, for him, going to God, no matter how beautifully described, would be no compensation for being separated from his parents, I would picture our whole family as eventually growing old, dying and going to live together in heaven, ignoring the age difference for the time being, until the child reached a more independent and understanding stage. For a nonreligious explanation, I myself would point out that death won't come for many years until we are all old and tired. And I would explain that we'll just stop breathing and moving and feeling (without drawing any comparison with sleep). If the occasion of the talk were the death of a child whom my child knew, I'd admit that once in a great while a child gets very sick or has an accident and dies, but I'd also emphasize (without getting so tense about it that my reassurance sounded forced) that most people don't die until they are very, very old. Then I'd grin and hug my child and tell him that we're all going to live together for a long, long, long time.

The tragic situation when a member of the immediate family dies presents quite different problems, which I'll discuss in the next chapter.

A DEATH IN THE FAMILY

*When a close relative dies, the child's sorrow is
often complicated by feelings of guilt.*

A DEATH of a member of the family — a parent, a brother or sister, a grandparent who has lived in the home — stirs up feelings in a young child which are quite different from those aroused by the death of a person who is not well known to the child, or by an impersonal discussion of death. In the latter case, as I have explained, the young child's main concern is in the possibility of his own death and whether this will separate him from his parents. But when a member of the household or someone close to it dies, the child's previous relationship with that person leaves a mixture of upset feelings which may last for many months.

First of all is the sense of loss. If a close brother or sister has gone, there is the repeated sharp sorrow which comes from wanting to share another experience with him and realizing again that he isn't there. If a parent has recently died the child will continue to want to turn to him or her a hundred times a day, when he needs knowledge, assistance, guidance, approval, comfort or reassurance. The anguish is fresh each time. This sense of bereavement we call mourning. In a healthy child (or adult) it heals gradually over the months as other attachments and interests fill the emptiness.

But there is a surprising difference between children in how much the mourning shows. One child — and it's more apt to be a girl — loses her joy in her usual pursuits, looks sad, and easily breaks into tears. Another child, even in the same family, may appear on the surface almost unaffected. We know that this appearance does not represent a true lack of feelings. Rather, the child has a personality which is expert in controlling, suppressing and denying them.

Most parents have noticed similar variations in how their different children react to everyday sorrows and worries. Feelings come to the surface so easily in some and are concealed so promptly by others. A majority of girls who have had a pleasant life feel free to shed a few tears of disappointment when a treat has to be canceled, or of sorrow during the sad part of a story. Most boys — in America at least — are learning to keep a stiff upper lip by the time they are six or eight.

There is the same contrast in regard to other feelings too, (as I explained in the chapter. "Some Differences Between the Sexes"). Girls when really overjoyed may squeal with delight. But boys are more apt to maintain a partial dignity and use some conventional expression, like "Gee, that's swell." When fighting, most boys try to battle silently and to use only their fists.

This usual difference between the sexes is not primarily a glandular matter. In some other parts of the world — even the Western world — men may scream at each other when mad. When a death occurs they not only permit themselves to cry; it appears to an embarrassed American as if they were encouraging themselves to become hysterical. So it seems that the male pattern in our country is mainly taught. It's partly done with words: "Don't cry"; "Fight like a man"; "Don't be a sissy." More important still is the example set by the father and other men and boys.

But I'm bringing out the usual contrast between boy and girl primarily to explain how even in the same sex there can be marked differences. A girl in America may appear to be as untouched by distressing situations as the average boy. Perhaps she grew up in a family where mother was just as self-controlled as father. Or she may have taken as her model in this respect not her mother but her father. We see, in child-guidance work, the girl who has had some difficult emotional problem ever since childhood (such as prolonged toilet-training conflict, severe jealousy of sibling or resentment of parent) who learned to protect herself from the painfulness of her feelings by drastically suppressing or denying them. It's a form of self-defense. In such a child (or adult) the feelings still exist, buried deep, but they show only in some disguised form — in bodily symptoms, for instance or in inappropriate behavior. Conversely, a boy may show more emotion than is conventional for his sex — because, for instance, his father sets a similar example, or the boy is taking after his mother in this respect.

So far we have been talking about the bereavement a child will suffer and may or may not show. But there is another feeling which is just as important. It may be more upsetting and last a lot longer. You might be skeptical at first that it even exists. I am thinking of guilt.

That a child might feel guilty about the death of a close relative was recognized only rarely before psychiatrists began to understand the hidden feelings of people of all ages who were miserable or nervous or mentally ill. It was first realized that an occasional adult would react to the death of a member of the family not just with mourning but with a more complex depression that lasted for many months. He would cover himself with reproaches: that he had not sought medical care early enough; or that he had not been as dutiful as he should have been during the last illness; or even that he had brought on the sickness, through his inconsiderate behavior for many years back. His relatives would call these self-accusations entirely unjustified, the very opposite of the truth. It was discovered that such a person was feeling terribly guilty not so much about the things he had actually done or left undone, which were largely imaginary, but about unkind feelings and wishes that he had harbored at times toward the deceased. Deep inside he assumed that these feelings, in some magical way, had done harm.

In some parts of the world, where science is unknown, a person believes that he has fallen ill because someone is using black magic against him, or he seeks revenge by sticking pins into a clay statue of the one he thinks is his enemy.

It isn't just mentally ill people or savages or ignoramuses who believe in the harmful effects of bad thoughts. Most of us pride ourselves on our rationality, which comes from a sensible upbringing and long education. But almost all of us are a bit superstitious about the power of our thoughts and words, even if we decline to admit it publicly. We step over cracks in the sidewalk or throw salt over our shoulder or knock on wood. We believe in magic, not because we aren't educated enough but because each of us still has inside him traces of the child he once was.

When psychoanalysts began to treat unhappy children they learned how guilty children feel — not only about their hostile acts, but about their hostile wishes even when there are no acts. This is not surprising, when you think about it. Children get plenty of chances to feel angry every day, what with the crudeness of other children, and the frequency of parental correction and irritation.

Young children carry most of their anger toward others directly into action and they see the effects of it in the tears of brothers and sisters and friends, in the disapproval of their parents. You might say that it takes them a number of years of growing up before they realize that the hostile wish which doesn't get carried out doesn't hurt anybody.

Parents in their efforts to curb open hostilities frequently warn of the possibility of serious consequences from anger: "You might break his leg" (or put his eye out or even kill him). Without realizing it, parents also often teach children that even illness comes from meanness and disobedience. "Your fighting has given mother a headache." . . . "You got the earache because you didn't wear your rubbers as I told you to." . . . "When you splash water on him like that you might make him catch cold." So children all get the idea, in one way or another, that their anger could do serious harm. This doesn't really surprise them too much, knowing as they do the unrestrained vigor of their feelings. Even in their cooler quarrels young children can threaten to kill each other, over an issue that would provoke an older child or adult only to the point of shouting, "I'm going to report you."

When a brother, sister or parent dies from any cause, there is stirred up in the child the guilt left over from all the times he actually did hurt him or wanted to hurt him or wished that some other misfortune would befall him. So the primitive part of his conscience, which was forming at two and three and four years, tells him that it was his evil wishes that brought about the death.

The amount of guilt will be quite different, of course, in different children. A child who has had a very predominately loving relationship with the relative who died will have much less guilt than the one who felt a lot of hostility. The child whose parent used heavy moral disapproval will have a heavier conscience than the one whose parent used a more direct and casual sort of control. And, other things being equal, the older the child, the more his knowledge of the true causes of death will counteract the primitive sense that his own evil wishes did the harm.

What are the applications of this knowledge — that children feel guilty about a death in the family? The Romans used to say "De mortuis nihil nisi bonum," meaning "Don't say anything but good about the dead." This may be an ideal for grownups to strive for (in the sense of avoiding unfair or senseless defamation), but it would be too hard on children. If, in family discussions, a departed child is pictured as an angel without fault, it makes the living children feel inexcusably evil to have ever been angry at him or to have wished him any harm. So when the family is talking about how much they miss him and how humorous or helpful or smart or loving he was, it might be good for the parent to add — understandingly, not accusingly — that he was sometimes irritating too, because of his obstinacy or selfishness or whatever. "I certainly used to get mad at him at times." Such remarks, in a tolerant spirit, not only keep the memory of the departed from becoming oppressively pure; they show the children that if a parent can admit irritation without guilt, they too can be a bit less uncomfortable about their own antagonistic feelings, more able to talk about them.

Even in the case where a parent has died I think it is possible for the other parent, without disloyalty, to admit casually that he had his failings like everyone else. "Do you remember, Jackie, how cross Daddy used to get when you left your bike out?" (or used his tools or whined or wouldn't eat). "He was more crotchety about that than most fathers. It must have made you mad sometimes."

Perhaps we should bring up the broader subject of whether the dead should be talked about at all. I think that most parents would be surprised at the question, assuming that such conversation would be inevitable, natural and proper. Yet there are some for whom this is so painful that they almost never mention the dead relative themselves, and either act disapproving or at least change the subject if the children speak of him. You can imagine that if a child is consciously or unconsciously holding himself responsible to some degree for the death, a parent's stern refusal to let the death be mentioned might intensify the child's feeling that unspeakable evil (including his own) had played a part.

Sometimes a parent not only overidealizes a dead child, but uses this image quite purposefully to bring brothers and sisters into line. "Surely you want to be a helpful" (or honest or pure or studious) "person like Harriet was. What would she be thinking if she knew what you did today?" This is unfair, of course, to Harriet as well as to the erring child, because the latter, in addition to guilt, can't help feeling an increasing antipathy to this apparently smug and preferred sibling.

Once in a great while, parents who have been unable to become reconciled to the death of one child may expect a subsequent child (or adopted child) to fulfill not only all the actual achievement of the first, but also the future hopes they had had for him. (They may even name the new child after the dead one.) Such expectations, being impossible for anyone to achieve, will compel the living child to feel a failure sooner or later — in his parents' eyes and in his own.

It not only helps children in their adjustment to the death of a child or parent to be able to talk naturally about their former relationship to him, it should help the parent in the long run, however painful it is to him at the moment.

Needless to say, the child who shows more than the expected amount of grief, and little tendency to recover from it, and particularly the child who reacts with fear, guiltiness or other personality change, should have the help of a child-guidance clinic or family social agency.

THE QUESTION OF NUDITY

*It's not just the question of how much skin should
be bare, but of the child's stage of development
and the parent's attitude.*

How MUCH nudity or how much modesty is wholesome in the
family? The only thing I am sure of is that there's no simple
answer.

Back in the earlier years of this century it was thought
by many people, influenced by the studies of Freud, that the
answer *was* simple. Freud had pointed out that many neuroses
(such as phobias, hysterias, compulsions) and sexual maladjustments occurred in people who in their childhood had been
severely inhibited or mixed up about the facts of life. Of course
Freud and the other early psychoanalysts in general had patients
who had grown up toward the end of the Victorian era, which
was an unusually prudish period. Among polite people it was
not admitted publicly that women had legs, they had only
limbs. A woman who was pregnant was said to be "in a delicate
condition."

When Freud first called attention to the fact that most children of three and four and five showed considerable interest —
of a childish kind — in the facts of life, conservative people were
shocked and called him an evil-minded man. Nowadays, when
we aren't so afraid of sex, almost any parent with an open mind
and with a young child can see evidences of this interest.

Anyway, it was quite logical for the people who were impressed with Freud's studies, people who were concerned with

preventing neuroses and marital problems, to come to the conclusion that less secrecy and less shame would be a lot more
wholesome for the growing generation. They emphasized the
importance of parents being franker in answering their children's
questions. Some of those who were most impatient of modesty
deliberately practiced some degree of nudity at home, feeling
that they were conscientiously aiding their children's education.

As the years have gone by and more experience his accumu-
lated, it has become clear that the prevention of neuroses and
sexual maladjustments is not nearly so simple as that. Some
children have even been upset by too much parental nudity
which had the wrong spirit behind it.

How complicated the matter of dress and undress is, what
effect it has on other people, can be realized if we stop to think
how different the customs are in different parts of the world —
and what illogical rules we have even in our own country. In
some Moslem countries it is immodest for a woman not to keep
her face veiled. It's certainly hard for us to think of a face as
being shameful or too exciting. In Bali, women go bare to the
waist, but I doubt that this keeps the men of Bali in a constant
dither.

At the present day in America it is invariable on the beach for
men to be bare to the waist, even though many of them *look*
awful, whereas fifty years ago it would have *been* awful. Women
on the beach only have to wear bra and shorts. But the women on
the beach whom the men can't help watching are not necessarily
the ones showing more skin, and not all the ones who have good
figures (what a Victorian word!), but the ones with figures who
want men to watch them and are bold enough to show this in
their manner. The amount of leg that draws no attention at all
on the beach would alert every man in the room at a social
gathering, especially if revealed by a hussy type.

My choice of examples might give you the impression that
it's only women who want to attract attention to themselves.

Actually, men have some of the same urge. But our particular civilization makes fun of men who try too hard. Besides, women, being more sensible by nature, aren't nearly so impressed with bodies as men usually are. The young men who hopefully throw a volleyball back and forth for hours at the beach to show their muscles don't draw much of an audience.

These examples arc enough to show that nudity itself isn't necessarily disturbing. You might say, thinking of the different customs at beach and in parlor, that it's what we are used to that makes the difference. That's part of it. But really the more important question is what we are trying to do with our nudity or with our clothing, and whether we are trying to attract attention in an exciting way. And of course, it isn't simply the question of what we are trying to do consciously, knowing it and admitting it, but what we are trying to do unconsciously, without realizing it.

You may have got the idea that I've been implying that it's wrong for us to attract attention to ourselves. I don't mean that. It's a normal part of human nature. It's the main reason why we look for clothes that fit and suit us. It's the main reason why women's styles keep changing and why women's clothes are always partly revealing, partly concealing. We use our clothes and our manner of wearing them most deliberately to attract the people of the opposite sex who appeal to us, especially before marriage. But even afterwards, none of us is so prim that we want to stop looking reasonably attractive. It's really a matter of both degree and intention. Satin dresses off-the-shoulders and an extra-charming manner are all right at a dance, when alluringncss is considered fair and respectable all around, but the same amount of clothes appeal and coquettishness in an office or shopping center is frowned on as out of bounds.

The same matter of degree and intention applies to the effect we have on our children with our clothes or lack of them. A wholesome mother is pleased if her five-year-old son, seeing her dressed in a formal gown, tells her she looks beautiful. The same mother might buy an alluring nightgown because she thought it would please her husband, but she wouldn't parade around in it for her son's benefit.

But one complication is that some people have a greater-than-average urge to make the opposite sex look at them, by means of clothes or the lack of them. Certain of these people know it. Others of them don't admit it at all, even to themselves. And some of them, without realizing it, may enjoy showing off a bit too much to their children. They may think, quite sincerely, that they are just trying to give their children a wholesome education. It was an occasional case of this sort, in a very mixed-up family, that particularly alerted psychiatrists to the possibility that parental nudity could be quite upsetting to a child.

Another somewhat separate aspect of the question — of how much nudity — has to do with young children's tendency to worry at least slightly about genital differences, the differences between boys and girls and the differences between children and adults. It seems to be the nature of most children to begin to notice intently the difference between boys and girls, men and women, quite early in childhood if they have the opportunity: a few at two and a half, more at three, most by three and a half. They act quite surprised at first and then, instead of accepting the difference, they usually show some concern. A little girl who has had no previous experience and who observes a boy's penis for the first time when he's being dressed on the beach is first apt to say, pointing, "What's that?" and then after a few moments, in a worried or resentful tone, "Why haven't I got one?" or "What happened to mine?" A boy, far from being reassured to see that he has more visible equipment, is apt to ask tensely, "What happened to her wee-wee?" And then, unless he can be reassured, he is likely to start worrying about whether some injury might happen to his penis, as he assumes it has happened to the girl's.

We think nowadays that if parents realize that these are

normal questions and normal fears at this age, they can be ready to help their children with sensible, comforting answers when the questions come, ("Boys are meant to be different from girls" . . . "You are made like mommy" . . . "Boys have penises but only we girls and women can have babies," and so on.) However, the fact is that even the most reassuring answer doesn't seem to allay the worry altogether.

There is evidence that it's somewhat easier for most children to come to sensible conclusions about the differences between male and female from seeing other young children than from constantly observing the parents. The main reason for this is that feelings toward parents — of love, of jealousy, of guilt — are much more intense than feelings toward other children. Such strong feelings are apt to interfere with reasoning about any subject.

The difference between grownups and children can be an equally confusing factor for the small child. The pubic hair of adults is apt to puzzle the child. And the pubic hair of women conceals the nature of the genitals. We have learned that young children often imagine, illogical as it may sound to us, that the woman may have male genitals under the hair. This thought comes from the same mistaken idea that everybody is meant to be made similarly. The child hopes that this is true so that he won't have to worry about his other mistaken idea that injury may be the explanation of why girls don't have penises.

Then there is the rivalry about size that boys, especially, feel toward their fathers. Even though they love and admire their fathers, it irritates them to have to be so much smaller. They've heard many times that they'll be as big as their fathers someday, but that day never seems to come. I've been told several times by parents that if the father, for instance, is in the habit of shaving naked in the morning and his son wants to be with him at these times, the boy after a few minutes may show signs of irritation at the father's larger equipment, by half-joking remarks or teasing gestures.

This kind of rivalry may sound farfetched to women, but men

and boys know how frequent the kidding is, either envious or belittling, that goes on in locker rooms and swimming places. In other words, males tend to compare themselves, uneasily, about genital size even more than about total height. This kind of rivalry begins surprisingly young and it may be upsetting to the small boy who is just beginning to try to figure things out. When a small boy compares himself with another small boy there isn't so much difference to worry about.

There's one more aspect of nudity that we ought to consider before trying to come to some set of conclusions, and that's the degree of modesty in relation to different stages of development.

In the three-to-six-year-old period there is often only a mild inclination on the part of children to be modest unless it has been drilled into them. In fact, it's an "exhibitionistic" age, to use the psychological term. They rather enjoy showing off their bodies on occasion. But around the age of six or seven they are going into a different phase in many respects, and one of these is a sharp turn toward modesty, at least at certain moments, even in the family that acts in the home like a nudist colony. A boy of this age, asked to undress in the doctor's office, is apt to look nervously at the open door that leads to the secretary's office and to ask if he can close it. And the mother may give the doctor a grin, meaning she doesn't know where all this modesty comes from, because it's not from the family. At this age, spontaneous modesty is likely to be a very variable matter. One day the child bellows indignantly when someone starts to come into the bathroom where he's taking a bath. The next day he takes off everything without a qualm even though half the family happens to be in his room at the time. So, after six or seven I think the best guide for parents is to assume that children of opposite sexes will gradually want more privacy and to help them get it as far as possible.

In adolescence the picture is more complicated. Normal sexual development gradually increases the urge to attract attention, but most youngsters dare do this at first only by talking noisily when passing a group of the opposite sex. The desire to be grown up is strong; but stronger still, in most of them, are self-consciousness about the changing body, uneasiness about being able to act the part of the adult, mixed feelings of attachment and antagonism toward the parents. The balance for most early adolescents swings strongly toward modesty, and this should be respected and fostered.

What does it all add up to as far as the parents' own behavior is concerned?

Every sensible professional person in the children's field agrees today that parents who are naturally modest should stay modest with their children. A modest parent trying to be a nudist for a child's education can't help being an embarrassed nudist, and this is more likely to trouble than to help the child.

On the other hand, it's not necessary or wholesome for a parent who is discovered by the child, accidentally, in the bathroom or undressed to scream or act as if the child had committed a crime. Overemphasizing the "badness" of nudity only produces morbid shame and, sometimes, morbid curiosity. It's only necessary to ask the child to go out until you are ready, which is simply asking that he respect your feelings.

Now to shift to the family that tends toward nudity at home. Since there are some parents with more of a tendency to show themselves off than they are aware of (they may be quite sensible in other respects), and since most psychiatrists have decided from professional experience that parental nudity is always *somewhat* bothersome to a child, I'm inclined to suggest to all parents that they give the child the benefit of the doubt and keep themselves reasonably covered when around him, without making a fuss about it, and without worrying about accidental lapses. But I think that the parents' *general* attitudes toward nudity, toward sex and toward their children are the most important factors, and that the number of minutes and the number of inches of body exposure are secondary.

Most professionals in this field (including myself) believe that it's wholesome for brothers and sisters under six years to get used to seeing each other undressed casually at the times of day when this is natural, that the same applies to friends (in changing at the beach, for instance), that boys and girls can be allowed to use the same bathroom in a nursery school where an adult is not far away. At the same time, it's well to remember that somewhere around two and a half to three and a half years the child's increasing maturity will raise questions and probably some worries in his mind about differences, and the parent should be ready to understand and reassure him.

You may raise the theoretical question whether it's advisable for even young brothers and sisters to observe each other, since even this is said to arouse some degree of concern. The only answer I know is that life is bound to create a variety of unpleasant tensions in the happiest of children: occasional resentment at parents, jealousy of brothers and sisters, disappointment in friends, trouble with lessons. Children who never have a chance to observe the opposite sex still have feelings, curiosity and the capacity for morbid imagination. A few I've talked with after they've grown up have felt that their ignorance wasn't bliss, but had had a rather unpleasant effect both in childhood and in adulthood. So there is no such thing as taking all the worry out of the facts of life. There is only the practical question of how you can keep it to a reasonable minimum. It is believed that the moderate degree of inhibition which we all received in our own childhoods and pass on to our offspring plays a constructive part in freeing a child's mind, during the school years, for such impersonal interests as the three R's. In adolescence and adulthood normal inhibitions contribute to the romantic and altruistic quality of love, the appreciation of literature and the arts, the ambition to do great things in the world. In other words, inhibitions about sexuality and nudity are a normal, constructive part of human nature. It is only when they are excessively severe and worrisome that they create problems.

Come to think of it, all of us as human beings want a certain amount of privacy in all aspects of life, in order to preserve our dignity as individuals: privacy in keeping some of our thoughts to ourselves; privacy for particularly precious possessions to prevent their being broken or lost; privacy in some of our hobbies; privacy about parts of our bodies which we think are homely (such as skinny arms or bowlegs), apart from any sexual aspect. It needs no apology. It's an admirable side of human nature.

TEEN-AGERS AND THE
FACTS OF LIFE

They still need your guidance.

❪ WHY IT'S HARD TO TALK WITH THEM

ANYONE WHO THINKS it's easy to talk to adolescents about love and dates and sex probably hasn't tried it. We Americans consider ourselves enlightened in regard to sex education; and perhaps we are, compared with many other countries and compared with our own country in past centuries. But surveys show that relatively few adolescents here receive much knowledge at home even today. Most of them say they learn from friends, books and experience. There are real reasons why communication is difficult — for the parent and for the adolescent. In human beings, unlike other creatures, sexuality always involves to some degree feelings of modesty, embarrassment, guilt, even in parts of the world where customs and attitudes are very different from ours. This isn't a minor difference between human beings and other species. From what we've learned through psychoanalysis, we assume that these feelings of constraint were built into the human race as a basic part of its nature, through the process of evolution, and that they are built into each individual, partly through his inherited instincts, partly through the typical experiences of growing up in a family. In all other species the period of dependence in the young is relatively brief, and leads right up to full sexual maturity. There is no taboo in adulthood which tells them that sex is an embarrassing matter or that sexual relations between certain individuals is wrong. Humans, by comparison, go through an amazingly prolonged and zig-zagging course of emotional development.

There is a whole year of almost complete helplessness in infancy. Then there are two years during which they discover they are separate beings, though still very dependent, and assert their puny independence. From three to six they turn back much more positively toward their parents. A boy in this stage develops his manly ideals through his devotion to his father. He develops his basic ideals about women and marriage by becoming romantically very attached to his mother. But human romantic love is intense and possessive. We believe that it stirs up in a little boy of four and five hidden feelings of rivalry and resentment toward his father, and makes him worry that his father is similarly rivalrous and angry with him. The little girl, feeling competitive with her mother for her father's attention, imagines that her mother is resentful. Parental disapproval of touching the genitals, which is frequently shown at this age, reinforces the child's idea that the parent is angry about *all* his sexual and romantic wishes. These ideas are so worrisome to small children that they don't want to think about them, but quickly repress them into the unconscious levels of their minds.

We believe, from the psychoanalysis of thousands of adults and children, and from the dramatic play situations that children create for themselves and for their dolls, and from the frightening dreams which become more frequent at this age, that this fear of the parents' anger about sexuality is universal in children at four and five years. As the anxiety builds up, it eventually causes every normal child to strive to suppress his romantic and sexual feelings altogether at about five, six, seven years of age, especially in regard to members of the family. And these feelings stay suppressed for the next half dozen years. This is the age when the boy claims girls are repulsive, scorns talk or movies about love, no longer wants tender treatment from his mother, and turns his interests toward schoolwork and other impersonal matters. A comparable process takes place in girls, but they do not usually feel the same degree of fear and do not suppress their romantic interests so deeply. We believe that it is a biological necessity that this suppression take place, in a species which loves so intensely and in which it is necessary for children to be dependent on their parents for fifteen to twenty years, while they learn how to get along in the world. Otherwise they'd be acting like sexual delinquents instead of docilely attending school. And families would be disrupted by jealousies before the children were ready to be on their own.

It is the glandular changes of early adolescence which bring to an end this comfortable middle-childhood assumption that the opposite sex can be ignored. The newly stirred up sexual and romantic feelings have a tendency to go out toward the parents again — unconsciously, as dreams often show — but the adolescent fights off any recognition of this, sometimes by being unbearably disagreeable to the parent of the opposite sex. A boy is apt to become even more intolerant of his mother's physical affection. A girl may beg her mother not to mention to her father that her periods have begun. The old rivalry with the parent of the same sex is revived — with a new intensity because the child really is approaching maturity and competition with adults. The boy, however reasonable he may be on the surface, doesn't really like to be bossed by his father. He feels that he should have the car when he needs it. The girl feels that it's now her turn to have the beautiful clothes, use the cosmetics, be the romantic queen. Time for her mother to take a back seat.

When a child was three or four he had an unembarrassed, eager curiosity about such questions as where babies come from, which made it fairly easy for the parent to explain. Between six and twelve, when a child's romantic interests became strongly repressed, he was able to look at the biological aspects of reproduction quite impersonally, like a scientist, and this helped the parent to take the same tone. Then when adolescence forces him to become acutely conscious of his own sexuality, the strong taboos of the previous six years make him feel acutely uncomfortable. They also make him want to deny that his parents are sexual beings. (The embarrassed teen-age daughter of a pregnant mother may make indignant remarks such as, "I thought my mother was way beyond that sort of thing!") So in one sense the parent is the last person a young adolescent wants to reveal his sexual concerns to, or hear about sex from, particularly in the case of the boy. Many a parent has found, when he tries to suggest a discussion, that the child hastily says, "I know all about it," and looks around desperately for a means of escape. This makes the parent as self-conscious as if he were telling off-color stories in very proper company.

I'm only warning parents, sympathetically, that they've got to brace themselves, as if they were giving unpleasant medicine to a small child. It's usually considered preferable for mothers to talk with daughters, and fathers with sons. But when fathers, many of whom are even shyer than mothers on this topic, can't bring themselves to talk with sons, it's better for the mothers to do it than no one. A few people have advocated that mothers talk with sons, fathers with daughters. Obviously families are different, and what seems most comfortable is usually the best.

The relatively few sessions in any family devoted to serious discussion of love and sex are less important than the way the parents and children have lived together all along. Children get their basic feelings about just what it means to be a man or a woman — and the relationships between them — from the way their parents treat each other. When there is mutual devotion and tenderness and respect, the sons and daughters grow up expecting this sort of relationship for themselves. They'll instinctively shy away from contemporaries who are looking for something else. But as children go through the teen years it also helps them to crystallize their standards further if they can discuss casually with their parents — at mealtimes, for instance — questions about the everyday behavior of classmates and themselves. They really respect their parents' judgment and want their guidance, even though they don't always show it. But they hate to be scolded or belittled. So parents have to listen understandingly to what an adolescent is trying to tell them or ask them. They can show by their manner that they respect the fact that he is now having to make his own decisions when away from home, and that they are advising him sympathetically so that he will not get into situations that might make him look foolish or lose him the respect of schoolmates he admires.

Another factor which makes discussion difficult today between American teen-agers and their parents is that dating practices have been changing so fast. There has been a progressive relaxation in sexual behavior since World War I, which has gone along with other profound social changes. In earlier centuries the church, the state, respectable society and the elders in one's own family spoke in one voice on questions of morality. It was not that everybody behaved accordingly, but they knew what the rules were. In the twentieth century these authorities have lost part of their influence for many people. Nowadays psychologists and sociologists report on what people are really like. And there is so much respect for "science" and "normality" that some people, after reading the reports, are inclined to select their own standards from the statistics. There are many conscientious parents today who, fearing that they may be old-fashioned or too strict, hesitate to give their children any firm guidance. Even teen-agers themselves complain of this. It's not that all parents will have the same standards. But they should make clear to their children what they do believe.

I think myself that the realistic understanding that we have gained about human nature need not paralyze us in counseling our children. In fact, it provides us with information and advice

which, because it is realistic as well as moralistic, will not lead
to disillusionment.

A basic question that naturally troubles all well-brought-up
adolescents is whether sexuality in some or all of its forms is
"bad." They see very contradictory attitudes on the part of the
adult world. It's all very well for parents to answer that the
sexuality which is part of a good marriage is good. But the
adolescent doesn't have a marriage and he certainly has sexual
urges.

I think it will help an adolescent to hear his parent say that
psychologists believe that shame about sexuality is a built-in part
of human nature which all peoples everywhere experience. It
is there to keep sex under control in the complex and close-knit
kind of life that mankind has to live. The guilt is especially
strong in adolescence because sexuality comes so suddenly then.
It can't be reasoned away, any more than guilt about stealing
or hurting another person can be reasoned away. It gradually
lessens as a result of the enlightenment that comes with growing
up and the experience of marriage.

I'd also explain that it's our religious and family ideals which
then guide us specifically as to which aspects of sex are wholesome and noble, and which are considered wrong in the sense
that they are upsetting to other people or to the individual himself.

(HELPING THEM TO UNDERSTAND
   LOVE AND SEX

The young adolescent has to wrestle with conflicts in many
spheres. But these struggles are particularly intense in regard to
sex. Desire has come abruptly. It is more insistent, especially
in boys, than at any later stage. When the young person reaches
greater maturity he will have a much better sense of the kind of
person of the opposite sex he really gets along with. Then the
sexual drive will be blended with, and controlled by, other

aspects of man-woman relationships: deep companionship and respect, common interests and ideals, plans for the future. But in early adolescence it is suddenly there, unconnected with other interests, calling attention to itself in an embarrassing way, buffeting the inexperienced boy and girl around. It's partly pleasant, it's exciting. At the same time it can bring about self-consciousness, loss of assurance, anxiety and guiltiness.

One aspect of sex which is particularly confusing to an adolescent in America is that many adults show contradictory attitudes toward it. At one time they will talk about it as if it were almost sacred, then as if it were shameful, and then again as if it were a joke to snicker at. This gives him the impression that adults are hypocrites and makes his own understanding of sex more difficult. It seems to be hard for us Americans to think of sex as both natural and noble. This is partly due to the fact that we started as an intensely puritanical country and are having trouble outgrowing this attitude in a scientific age. Lately some teen-agers have tried to settle the conflict in their own minds by concluding that sex and love are just a matter of biology, of glands. This is true only of such animals as insects and fishes and rabbits. We know for a fact that some of the finest aspects of boys and girls, their idealism, their creativity, are outgrowths of their capacity of true love of each other. If they try to deny the spiritual aspects of love they will surely get more mixed up; they'll end up being disappointed in themselves and in each other, in dating and later on in marriage.

It is good to be clear at the start about the differences between male and female in respect to the nature of their sexual drives. Back in Victorian times it was a conventional belief that men had all the sexual instincts and that good women were innocent of any such desire. Then, in the revolt against prudery and the double standard, the pendulum swung in the opposite direction. Some people claimed that women had just the same impulses and outlook as men. Nowadays sensible people point out the differences again.

In general, physical desire in boys and men is considerably more insistent. It is less discriminating in its choice. It responds easily, of course, to an attractive, appropriate and appreciative girl. But a boy's sexual interest can also be stirred up by a good figure alone (especially if it's seductively clothed) or a pretty face, even though the girl's personality has no special appeal. He can be aroused by pictures, by stories, by thoughts.

This does not mean that a boy lacks the capacity for the other aspects of love. It depends a good deal on the kind of family he grows up in. If his father shows not only ardor but tenderness, protectiveness, admiration for his mother, it powerfully molds a boy's expectations of what he himself will offer to girls as he grows up. We also know that a boy's capacity to love spiritually is developed way back in early childhood through his intense devotion to a good mother, when she was the most wonderful and important person in the world to him. This is what inspires him, years later in adolescence, to fall in love with a girl who seems to have just the right combination of qualities.

This expression "falling in love" means that his attitude toward her becomes romantic and chivalrous and adoring, as well as physically desirous. He is ready to idealize her, to invest her with wonderful attributes (which may be hard for her to live up to). His greatest desire is to please her in all respects, to achieve success in school or in the world for her sake, to protect her, to give her gifts. Even his physical desire, as he matures, is largely aimed at pleasing her sensually; he receives his most intense gratification only when she responds.

What all this means is that if a worthwhile boy begins to be attracted to a girl (and she to him), he is ready to offer her as many aspects of love as he is capable of. It is up to her to show what kind of appreciation she wants from him. If she's normal, she'll want to be physically attractive. But much more she'll want to be loved as a completely appealing person. It will take a long time, though, in adolescence for both of them to find out whether they really have the qualities that will satisfy each other's needs and ideals. If they do, they will feel a stronger and stronger love. But meanwhile the problem is that the boy's physical desire is strong enough so that, soon after he finds the girl, he will want to express it. If he has any boldness, he will probably try to do so. This is particularly apt to be true in the early part of adolescence when sexual desire is so new and separate. But if a girl allows petting to progress faster than the development of true affection, it is so exciting that it quickly becomes the main interest of their dates, especially for the boy. It gets in the way of their coming to love and respect each other more. Boys and girls who are responsible people sense this and try to keep their physical desire under control. But it is girls who are usually better able to do so.

Most girls have a less intense, less persistent physical desire. Their bodily response is relatively dormant until stirred up by a boy's approaches. A girl is not so apt to be carried away by a boy's appearance alone. She may be attracted by his face at first. But soon her good sense begins to operate. Then she responds primarily to the appeal of his total personality, his attitude toward her, and — most important of all — his suitability as a long-term partner.

All this does not mean that girls are not intensely interested in boys. In fact, it looks as though they spend more hours of the day than boys in thinking and talking together about members of the opposite sex, in sorting them out, partly on the basis of romantic appeal but also very realistically. (It is interesting to know that surveys have shown that, at election time, women in contrast to men judge a candidate more on the basis of what kind of family man he'd make, less on where he stands on the issues.) In the early years of adolescence — thirteen, fourteen and fifteen — the interest of girls in eligible boys is so great and the shyness of most boys is so disappointing that some girls are surprisingly aggressive in chasing the boys who appeal to them, or in arranging, in roundabout ways, to reveal their feelings.

It is necessary, though, for a girl to know early in adolescence that she has a capacity for strong physical desire. If she and an attractive boy spend hours together in privacy, over a period of weeks and months, the desire for greater physical intimacy will steadily increase. And each stage of intimacy creates a more intense desire for the next. Human nature was designed this way, so that the restraints which are essential in the human race can be gradually broken down between two people in preparation for marriage. The trouble is that Nature is working for a marriage at about fifteen or sixteen years. Early dating and going steady for months will encourage intimacy even before fifteen. But our society expects everyone to be in school until at least seventeen or eighteen, and for many people years longer.

There are other drives, aside from physical desire and the search for a suitable partner, which draw boys and girls together. There is a gnawing curiosity about what sex really means which becomes steadily more intense through adolescence. Outspoken boys and girls complain that lecturers in school and college, counselors, parents, books are quite inadequate. These reproaches are often true. But I think that even when literature or experienced friends are thoroughly revealing, the young person will inevitably continue to feel cheated in his knowledge until he has had a satisfactory sexual relationship himself.

In every boy (as in every man) there is a chronic anxiety about whether he will be a sufficiently virile male in general, and an adequate lover. It varies greatly in individuals. It isn't very conscious in the early part of adolescence. Then it becomes particularly insistent through the rest of that period until the young man has proved that he can win, satisfy and support a woman. But all their lives boys and men may show their uneasiness by such actions as taking crazy chances, boasting to females, making passes that are not appropriate, demanding a good table at a crowded restaurant, acting as if they were dashing young bucks when they should be old enough to know better.

In girls and women the corresponding anxiety is whether they will be sufficiently appealing to attract the kind of man they want, and whether they themselves will be able to respond fully. This concern will, of course, be greatest in adolescence when they have no basis for assurance yet. In most women, marriage relieves the major part of the uncertainty, though they continue to need the assurance that their husbands love them, and appreciate occasional evidences that other men still consider them attractive. A few women, though, remain so insecure in this respect that they must forever be trying to infatuate another male.

Another motive for dating which is unnaturally strong today is the desire of teen-agers to have a boyfriend or a girlfriend in order to be like everyone else. It's based on imitation and competition and the search for security in social life. It's now the convention in most places. It is almost a frenzy in some groups. Back in the days when few went steady until late adolescence, the shy ones and the less mature ones were free to take their time in growing up to dating. Nowadays some children who aren't at all ready are forcing themselves to compete for partners and to play the roles of people in love. There are girls who consider themselves old maids if they aren't married soon after graduation from college, or even school. Sometimes a mother will urge her daughter on, from a misguided desire to ensure her popularity, or because of her own ambitiousness or vicarious excitement. Girls who are too eager to have steady boyfriends are apt to remain pursuers all through adolescence. This brings out the wrong characteristics in both sexes and it isn't good for either.

Many girls are easily persuaded that they must be free in petting in order to win and hold their dates, even though they may not feel at all ready for this at the start. (Every time I see on the road a girl crowding against the boy who's driving the car, this reversal of sex roles startles me.) It's impossible for most boys not to take advantage of such invitations. The girls, in turn, learn gradually to overcome their natural reserve. When a boy gains physical intimacy with a girl without her asking for love and respect, he is sure to think less of her than before, even though he goes on asking for more favors. Girls should know, too, that boys who take advantage of girls who are easy marks show their scorn for them by joking together about them. An increasing intimacy, before a boy and girl have found out whether there are real admiration and tenderness between them, frequently leads to an unpleasant breaking up of the relationship, because at least one of the pair has come to dislike herself or himself for this purely physical sexuality. But it also leads quite often today to pregnancy. (In the past twenty years the rate of pregnancies in unmarried girls has tripled.)

Adolescents are apt to think that the worst result of an unmarried pregnancy is the shock it gives to their parents and the neighbors. (In fact, many of the girls who become pregnant by throwing caution to the winds are those who are at odds with their parents and unconsciously wish to embarrass them.) Some young couples who become involved in a pregnancy decide that the most gallant way to meet community disapproval is to act unashamed and defiant. This may impress their parents, classmates and neighbors, but it doesn't make the couple feel good for very long. They've misunderstood where the real harm is inflicted. The parents have their old friends who remain as loyal as ever, and they still have their respected place in the community. As soon as they can overcome their sense of shame, their life resumes as before. It is the boy and girl who suffer the most, whether they realize it or not. If they decide to make a marriage which is not based on love and mutual respect, the chances are high that it will soon end in divorce. Such a marriage and divorce will leave a worse taste in the mouth than one which started with high hopes. If there is no marriage, the girl has to go through the frightening experiences of the long, lonely, secret pregnancy and the childbirth, without the love and emotional support of a husband, without the encouragement of relatives. The pregnancy is likely to interrupt the education of one or both, and so it handicaps careers. Often the most painful experience is the isolation from former friends and classmates at an age when confidential friendships and group life are most precious. In the long run the worst harm for boy or girl, unless he was a callous person to start with, is the loss of self-respect — for having hurt his partner, his family and his ideal of himself. (And an individual's sense of his own worthiness is what he really depends on most to maintain his inner peace of mind from day to day, and to fire his enthusiasm for the future.) If the girl is a highly conscientious person she may remain excessively aware of what she considers her shame, avoid her old friends and neighbors if she continues to live in the same town, fear to fall in love with another boy in the future because she dreads that she will have to confess, worry about what she will tell her later children, feel guilty about the one whom she has given up.

Before I end this discussion of pregnancy I want to make sure it is understood that I have been talking about the dangers of increasing physical intimacy that start primarily with a young girl's belief that she must allow liberties to be taken with her person in order to gain and hold some boy's interest, before she knows whether there is any genuine love between them. She's trading her body and part of her soul in order to gain — for a brief period — a steady partner and a bit of social prestige. This is a miserable bargain.

The sequence is very different when a boy and girl have become mature enough in their feelings to be drawn to each other as people, and when the girl senses that her physical appealingness is a precious part of her total being. As they come to know each other better they may find incompatibilities and draw apart. Or they may fall more seriously in love. But the progress in stable people is usually gradual. The boy's physical desire increases, but so does his desire to cherish, protect and please. This gives the ultimate control of the expression of physical affection to the girl. If she becomes steadily more convinced that this is a person she can love and depend on, her readiness for physical responsiveness increases. But she is usually less impulsive than the boy. She is the one who set the limits. This does not make a boy who is in love lose interest. It increases, for him, every aspect of a girl's desirability.

Most young people who have been brought up in families with high ideals will not let themselves get to the point of intercourse until marriage, not because of lack of desire, not because they are timid, but because the girl, knowing herself, knows that she would lose some of her respect for herself. And the boy loves her too much to be willing to make her unhappy. Other couples will at least wait until they are sure enough of each other to make the commitment of formal engagement. And then, out of respect for the reputation of their families and of their own future marriage, they will take no careless chances.

I've been talking as though there were only the very foolish young people and the very wise ones. Actually, of course, the great majority are in between. In most early and middle adolescents the feelings about self and others are usually so changeable that they can't be counted on.

So I think a sensible parent's advice to daughter or son should always be: Go slow, don't wear your heart on your sleeve or throw yourself at others; don't let yourself be rushed by your own impatience to be popular or by your date's pleas; when in doubt, trust your cautious feelings because they are the ones that usually prove right in the long run. A parent from his or her own knowledge of the world can tell a child, especially a daughter, that some of the individuals most dated in the early teens may be quite neglected or laughed at a few years later, and that the ones who keep their self-respect are more apt to have the worthwhile partners in the end. This advice sounds stodgy. But it's really smart, as most older adolescents and adults will agree, both those who were wise themselves and those who were foolish.

❨ THE PRACTICAL PROBLEMS THEY FACE

In tackling some of the specific problems that young adolescents run into and the questions they ask, I realize that different parents' answers will vary greatly, depending on how they themselves were raised, the particular ideals they adhere to, the neighborhoods in which they live. I don't want to impose my own ideas. They will sound too puritanical to some people. But I think I can be most useful to those parents whose standards are high and who have difficulty making them sound reasonable to children who are growing up in a permissive period.

The commonest protest of a girl to her mother is that she is compelled to let boys take liberties beyond what she would like because otherwise she will be hopelessly unpopular and isolated. Part of this objection comes from the fact that her own instincts, curiosity, doubts about her attractiveness, are naturally urging her to experiment and she would feel more comfortable if her mother would agree that she has to give in. At the same time, the self-respecting and idealistic part of her personality really wants the backing of her mother's wisdom, even if she argues indignantly against her advice. I would tell a daughter flatly never to let a boy go a step beyond what seems right to her. There are all kinds of boys. Her need is not to please a lot of them but to find the few whom she can really be fond of. A boy who feels drawn to her as a person and who is likely to appeal to her in the long run will surely not be put off by her wish not to pet. Though his physical desire and his need to prove himself a man are urging him to try, the idealistic side of him that admires her will actually be glad to find that she is not cheap to get. Her privacy about her physical self when combined with her responsiveness to him as a person is just what enhances her appeal. It challenges him to win her totally. If a girl can understand this two-sidedness of the male, she's well on the way to becoming a woman of the world.

What is most difficult for the young girl (though it comes easily to the older one) is how to keep her physical reserve without seeming to reject the boy as a person. A boy is apt to think that on a date with a new girl he should make some kind of advances so that the girl, if she is expecting this, won't think he is a timid mouse. (This is an aspect of his worry about whether he is masculine enough.) He assumes she will stop him if she doesn't want this. On the other hand, he dreads being rebuffed. A young boy's hesitancy may have kept him debating with himself for hours or even for days. In desperation he may suddenly make an awkward pass or a lunge. A girl taken by surprise is apt to recoil in alarm or act outraged. Even in her later teen years a girl may find that a boy who had never tried anything before is suddenly wrestling with her, especially if he has been drinking to get his courage up. The girl's job is to make it clear that she does not want the advances but that she still feels friendly toward him, appreciates his interest in her. If he is a sensitive person it may be sufficient for her to take his hand gently off her shoulder. Or she can say in effect, "No, please don't," or "I'm sorry, I don't feel that way now," without reproaching him or getting angry. She acts as if it were due to a misunderstanding, perhaps partly her fault, rather than to his crudeness. A boy who really likes a girl and wants to know her better will be relieved to learn clearly what she wants and doesn't want.

But a young girl also needs to know that a boy may keep persisting for a while, or argue and act indignant, to cover up his hurt pride. He may try to convince her that she's a prude, or that she was leading him on. She shouldn't feel obliged to defend her reasons or to make long speeches. That only prolongs the uncomfortable argument. If he has no sense, she may have to become really angry. To get away from the arguments, she can try to start up the conversation again where it left off, or to let him know how much she enjoys his company in other situations. If she feels like it, she can show that she still is friendly in a physical sense to the degree of wanting to hold his hand. This helps to ease his guilty fear that he has completely alienated her. The next step will probably be to suggest that it's time to rejoin the gang or to be getting home.

More basically a girl protects herself from unpleasant experiences by her general reputation, by not going on dates with a boy alone until she has gotten to know him in groups (and given him a chance to know her), by not agreeing to drive with him to secluded places, by immediately insisting that she must be getting home if he starts to park somewhere. It's important for a young girl to know that most boys brought up like herself, though they would like to think of themselves as irresistible cavemen, are actually quite cautious most of the time about not getting into situations in which they will be rebuffed and embarrassed. So they are always watching for signs and signals. The girl's job is to be careful that she is sending out the kind she means.

Romance is often painful in adolescence because young people are so frequently disappointed by those they have become fond of. A boy and girl are drawn together by mutual appeal and are delighted to find how many interests and aspirations they share. They begin to fall in love and promise devotion to each other. Then one of them loses enthusiasm and backs away, for no good reason that the other can see or — worse still — becomes more interested in somebody else. These disappointments can be terribly painful. They may make the hurt young person fearful of becoming involved with anyone else for a long time. Older people who have grown too far away from their own youth smile at these early love affairs, forgetting that the emotions are just as intense as any that come later. It isn't that the teen-ager is insincere or fickle in his love. There are other explanations. One is that the teen-ager's desire to find someone

to love intensely — and his own idealism — make him liable to
see wonderful qualities in the other person which are not there,
or make him temporarily ignore unattractive qualities which
really are there. Time forces him to be more realistic. Another
problem is that the adolescent is still developing rapidly — in
his character, in his tastes, in his aspirations. In a few months
he may completely outgrow a person who was right for him
yesterday. A parent could advise a teen-ager to protect himself
from being hurt by his beloved — or to keep from hurting his
beloved — by being cautious about admitting love, or at least
about declaring it. This is unrealistic though. The last thing a
person in love wants to be is cautious about telling the other.
Perhaps the best that parents can do is persuade young people
in love to promise to tell one another courageously if their feelings cool. This is painful too, but in the long run it is kinder to
the one who must be disappointed than to have to spend weeks
in anguished doubt.

Aside from the normal drives that draw boys and girls together, it is good for young people to realize that there are
mixed-up desires too. I am thinking first of the individuals who
use all their wiles to make conquests of members of the opposite
sex. When that is accomplished they lose interest in them and
drop them heartlessly. This is a selfish, hostile use of sex. Usually these are people who have felt neglected by their parents
and are unconsciously taking revenge on others instead. We are
apt to think of the males of this type, but there are the females
too. There is a trace of the enjoyment of conquest in most of us.
It is apt to be stronger in early adolescence, before tender feelings for special members of the opposite sex have had a chance
to develop. When girls compete for boyfriends by being easy
to make, it accentuates the conquest-seeking attitudes in these
girls and in the boys they make a play for.

There are dozens of other mixed-up (neurotic) patterns of
relationships between the sexes which show up clearly in marriages but which cause difficulties in dating too: the excessively

jealous person or the one who is compelled unconsciously to make his beloved jealous, the one who must always be quarreling, the individual who is constantly hurting feelings or teasing, or who is asking to be hurt or teased, the dominator, the submitter, the person who can only fall in love with someone who already belongs to another (and loses interest as soon as the beloved becomes available), or the one who can only fall in love with someone who is indifferent to him (and instinctively pulls back as soon as he finds any responsiveness), the individual who can feel sexual attraction only toward those whom he does not respect morally or socially. If an adolescent has been disappointed and hurt by finding an attitude such as one of these in the person with whom he has fallen in love, it may help him to free himself if he can realize clearly that the unhappy experience may not have been due to some misunderstanding between them but to an ingrained trait. If an individual finds that he is falling in love with one person after another, each of whom disappoints him in the same way, then there is something in himself which is leading him into these repeated frustrations. He can get help from a psychiatrist.

An aspect of sex which is apt to be troublesome to adolescents is masturbation. Studies have shown that most adolescents succumb to the urge at least occasionally, but also that it is *much* less frequent in those who become involved in sexual relations. So it is really a substitute outlet for young people in our kind of civilization who must postpone the more direct expression of their instincts. It continues to be a problem much longer for the individuals who are unusually slow in getting around to dating and marriage. It's of some comfort to an adolescent to have his parent explain that few people his age can resist the temptation altogether and that it is not physically or psychologically harmful. The very frank teen-ager may insist on asking, "But is it wrong?" Each parent has to answer on the basis of his religious and personal beliefs, which is as it must be if parent and child are to feel right about each other. But even when the parent answers, "No, it's not wrong," this will not make a child with high ideals feel entirely comfortable about the habit. Incidentally, I think it is a mistake for a parent to say that masturbation is not harmful "if not practiced too often." There is no medical basis for this distinction, and it only shifts the worry of the child to the question of what is "too often."

All teen-agers have concerns at times about whether they are normal or abnormal — physically, medically, psychologically, socially. The slightest difference from others, real or imaginary, may cause anxiety or despondency. The fantasies (daydreams) about sexual intimacies which their instincts create in their imaginations, and which are often more strange and "indecent" than anything they have ever heard about, are apt to be particularly disconcerting. They can be reassured that most such fantasies are normal. (The principal exception is fantasies that involve harming or taking advantage of an unwilling person. These should be discussed with a psychiatrist.)

There are temptations which come particularly strongly to boys who are slower than average in regard to the direct approach to girls, such as peeping in windows, making passes at strange girls in movie houses, involving young children in sex play. It's sensible for parents to seek psychiatric advice when a child has special problems like these. But it's important for all adolescent boys to realize clearly that these temptations are common and that, since the law and other parents are severe about such activities, they must firmly resist these temptations in order to avoid getting into real trouble.

Boys need to know that "nocturnal emissions" (discharge of seminal fluid during sexual dreams) are normal, and occur in all males who are not regularly having intercourse. Their frequency or infrequency has no significance.

There are a few realistic points that need to be made about venereal diseases. Their frequency in young people has shot upward in recent years because of the general relaxation of sexual behavior. These diseases do not come from doing what's forbidden. They are caught by having intercourse with individuals who are infected. The people who are most likely to be infected are those who are having intercourse promiscuously — not being particular with whom or how many. Gonorrhea shows itself by a discharge of irritating pus from the penis or vagina. This discharge, which usually begins about five to seven days after the contact, is first yellowish and then turns somewhat greenish. It is quite different from the common vaginal discharge which is white and not irritating. The first stage of syphilis, which takes several weeks to develop, is a sore which is usually on the end of the penis in the boy but which may be invisible in the vagina in the girl. It takes weeks more before the rash of syphilis appears, which most often looks something like measles, pink spots all over the body including the abdomen, sides, limbs. It is not like acne which consists of a relatively few raised pimples on the face and shoulders alone. The most important point of all is that gonorrhea and syphilis can both be treated successfully but they should be treated promptly and thoroughly. Adolescents should realize that if they are in trouble their parents will want to know and help. But if they can't bear to tell their parents, they should go to their family doctor whom they can trust, not to an unknown doctor who may be a quack.

In view of the tensions and pitfalls of sex in adolescence, what general advice can parents give to their children?

I think myself that we've had enough experience with the recent social customs of early dating and going steady to say that their disadvantages outweigh any advantages. They make young adolescents compete for partners before they have a genuine need of each other, which belittles the idea of love. They often encourage physical intimacy long before teen-agers are capable of knowing what partners are right for them or what lasting love means. Sometimes they lead to premature marriages or illegitimate pregnancies which interfere with healthy personality growth and shatter educational plans — in a country where the importance of continuing education is greater every year.

I think it's the duty of parents who disapprove of these customs to present their views convincingly to their children. That's what parental experience and wisdom are meant to be for. But to reverse these customs will take a lot of doing. Parents will need to get what cooperation they can from the neighbors who agree with them, and the school people. This is an ideal topic for PTA discussions in junior high school. In some communities a majority of the parents may be very much in favor of a co-operative effort. Even if only a minority of parents agree, each of their children will know that there are some other young people in the same situation as himself. It will be much easier to start with children just on the threshold of adolescence than to try to change the rules for those in the middle.

A parent can explain to a child — especially a mother to her daughter — that she considers it unwise to agree to go steady until one has known a person for a long time and is ready to think about engagement and marriage. This does not mean that a boy and girl can't see a lot of each other and, as they grow older and fonder, have repeated dates. The disadvantages of really going steady lie in the agreement not to date others, not to dance with others, the obligation to have regular dates and to attend all possible social functions together. Youth is meant to be the time to get to know a lot of people and oneself, not to retire from circulation and spend all free time together, like a married couple. A mother can also explain that she doesn't consider it wise for a girl to go on single dates until she is several years older. There will be plenty of opportunities to get to know boys at parties in homes and school and church, and later, perhaps, in movie parties made up of several couples (with parents driving the cars).

Parents can show by their friendly manner that they are not old fogies or killjoys. They want their children to have the full benefit and fun of adolescence. They want to keep them from getting into situations where they might look foolish or be miserable. Parents can also show that they will always be ready to discuss the rules — and changes in them — as the child grows in experience and wisdom.

Even in the later teen years I think a mother should encourage her daughter to have most of her fun at parties or on double dates, to keep to public places when she is on single dates, and to avoid prolonged parking and petting until she is old enough and sure enough to be thinking of an engagement.

What happens to sexual energy which is denied direct expression? What outlets are available to carefully reared children? Ordinary social contact between boys and girls in school, at parties, at dances, probably relieves tension to a degree, even though there is no direct expression of sexuality. It's a common observation in boarding schools for boys or girls that the complete absence of the opposite sex often leads to a constant and intense preoccupation with them. Soldiers stationed in uninhabited areas of the Pacific often talked about nothing but women. I also remember vividly, when I was still in pediatric practice during the war, that some girls whose fathers were overseas when they themselves were four and five, the age at which they are more intensely attached to their fathers, would hurl themselves on me during a house visit as if they were desperate for male company and affection.

Boys in boarding schools and colleges have always been exhorted to engage vigorously in athletics and other extracurricular activities to keep their minds off sex. A lot of fun has been poked at this simple-sounding solution, but there is probably considerable truth in it. Most married couples can testify that preoccupation with family and business problems distracts attention from sex to a degree, and that a leisurely, secluded vacation increases desire.

Certainly we know today that the emotional energy which makes an adolescent dream idealistically about his future, the emotional energy which spurs him forward in the study of science or technology or the humanities or the arts, comes in large part from a transformation of his sexual drives. (The psychological term for this deflecting of instinct is sublimation.) Statistics show that it is the adolescents who are more inhibited in the direct expression of their sexuality who, on the average, go farther in their schooling and careers, and that when adolescents marry young or have regular sexual relations, their interest in studies and ideas are apt to decline greatly.

Though we've been discussing the particular problems of early adolescents it might be well to end up with a word on the relation between studying and sex at the college level. The conflict between education and a full sexual life is not so sharp when real maturity is reached. The ex-soldiers who were already married and who returned to college after World War II with a determination to gain all the benefits of education were generally a delight to their instructors. But nowadays the picture is a mixed one in regard to married college students. When a marriage has been a well-considered one between two unusually mature people it may give greater purpose to their studies. But a less stable marriage can play hob with education. It is not simply the distraction of sex. The problems of mutual adjustment, which are inevitable in all marriages, may reach stormy levels so much of the time that concentration is impossible. Economic need sometimes compels the wife to go to work. The unplanned arrival of children compounds the problems of finances, concentration and marital adjustment.

In today's atmosphere of greater sexual freedom, unmarried college students who are not ready to fall seriously in love nor to have an affair are sometimes made to feel, by their less inhibited girl and boy friends, that they are therefore abnormal. It would be a great mistake for such individuals to be persuaded by this bogus reasoning. College counselors are impressed with how disturbing sexual affairs may be. They seriously detract interest and time from studies, extracurricular activities, the forming of friendships, the broadening of perspectives, which only the college years can provide so richly. The fear of pregnancy and of detection, the sense of guilt, create a constant strain in all but the most blasé. I think that the college student who wants to be very sure that he or she is ready for marriage, and has found the right person before becoming involved, is to be admired and congratulated.

VI

Divorce, Widowhood, and Remarriage

TO DIVORCE OR NOT TO DIVORCE

*What's better for the child depends on
what's gone wrong with the marriage.*

HERE ARE excerpts from a mother's letter:

I need advice on an unhappy marriage and its effect on children. I realized from the beginning that our marriage was a mistake. Before the birth of our son, three years ago, we managed to present a mask of compatibility in public. Now I am wondering if you would consider divorce less damaging to the boy. I suggested consulting a marriage counselor, but my husband opposed the idea. He is completely selfish, miserly and antisocial. I have yet to see him do a kindly, unmotivated act for another person. His only interest is driving a big car. He showed no interest in the baby during the infant period, although the past year he has developed a sort of top-sergeant affection for him. When he comes home, he turns on the TV and gets himself a drink. Then the dialogue goes something like this: "Peter, come here, give daddy a kiss." This is delivered in a disciplinarian tone, and if the boy is reluctant he is in for a hard time. If we get past the homecoming greeting without conflict, things are quiet for a short while. Then while the youngster is sitting quietly, playing or watching television, my husband will start to tease him. He'll give him a little kick with his shoe or pull his hair. Peter either gets irritated or, if he decides it is a game, he starts to roughhouse. At this point my husband will decide to give his attention to his newspaper or television and he promptly gets angry and gives the child a cuff and tells him to be quiet.

I realize that I, too, have faults, but without cooperation from my husband I am unable to resolve our problems. I am thirty-five years old, and it would be financially necessary for me to work and put my son in a nursery until he is school age. Do you think there is any age when divorce is less harmful to a child?

It's impossible to make any flat statement about the desirability of divorce for a child's sake. Almost all marriages involve some conflict, and children always sense it, so there is no escaping it altogether. On the average we find more disturbed children where there is severe parental conflict, and there is every reason to try to remedy such situations. But divorce is not necessarily a solution.

Young children are upset at least temporarily when parents separate. They know — to the marrow of their bones — that they want both a mother and a father. They almost invariably protest against a separation, unless one parent is behaving outrageously. When they live with a divorced mother they are usually begging her to remarry. Surveys of divorced women with children have shown that many of those who have not remarried find life grim: a job of necessity, not by choice; a tighter budget; a great diminution of social contact with old married friends; the difficulty of finding satisfactory care for the children; the obligation to spend evenings and weekends with them without the companionship of another adult who shares the responsibility and the pride; the anxiety about whether one parent can satisfy the child's need for two; often an over-all sense of going round and round in a squirrel cage without any promising destination. This doesn't mean that it's impossible for a mother alone to bring up children successfully, for many do it. The outcome will depend partly on the mother's ability to find satisfaction in her job and in a new social life, partly on her capacity to remain a wholesome mother to them despite natural impulses toward resentfulness, guiltiness, permissiveness, possessiveness.

As for remarriage, when parents enter it maturely and make a go of it, most of the children achieve a satisfactory adjustment. On the other hand, a disturbing proportion of second marriages runs into serious trouble too. This means, of course, that there is something persistently out of kilter in these individuals — either in personality or in their unconscious reaction to marriage.

Since there are serious hazards either in continuing or in terminating a strained marriage, parents owe it to their children as well as themselves to consult, in good faith, a psychiatrist (or two psychiatrists), a family social agency, a marriage-counseling service, or a minister. This is to get professional help in evaluating not just their mutual complaints but their underlying problem and the possibility of its solution. Ideally, after thorough consultation, it becomes clear to both partners in one case that they have a potentially good marriage and they want to preserve it; in another situation it becomes increasingly apparent that it was an unhealthy marriage, doomed from the start. In either case the husband and wife should be able to learn more about themselves so that there will be a better chance of future stability — in the present marriage or in new ones.

The hitch is that many couples balk at the idea of counseling. So often one parent, at least, is feeling thoroughly fed up, convinced that the other spouse deserves the lion's share of the blame. He or she believes that the last thing in the world he wants is to find a way to continue the marriage. To go to a counselor seems like admitting guilt — or at least it seems like admitting doubt. It's generally true that refusal to discuss a fateful choice indicates a secret fear of being proved wrong (more men than women are susceptible to this fear).

Even if one spouse refuses altogether to take part in counseling, it should be very worth while for the other to go ahead anyway. In any chronic conflict between two people there is always some kind of fit, some particular matching between the two personalities that keeps it going. The old saying is that it takes two to make a quarrel. This doesn't necessarily mean that there is equal fault in a legal sense or in a moral sense.

I'll give you an oversimplified outline of a common type of emotional disturbance in marriage in which the partners play interlocking roles that neither understands consciously. Individuals who grow up in families where there is more than average teasing and quarreling and meanness may reach the stage by adulthood where they not only expect this in all their close human relationships, but unconsciously seek it. What was originally painful becomes — in a perverse way — grimly pleasurable. These individuals unconsciously expect their own marriages to be largely composed of teasing or sneering or yelling or blows, and they seem to find spouses who'll fit this pattern. (Less scrappy types appear dull and flavorless to them.) One spouse may play a more aggressive part and the other a more submissive one. But if you observe their quarrels closely you see that they are both provoking each other. The wife who shouts "Don't you hit me, you thug!" before this idea has occurred to her husband is an obvious example. Each spouse is indignant about the retaliation of the other, but fails to see his own needling. The close tie between negative and positive feelings is shown in these marriages by the frequency with which lovemaking is preceded by a violent quarrel.

Psychiatrists use the term sadomasochistic for these relationships. To a mild degree all of us have the capacity to get a bit of pleasure from aggressiveness or submission. This is what makes us able to enjoy giving and taking "good-natured" teasing, or trouncing an opponent in a game, or working like a dog on a committee for a demanding chairman. So we are discussing tendencies that are not abnormal in themselves but which, if accentuated through a person's upbringing, may dominate and warp his marriage. Often when marriages have begun to go wrong for other reasons, and the partners have become resentful of each other's faults and secretly guilty about their own, they may drift deeper and deeper into mutual provocation.

A marriage of this sort is hard on a child even if the parents leave him out of the fights. More frequently, without realizing it, they use him as a pawn, one teasing him as a way of getting at the other, the other exaggerating the child's plight in order to justify his own anger. If the mother and father stay together because basically they get more satisfaction than dissatisfaction from quarreling — however vehemently they deny it — the child's attitude toward them and toward his own eventual marriage is going to be distorted to some degree. But if they are divorced and if the mother has too deep a tendency to seek quarrels, there is a chance she may involve herself, and her child, in another marriage of a similar pattern.

If you will look back at the letter from which I quoted you can see why I suspect that the real issue is quite different from the mother's question whether to divorce or not. The flavor of the letter suggests that father and mother have been locked in an endless tease-and-be-teased relationship and that they are involving the boy. The mother feels that the father comes home all set to be mean, which I have no doubt he does. But if he were asked his view of the conflict he might say that she watches him resentfully from the minute he enters, puts the worst interpretation on everything he does with the boy, until he gets so mad that he sometimes does pick on him. Another indication that the mother doesn't understand what's gone wrong is her statement that her husband is totally lacking in admirable qualities and that she discovered this just as soon as they were married. If true, why did she not suspect it before they were married? (This doesn't sound like the whirlwind marriage of impulsive teen-agers.) Two grown people don't fool each other that easily, though they may fool themselves. And if he was that bad, why did she go on living with him when there was no child to consider, and why did she then have a child by him? I sound like a district attorney. It's not that I'm critical of her as a person. If I'd heard the father's story instead, I'd be just as skeptical of his interpretation. I'm only emphasizing the point again that when two people, who were once enough in love to marry, reach the stage of considering each other scoundrels, and if they can't talk things out together, they need to talk them over with someone else.

I've concentrated on one type of marital problem because it's so common and because it brings out the issue of the child's welfare. But psychiatrists and other counselors have found dozens of other psychological factors which work to undermine marriages. Some are superficial, but many are complex and hidden from view in the unconscious. Infidelity is often basically caused by self-doubt or resentment toward the spouse rather than by true infatuation. A couple who have married supposedly for a partnership of mutual cooperation may reveal by their subsequent behavior that each is unconsciously expecting to be totally dependent on the other, like a small child. A woman who is well adjusted in most respects but who is overcompetitive with men may, without any realization of it, respond to and marry a man whose forcefulness is inhibited already, and then fail to express any confidence in him in whatever success he may achieve afterward. And a man, because of forgotten hurts in his own childhood, may be impelled to undermine his wife's serenity. Romantic attitudes and sexual responsiveness which seemed ideal during courtship may disappear after the wedding, because certain attitudes toward sex and marriage deeply absorbed during childhood sometimes play cruel tricks with adult feelings.

Though I've urged professional consultation, I don't want to leave the impression that it's a quick-and-easy solution. If there is good will on the part of both parents and if the roots of their problem do not go very deep, they may be able to achieve considerable understanding and harmony in a few months' time. If the conflicts are severe and have their main origins buried in the unconscious, they may be satisfactorily coped with only through intensive psychoanalysis.

However, it would be compounding an American misconception, I think, to imply that a marriage can be a success only if both partners are ideally adjusted. The general spirit in which a marriage is lived is more crucial than any of its specific aspects. For example, despite the importance of a good sexual adjustment in most marriages, there are instances which show that its absence may not cause failure if the partners have great devotion to each other and to their joint endeavors.

Visitors from foreign lands and anthropologists who've studied marriage in other parts of the world are always impressed with the extraordinary emphasis on romantic love in America, the widespread acceptance of the notion that love strikes two people like a bolt of lightning and that this mutual attraction automatically assures their living happily ever after. This despite the fact that we have one of the highest divorce rates in the world. It's not that there isn't a large kernel of truth in the magic power of love. Even in countries where marriages are arranged without the participation of the young people it is assumed that they will come to love each other. But in most parts of the world marriage is heavily invested with other purposes and obligations, too, which are taken very seriously: the fulfillment of God's design; the rearing of children to carry out the work of the family or to perpetuate its honor or to serve the nation; the selfless cooperation of the couple themselves in their daily toil, which is vital in most countries just to keep a family alive. In America such considerations are not ignored altogether, especially by the parents of the bride and groom. But with our indulgence of the young, the ease with which we make a living, and our official credo that love conquers all, I think we let many children grow up assuming that everyone is entitled to receive happiness in marriage as a gift (like a wedding present from Cupid). Then if it's not forthcoming they assume that it has been snatched away by a spouse who was hiding his selfish nature during the courtship.

Anybody who has been at least moderately successful in his marriage knows that it doesn't take care of itself, any more than a business or garden does. A great deal has to be learned at first about one's spouse and oneself. Countless adjustments and accommodations have to be made in a hurry. As the years unroll it becomes evident that a mutual desire to please is still necessary, in the sense of discussion, consideration and graciousness. Even with these benefits a marriage may lose some of its sense of meaning unless the couple share a genuine devotion to the rearing of their children, and to other causes. The happiness that comes from marriage is, of course, simply a by-product of the effort and love that are invested in it.

We assume that our children will come to understand the spiritual, altruistic and realistic aspects of marriage from the example we try to set, as well as from the teachings of church and literature. If there is no example they surely won't learn it through words. But perhaps as parents we should make more of an effort to be explicit in words, too, especially during our children's adolescence, when their capacity for idealism is high but when, at the same time, they have an inclination to be excessively romantic and also self-centered.

PROTECTING THE CHILD
IN DIVORCE

*The hardest job for the parents is to subordinate their
mutual antagonism to the child's needs.*

WHEN conscientious parents feel that they have made every
effort to rescue their marriage but have failed, one of the next
questions is when to tell the children. They are naturally reluctant to come to this step. I remember an extreme example in
which, ten months after the divorce had occurred and the father
had left home, the mother still could not bring herself to tell
the nine-year-old boy what had happened. This situation had
come to light in the school because the boy was so preoccupied
with his own worries that he was failing most of his subjects.
Why didn't he ask his mother where his father had gone? A
majority of children would, of course, because they know their
parents will answer. But children also sense what kind of things
their parents are too uncomfortable to talk about. Serious family matters should be explained to them, in simple terms, because
they always feel disturbances in their parents' moods. They are
wiser than adults in this respect. On the other hand their inexperience in the ways of the world and their own troubled
feelings in times of crisis make them imagine situations that are
far more fearsome than the actual fact.

However, it would be a cruel mistake to announce to a child
a divorce which was only decided on the night before during a
violent quarrel. In all probability the parents will cool off in a
matter of hours or days and reconsider. Nowadays, parents who

have no serious thought of separating may be surprised by having their child ask them if they are getting a divorce, because he has stumbled on an ordinary quarrel or because he has heard the word divorce bandied about in anger. Of course he should be promptly reassured that they have no such intention. But if after months of discussion and counseling, parents have come to a firm decision, it should soon be discussed with the child so that he can understand the causes and the consequences of the tension in which he has been living, and begin the long process of making his adjustment.

When divorce is imminent, how are the parents to present it? It depends somewhat on the age of the child, the actual reasons, and the attitudes of father and mother. If they have been seeing a marriage counselor, psychiatrist or minister they will have had a chance to discuss the handling of the child's angle too. If not, it would be wise for them to consult a child psychiatrist or family social agency at this point anyway. Even without professional help they may be able to plan together the discussion with the child, and his future, if they are mature people who can subordinate their own resentments to his welfare.

It's a basic desire of every child to have a mother and a father who are in fundamental agreement, because they are the two most important parts of his world. He wants his world to be in one piece, not flying apart. But if his parents can't remain together, then at the very least he must still be allowed to continue to believe in both. For he realizes that he is made of both — physically and psychologically. They have been his ideals. If a boy becomes convinced that there is something wrong with his father, then there must be something wrong with himself because he is patterned in his image. If he comes to believe that his mother, on whom he has been so dependent, is bad, then he loses faith in her, in himself, and in all women, to some degree. Child-guidance experience has proved this again and again.

A child would not be enlightened, he would only be harmed, if his mother told him that she was divorcing his father because of infidelity, or if his father explained that he felt justified in having affairs because his wife was unresponsive or generally belittling. And what could a young child make of a father's claim that his wife is too attached to her parents, or her counterclaim that he is irresponsible? He has no basis for understanding the complex factors that contribute to such situations. All that he could grasp would be that his ideals and his trust were shattered.

When a child asks, "Why are you getting divorced?" he is not asking for charges and countercharges. These would only distress him. He is really protesting, "I can't believe there is any reason important enough to justify this tragedy." So the parents' job is to make clear, not once but a number of times, that they have been considering this for a period of years, made many efforts to turn over a new leaf, and are now finally convinced that they cannot possibly go on together any longer. They can talk about arguing and fighting and being miserable all the time. They may want to add something, for a persistent older child, about conflict over money matters, or getting along with the grandparents, or their social life, just to define the general area.

Keeping the emphasis on the broad problem of the parents' inability to solve their incompatibility is not an evasion of the truth, since all the specific causes of marital conflict have been ironed out in many families in the past. This approach is fairer to the child because it keeps the blame on both parents together, for their joint failure, instead of their having to blacken each other's characters in detail, or asking the child to judge between their weaknesses.

The child needs to be reminded again and again that he will continue to have two parents even though one may live far away, that both will continue to love him, that the absent parent will see him as often as possible. These points may seem to an adult too self-evident to need mentioning to a child. But experience shows that a young child may assume that in the split-up he loses at least one parent totally and for all time. In his panic he may ask, "Do I have to be divorced too?" By this he may mean, "Will I lose both parents and be left on my own?" Even if he knows he will live with his mother now, he may fear that if incompatibilities later develop between her and himself, she might divorce him too. It's important during divorce to give a child opportunities to voice his questions, fantasies and fears — and he will come back to them again and again — so that the explanations given him will fit his particular worries.

It is often necessary to deny specifically that the child is the cause of the separation. Most children have an ever present and simple-minded sense of guilt. This is because most of them are scolded frequently and because they are not nearly as successful as adults in shifting the blame to someone else. So when they hear parents using their names during arguments, or using phrases like "If it weren't for the children . . ." they are apt to conclude that they have brought about the crisis. When a child is imploring a kindhearted parent not to go through with a divorce, the latter may be tempted to pretend that there is a possibility of reconciliation. This only prolongs the agony.

Up to this point we have been talking as if people are rational, as if all that separating parents need is to understand the child's point of view, and then automatically act in accordance with his best interests. This is true in some cases. But in many others the bitterness between the parents reaches such a point that it blinds them to their child's welfare. Though they may know in theory how vital it is for his future development that he be allowed to maintain his trust in both parents, they ignore this repeatedly in explaining to him the reasons for the divorce, in their wrangling over the custody and visiting agreement, in their relationships with the child and with each other in the years afterwards. The angry mother, if she is the one who has custody, may act utterly mistrustful of the father's character and persist in trying to interfere with his contacts with the child. Either parent may keep insisting, in all discussions with the child, that the other parent is bad, and encouraging the child to criticize him. Worse still is the situation where one parent is out to get the child away from the other, not because he or she particularly enjoys him, but just to deprive and hurt the other parent.

When we stop to think about this fuming resentment between two people who once were in love we can see that it is no ordinary dislike. During the deterioration of the marriage they may have fallen into the neurotic pattern of unconsciously enjoying the teasing of each other, the mutual hurting and being hurt, of which I wrote in the preceding chapter. When the time arrives when there are no more reconciliations, part of the sense of outrage comes from the fact that each had once given a lot to the other, expected and received a lot, so now he feels cheated. The sense of outrage is tremendously intensified when one and then the other goes to a lawyer, to tattle and complain outside the family, and when the lawyers do their job by wording the accusations to sound as dastardly and as one-sided as possible. When the mutual recriminations are publicized to the widening circle of lawyers, court and the community, each contestant has an increasing need to believe and prove that he is innocent. But most important of all, I think, is that each partner feels unconscious guilt (in addition to that which he can admit) for the part that he has played in the failure and for the pain he has caused his spouse and children. He cannot really face this. (None of us can face our most serious faults completely — we'd become too depressed. Instead we find employers, friends, spouses who will put up with them.) He uses all his wits to shift just as much of the blame as he can manage — to convince himself as well as others. He has an eagle eye for each of his ex-spouse's actual failings. The more faults he can find and the worse the interpretation he can put on them the more relieved he can feel. He is apt to go farther than this — without any realization of what he is doing — and keep provoking the ex-spouse to behave badly. Then he can say to himself and his friends, "See what I mean?" He may talk self-pityingly about how badly he has been treated to all who will listen, hoping that they will agree that he is an innocent victim.

When a person has no reason to feel any guilt about some painful crisis through which he has passed, he does not keep chewing it over, justifying himself, repeating accusations, looking for opportunities to reopen the issue. He is thankful to let bygones be bygones.

You may think I have been exaggerating the inappropriateness of the behavior of certain parents in divorce. But I think you will find that the lawyers and judges who work in divorce courts agree. How else can you account for the appalling things that people do to each other in divorce, people who are considered decent, considerate, rational individuals in their ordinary relationships with friends and business associates?

The greatest sources of bitter wrangling are the custody and visitation rights, and support payments, both during the divorce proceedings and for years afterwards. Usually custody of the children is given to the mother (at least up to adolescence, when there may be a provision that the children can choose). So there are arguments about the children's visits with the father. Resentful mothers commonly try to restrict the visits for various reasons, such as the children are unhappy about the visits, are not cared for properly, spend their time in unsuitable places with unsuitable people, become overtired and catch infections. They complain that the fathers overindulge them, neglect them, poison their minds against their mothers, fail to come when expected or bring the children back late. There is often at least a grain of truth in certain of the more specific reproaches. It is frequently difficult for a father to find appropriate things to do with his child for a few hours or a few days, unless he has remarried and has a real home. But a mother who is looking for trouble can easily exaggerate the perils her child is exposed to, with bits of information she extracts from the child. When the father gives his side of the story he is apt to complain that the mother is entirely uncooperative in accommodating to unavoidable delays and changes in his schedule; that she claims the child is too sick to leave home when he isn't sick at all; that he has evidence she is trying to turn the child against him; that she is so disagreeable when he goes to her home that he can hardly bear the humiliation, especially in the presence of his children.

If mothers frequently take out their resentment against their ex-husbands by making unnecessary trouble about visits, many fathers retaliate, consciously or unconsciously, by falling behind in their support payments. This encourages a mother to be more difficult still, which further hardens the father's heart. This bitter contest between the parents has a certain harsh logic for them, but it is entirely unfair to the child. He needs his father's company and attention whether or not that parent is financially responsible. He needs to trust his mother even if she is tormenting her ex-husband. Certainly it is improper for the mother to ask the child to try to collect the money from the father or for the father to send angry messages to the mother through the child.

I want to emphasize again that the divorcing parents, in order to protect their child against their hostility toward each other — during the divorce proceedings and for the future — should consult some professional person whom they both still trust, a social worker in a family agency, a child psychiatrist, the child's doctor, the minister, or a wise friend. This person, who will be thinking primarily of the child's welfare, can advise them about the custody and visitation provisions of the separation agreement. It would be judicious to name this person in the agreement, for future consultation of either or both parents, and also to name an arbitrator for disputes which cannot be resolved in the previous manner.

A separation agreement, to be effective, must combine definiteness with some flexibility since circumstances will change for every family. One parent may move out of town. The child grows and must be gradually allowed at least an expression of feeling as to how his weekends and vacations are spent. A previous schedule of visits every week or two may no longer suit anybody. When the question of modification of the agreement comes up, it may raise hostilities and suspicions to the boiling point again, with each parent thinking primarily in terms of *his* rights. The parents may have to be reminded that the original agreement and any changes should be for the child's benefit, directly or indirectly.

Young children should see the father often to keep the relationship alive, every week or every other week if practical. At one or two years of age the visits might start with brief walks or rides or trips to a playground, which gradually increase in duration. After the child is three or four years old it is often good for him to spend Friday or Saturday night at the father's residence, at least every other weekend. If possible the child who is four or older should be able to spend part of summer vacation and alternate holiday vacations with the father. There should be a provision that the father is consulted about school and college plans and about serious illnesses. Though the well-drawn separation agreement will diminish the area of conflict, it will not protect the child unless the parents resolve and remember to carry it out with good will.

There are often difficulties in working out the visits with the father even when both parents are trying hard. Unless good sense is used the father will be tempted to put too much reliance on presents, excursions, treats, in his efforts to compensate for not being in the home. It's not that these will win the child's greater allegiance to the father, as the mother fears. Every child certainly is greedy for such favors and may report to the mother those he receives from the father, in hopes of extracting the same from her. But deep down he appreciates that the parent's devotion and guidance are much more vital to him. In fact we learn from child-guidance work, in cases where a parent has no love to give and offers gifts and privileges instead, that the child scorns these even while he demands them. If I were a separated father who had a visit every week or two, I'd feel I was apologizing for something if I bought a present or arranged an unusual treat each time. I'd prefer to save these for special occasions, and act as if the visit itself was the main satisfaction for both of us. More important, visits that are mainly used for excursions give too little opportunity for child and father to become reacquainted in the relaxed manner of family living. (It takes time and a natural setting to resume a relationship even after a week's separation.) It's good if they can share household chores, a hobby, a book they both enjoy. But no two people even of the same age can stand mutual entertainment for an indefinite period, so there should be times when each can read or putter by himself, though in the same place. It helps if the child can have his own toys, projects, regular playmates at his father's residence, to come back to at each visit. It's carrying casualness too far, though, if the father just parks a young child in his office or car while he transacts business, unless the child has some special activity that he really enjoys. Just as in unbroken homes, it's sometimes more enjoyable for both ages if father and child team up with another father and child or a whole family for excursions, picnics, vacation trips.

When the father lives far from his child the visiting schedule will have to be influenced by distances and finances. Distance doesn't make a child need his father less, but it does provide a believable excuse to the child, if it's not stretched too far. More use has to be made of vacation times. Meanwhile, it is important that the father send some kind of message weekly — a letter, a postcard, a joke — any reminder that the child is in his heart and mind. Birthdays, Christmas, even Valentine's Day, should be honored scrupulously.

Of greatest importance to the child is the dependability of the father's visits — whether or not they can be frequent or regular — for it always upsets the child and lessens his trust if the father fails to appear when expected. To be sure, some fathers whose business obligations intrude into the weekend have a partial excuse. Even so, if a father realizes how much his child counts on seeing him, this should make him firmly resist breaking appointments with him or being late for them. (Young children can't stand waiting under any circumstances.) The fact that a father may call off appointments doesn't usually mean that he is lacking in affection for the child. Some fathers find excuses to cancel their visits because they haven't found out how to make them naturally enjoyable. More commonly what's getting in the way are all the old antagonisms toward the ex-wife and guiltiness toward her and the child. The father shrinks from the encounter with his ex-wife because it reminds him of all the past bitterness, his failure, his undignified position on the edge of the family, perhaps his tardiness with payments, or because she uses the occasion to vent her resentments.

I think it's the mother's job, if the child is being frequently disappointed by the father, to let the father know how much his visits mean. But if the father won't admit the importance of visits and stays away for months, the mother can explain to the child that lack of love is not the cause, but perhaps his crossness at her, his feeling bad that he couldn't learn how to live with his wife and child, his effort to forget the things he feels sorry about.

I hope that no one has been misled by the fact that I have called the child of divorce "he." It is easy to understand that a boy's picture of his father is what he has largely identified himself with and that he must be allowed to see and hear the best of him, in order to have a good model. A girl derives different values than a boy from her father. But they are no less vital. Her future relationship with the male sex, with whom she will have to deal the rest of her life and with one of whom (we hope) she will live her adulthood, will be crucially influenced by her experiences with her own father, and by the image of him created out of what she hears of him. When he disappoints her or when she is persuaded to think ill of him, what is harmed most is her future ability to find a good husband and to trust him.

All this does not mean that children of divorced parents cannot grow up secure and make good marriages of their own. Many of them do. But it should be apparent that it takes unusual effort, thoughtfulness, and a generous spirit on the part of both parents.*

* Two valuable books are:
   Children of Divorce by J. Louise Despert, M.D. New York: Doubleday & Co., Inc., 1953. $3.95.
   Parents Without Partners by Jim Egleson and Janet Frank Egleson. New York: E. P. Dutton & Co., Inc., 1961. $4.50.

THE CHILD WHOSE FATHER
HAS DESERTED HIM

Paradoxically he needs help most in
believing in his father's love.

I HAVE a little boy who is now twenty-two months old and progressing beautifully. About a month before he was born, my husband announced to me that he wanted a divorce and never wanted to see me again or the baby either. I cannot tell you how stunned I was, or how I got through that difficult time. Now I feel reasonably whole again and am naturally finding great joy in my baby.

What I should like you to discuss is how you tell your child that his daddy does not want to see him and why he does not. How do you go about protecting him from the inevitable questions other children will ask, and possible taunts? I cannot conceive of the possibility of lying to him, and still I cannot tell him that he just plain *wasn't* wanted, until he is old enough to understand.

We do not know from this letter what led up to the desertion. The fact that it occurred shortly before the baby's birth reminds us that quite a few men (and women too) feel threatened by the approaching birth of their baby, unconsciously at least. In their own childhoods they developed more than the usual amount of dread that a new baby would rob them of their parents' love. They carry this over into adulthood, often without realizing it, and fear the loss of the spouse's love. Of course a great majority are promptly reassured by seeing that the spouse can love them and the baby at the same time.

But the problem of what to tell a child whose father is not coming back is much the same, irrespective of the cause of separation. It's a most difficult problem — for the child and for the mother, but for each in a very opposite way. The mother is probably bitter about the father's behavior, which led up to the divorce or desertion. She is understandably indignant at his failure to make any effort to keep in contact with the child. Yet the child — because he is a human being — craves a father's as well as a mother's love. The fact that the father is absent and doesn't even communicate only increases his yearning. (Those children placed because of their parents' neglect in either orphanages or foster homes have always talked constantly about how much their parents love them and how soon they are coming to visit, despite months and years of evidence to the contrary.)

It is not simply that the child has the desire for love or tokens of love from his father. He *must* believe he is loved if he is to develop a healthy personality. He will make every effort to cling to such a belief even if he has to dream up his reasons for thinking so. However, if he should finally become convinced that his father has never had any affection for him whatsoever, either because his mother has persuaded him or because the father himself has given incontrovertible proof, then harm is done in several ways. He will feel deeply resentful of him, and so will acquire a less trustful attitude toward people in general. More serious will be a depreciation, a belittling of himself. A child who is really convinced that he is not loved by a parent (and I don't mean the child who works on his parent by saying "You don't love me") cannot believe that he himself is a person entirely worthy of being loved. He feels that there must be something fundamental lacking in himself. As he grows up (and remember, I'm talking about girls as well as boys) he continues to have nagging doubts about whether people truly like him — no matter how many do love him in reality. This will be apt to get in the way of his relationships with friends, co-workers, bosses, dates, his spouse and children if he marries. His normal self-esteem is injured in another way too. He assumes that if he is the child of a scoundrel there must be some of the scoundrel in himself.

These same considerations apply if it is the mother who has deserted the family or who makes no effort, after divorce, to keep in touch with them.

You can see why a mother is quite right to be concerned about what she tells her son if his father has broken all contact with the family. And you may be as baffled as the mother who wrote the letter about what she can possibly say under the circumstances that will be reassuring.

Of course what I am leading up to is that the mother, who by now may feel nothing but scorn for the father, must present him to the child in the best possible light. She must put her love for her child above her resentment. This will require great effort and generosity, not just during one talk or two but throughout her lifetime. If she can't think of anything good to say she might start by recalling the qualities that made her fall in love with the father in the first place, and of the former evidences of his love for her. (The angry woman who claims that her ex-husband only deceived her into believing he had any good qualities or any love for her is surely exaggerating her gullibility in order to preserve her righteousness.) She will have to resist the temptation — after she has said some favorable things — to undo this good by hinting at his evil side. I certainly don't mean that she need to go to preposterous extremes in pretending he was an angel. She wouldn't sound sincere. Moreover, a child can't live up to a parent who has no ordinary human frailties. What she must avoid is accusing the father of being a basically mean, selfish, unaffectionate person.

To put it positively, what a child wants to know is that his father had qualities that made most people like him. What he needs most to hear is that his father loved him, still loves him.

The words that a mother will use and how far she will try
to go in any one talk will depend a great deal on the child's
age, and what questions he asks.

Here are some of the things a mother might include, on one
occasion or another, when her three- or four-year-old son asks
such questions as: Why don't we have a daddy? Where did he
go? Why doesn't he come back?

"Your daddy and I loved each other very much and we got
married. We wanted to have a little boy to take care of and to
love. Then you were born and I loved you very much and your
daddy loved you very much. But after a while your daddy and I
didn't get along so well. We began to have arguments and fights
just the way you and Tommy have arguments and fights. We
tried hard to be friends again, but we couldn't find out how to
do it. We kept on arguing and fighting. Finally your daddy got
so upset that he thought it would be better if he went away. He
thought he would feel better and I would feel better if there were
no more arguments around here. But he felt bad to leave you
because he loved you very much. He loved to hold you and play
with you. I'm sure he still thinks about you a lot and wishes he
could live with you. But I think he is afraid that if he came back
to see us the arguing and fighting would start all over again."

A mother who has been indignant about the father's lack of
affection for the child may think that some of these statements
about how he loved the child are a bit too thick. Maybe they
are, in a few cases. But there are *very* few fathers who don't
have these feelings, no matter how they may have denied them
in anger or failed to show them.

The mother whose husband deserted before the baby's birth
can't tell her child how much his father enjoyed him after his
birth. But she may be able to recall some evidence of his having
loved the baby in anticipation (since jealousy does not cancel
out love), or to imagine him now thinking of the child with
love (since most adults continue to mature). If he consciously
resented the baby from conception, she can lay the desertion to

quarrels, which is a correct enough answer for the time being. In any case, the benefit of any doubt should be given the father — not for his sake but for the child's.

As for what a child is to say to his playmates: he merely states that his parents are divorced. There are enough divorced people in most communities so that children accept this as one of the facts of life.

When the child is older, more understanding, he will probably ask why the father does not at least write letters or send presents. The mother may be able to explain that a man who has been so upset that he left his family is still apt to be feeling upset about it years later. He probably feels bad that he had to go away. When we feel bad about what we have done, we try not to think about it. When we have had trouble with people we love, we may feel too embarrassed to get in touch with them.

If the father's problem has been alcoholism, the mother can explain to the reasonable child of adolescent age that this is really a disease which is very difficult to get over. If the father became infatuated with another woman, or a philanderer with several, the mother can simply say to an adolescent that he fell in love with someone else and that he and the mother decided that the only thing they could do was get divorced.

In all these explanations the words are less important than the attitude. The mother should be playing the part not of the reproachful wronged one who seeks the child's sympathy for herself and indignation toward his father but of the wise person who understands, like a doctor or minister, something about the troubles that other people have.

THE FATHERLESS FAMILY

*The mother can't be father too but she can
keep his image strong for the children's benefit.*

FROM LETTERS, from interviews in the office, from social conversations, I've been impressed with the degree of apprehension
that women express when they talk about rearing children without a father. This is as true of widows as it is of divorcees, so it
isn't based on guilt about having pushed the father out of the
home. They often use the words, "It's an awful responsibility
to try to be both a mother and father."

Certainly it's true that a mother alone is compelled to take on
serious responsibilities that would ordinarily be the father's, or
shared with him — having to make fundamental decisions all
by herself, perhaps earning the living. And the role of bread-
winner will interfere with the time that she could use ideally
for mothering. But I think that part of the excessive worry is
based on a misunderstanding — the assumption that a woman
should somehow make the attempt to be father as well as
mother. It's as impossible psychologically as it is physically.

We know that a child wants both a father and a mother. A
young child who lacks one or the other keeps asking the re-
maining parent for a replacement. But the remarkable thing is
that he can create a parent who will serve many of his needs if
he has to. If he remembers the parent or sees him occasionally
he will keep his memory fresh. He will really commune with
him in spirit between visits. If he can't remember the parent
he will reconstruct him out of what he has been told, what he

admires in other adults of the same sex whom he has known, what he would like his parent to be. When fathers came home after the war and announced themselves to offspring who were too young to remember them, some of these children angrily denied that these men were their fathers. They pointed instead to photographs of their fathers with which they had connected all the stories they had heard. Even a child who has never known either parent — because of death, desertion or illegitimacy — will create vivid images of both, whom he can describe in detail, compounded from elements of the people he has known or read about, and from his own yearnings.

Children who have been adopted at birth because of illegitimacy, even when they grow up in ideal families, may daydream a great deal of their true parents, about whom it is usually impossible for them to know or find out anything. Sometimes, in adolescence or adulthood, they set out on quests to track down their true parents, even though they realize that they won't be able to join them.

So a human being is a creature who *must* have a father and mother, in his feelings, and will create them if necessary. Of course a real father who's a good one will be a lot more satisfactory than an image, on many scores. But if there isn't a real one, the mother's job is not to try to be one, and not necessarily to try to find one, but to maintain a wholesome environment for her child so that he can create a wholesome one in his imagination.

At this point we will have to very briefly review the progressive development of the average boy's and girl's relationships with their father and mother — at the conscious and unconscious levels — and how this shapes their respective characters. Then we can discuss what the implications will be for the guidance of a mother without a husband.

It's at about the age of six months that a baby begins to distinguish between the various individuals who pay attention to him — and to develop feelings for them as people. The mother (or her substitute) is the one who is overwhelmingly important for the next two years, and from whom the boy or girl derives most of his security. He won't develop nearly as much dependence on his father at this stage, unless he's around him a great deal. But he will learn how men are different in their manners, voices, play and discipline. He will learn how to adjust to and enjoy these differences.

It's between two and three years that a boy begins to realize more consciously that it's his destiny to become a man. From then until six he really sets to work to pattern himself after his father particularly, after older brothers if he has any, after other friendly males. He watches to see what occupations they are interested in, how they go about them, what they think is right and wrong in behavior, what their attitudes are to each other and to women, how they talk, what mannerisms they use, what feelings they have, which ones they express freely and which they try to conceal, what they are scared of. He plays all day at manly occupations, pushing toy cars, building structures, riding a horse, shooting pistols, driving a car or a plane, acting the father when he plays house. By three a boy begins to be aware of the feelings connected with genitals and may become involved in sex play with other children his age. Between three and four his love of his mother, which was mainly dependent before, now takes on an increasingly romantic quality. By about four he may declare that he is going to marry her. But the intense and possessive nature of his love — because he is a human being — stirs up feelings of rivalry and antagonism toward his beloved father. Since he assumes that his father reciprocates this jealousy, and because his father is so much bigger, stronger, smarter, he becomes increasingly uneasy about this uneven rivalry and keeps it out of the conscious part of his mind. By five or six he is uncomfortable enough in his deeper feelings and wise enough in the ways of the world so that he finally denies the wish to have his mother for himself. After this he doesn't want to be kissed by her, at least in public. He becomes increasingly intolerant of all girls and of love stories. It's a welcome change for him to become absorbed in impersonal matters such as the three R's, nature, science, making collections, games of skill. From now on he doesn't have to work to copy his father because he feels sure he is very much a chip off the old block. Instead of wanting to please his parents he becomes somewhat argumentative, messy, irritating. Now he wants to imitate the older boys — in his appearance and manners and occupations.

We believe that a boy's attraction to his mother in the three-to-six-year-old period is vital in establishing an idealistic romantic pattern for his future life as an adult. In this way his sexuality will be strongly linked to a deep love for a fine woman, who will also be a devoted mother to his children. (This is in contrast to most animals in whom sexual attraction is quite indiscriminate and flitting.) But we believe it is equally important that the little boy, in his yearning for his mother, not be allowed to become so closely attached to her in actuality that he cannot detach himself from her later. In the ordinary family he is prevented from feeling that he can have her all to himself by three interrelated factors: his awe of his father, his realization that his mother's romantic love belongs to her husband, her tactful refusal to let the boy become too intensely affectionate toward her in a physical sense.

We sometimes see situations in which a mother, without meaning to, encourages her son to become much too close to her. It may be because she and her husband have lost all affection for each other and she turns all her warmth toward her son instead. Or she may be an exaggeratedly flirtatious person, who tends, unconsciously, to act a bit seductive toward any male, of any age. (You know the type I mean.) Or she may be a woman who doesn't really appreciate a man or boy who is distinctly masculine in personality but will be responsive to one who can be persuaded to share her womanly interests. There are various ways in which these different kinds of mothers may permit their sons to become too strongly attached. If a woman's husband is a traveling man, she may allow her son to sleep in his father's bed, and this encourages him to daydream that he is really taking his father's place. Another may carelessly reveal too much of her body or act too coquettish toward him or dance with him, as if playfully pretending he is her husband. She may embrace him too ardently and too long, or not interfere tactfully when he does the same thing. Another may show that she enjoys her son's company and conversation a lot more than she enjoys her husband's. Another still, without realizing it, may be subtly discouraging her son from spending time with other boys or from interest in boyish activities; instead she is always trying to interest him in interior decoration or dressmaking or the arts. She may be making him her confidant, telling him about her friends, her troubles, as if he were another woman.

I want to explain quickly that I don't mean to scare normal mothers out of being warmly affectionate and companionable with their sons. For it's just as undesirable when mothers are standoffish with their sons as when they are too enveloping. I'm only calling attention to the definite differences in the natural relationships between mother and son, mother and husband, mother and woman friend.

It's obvious that when a mother has no husband it will be more difficult to keep her relationship with her son as ordinary as it would otherwise be. She is apt to be lonelier. No matter how normal she is in personality, she will have an inclination to make her son an intensely close companion, especially if she has no other children, and to lavish all her affection on him. But the situation is not as lacking in natural safeguards as it might appear. In the first place a boy's instinctive drive to play the part of a regular guy is powerful. It will keep him on the right track unless he's up against great pressures, and he will actually guide his mother, too. He will strive to keep alive what memory he has of his father and to fill out his image of him. Furthermore we learn from psychoanalytic investigation that he will be sufficiently in awe of this memory of his father so that he will not want to trespass on his father's preserve if the mother plays her part right. She does this by showing that she too keeps alive the memory of the boy's father, and respects him as the boy's father. For the sake of her son she doesn't belittle his father (whether divorced or dead), no matter what she secretly thinks of him in other respects. She also helps the boy to be respectful of the composite father figure he creates for himself out of the other men who come into his life — relatives, male teachers, doctor, tradesmen, neighbors, the mother's suitors. She does this by showing that her woman-to-man relationships with each of them, whether impersonal, cordial or romantic as the case might be, are all quite different in quality from the mother-child relationship. To put it another way, each of these men helps to keep the boy in his place as a child, just as his father would have done, provided his mother cooperates by treating them as men and treating him as a child.

I don't mean that a husbandless woman should be so afraid of treating her school-age son as a mature person that she refrains from explaining about their financial situation, or chatting freely with him, or going on trips with him, or giving him a hug, or letting him feel responsible about saving money or earning it. Rather it's that she should allow him to remember that he is still her son, however responsible, not her husband (or not her woman friend). She should keep up her own friendships and activities. When she and the boy go on excursions they can sometimes invite another boy and perhaps his parents. She should encourage her son to cultivate his own interests and friendships, to accept invitations without her (rather than act hurt when he leaves her). When he gets into adolescence she may have to remind herself not to act jealous about his girlfriends.

All of this will be easier for a mother if she has several children, because then everyone is reminded that there is an adult world and a children's world, however closely they meet in the family.

But there are still the natural fears of a mother of a fatherless boy that, because she's a woman, she won't know what his needs are, or whether he is making a good adjustment, or how to help him if he has problems. (The feeling may be a bit like that of the chicken who has hatched duck eggs.) In the first place I myself think it's a good sign when a mother confesses that boys are more mysterious to her than girls, in some respects; it means that she's very much a woman herself and has a respect for the male sex as somewhat different. The woman who feels she knows just how to manage the opposite sex may try to manage them too much and produce either rebellion or submission. When a mother can admit that she's only a woman it should foster the chivalrousness of her son, whether he's four or sixteen. His wish to please and help her should more than make up for any lack of knowledge on her part. If things are working out right her son will instinctively follow his boyish destiny without constant guidance from her. She will be reassured by his success at home, at school, in friendships. She need not worry about hidden trouble if no signs of it show. But even if things are going well, I think she is entitled to regular consultation with a family social agency for her own comfort. If problems arise she should certainly get advice from the school people, family social agency, a sensible male relative or a Child Guidance Clinic.

A mother's uncertainty is apt to be accentuated when her son gets well into adolescence. He will probably be more secretive about his friends, dates, activities, thoughts. ("Where are you going?" "Out.") He shows at least glimpses of stormy feelings. He has an itch to be rebellious against certain teachers or other authorities. He may make it clear that he feels his mother, being of another generation and sex, is hopelessly out of touch with his situation. His huge size reminds her that she is incapable of controlling him physically. Discipline now can only be exerted by moral suasion, which is like riding a bicycle without touching the handlebars. The romantic attachment to his mother which was so intense before he was six is now most often felt negatively — as an intolerance of closeness, a bristliness. Only a "mother's boy" can feel cozy with his mother at this age.

The husbandless mother is only feeling in exaggerated form the same management problems that all parents of adolescents face. It's hard to define the right course in positive terms — they just sound like platitudes. It's easier to start with some negative statements. We know that the parent can't manage the teen-ager by constant nagging or threatening or punishment. These just irritate him and provoke him to rebellion. Prying and suspicion and mistrust are worse; he feels, "If she thinks I'm that bad, I might as well have the fun of being bad." On the other hand, many well-meaning parents nowadays, in their fear of antagonizing the child, act as if they are pretending that they don't care what he does. Adolescents realize that they are inexperienced, that they want guidance and rules. They don't usually admit this to their parents. But they often complain to their friends or trusted adult counselors that they wish their parents would give them advice and regulations, as their friends' parents do. They sense that this is one aspect of parental love. So the husbandless mother should certainly show that she cares about the impression her son makes on the community (his and hers) and that she takes it for granted they'll talk together about behavior from time to time, not necessarily in long solemn sessions but in casual conversations. An adolescent likes these discussions to be on an adult-to-adult level which recognizes the fact that he is on his own most of the day and that therefore he himself must feel convinced — not just told — what is right. He is not upset when a parent is clear and emphatic. What irritates him is being talked down to. The fact that he may not agree verbally with his parent's advice doesn't mean that he rejects it.

If a mother can't persuade a teen-age son that her stand is

right — because he feels she is unable to understand a boy's position — and if she is as convinced as ever, she should stick to her opinion. Even if he should disobey her at the time, he will be helped in the long run by knowing what her attitude is. Meanwhile she can suggest that they get the advice of another man — his uncle, teacher, minister, counselor.

If a boy and his own father visit each other or can correspond, some of these unresolved conflicts may be referred to the father. But even if the father votes against the mother, she doesn't have to change her opinion. She might say, "You may decide to follow your father's advice, but I still do not think it is wise." The point I am trying to make is that though a mother cannot have as total a control of a full-grown son as she could of a small boy, nor as much authority as the father would have if he were in the home, she can still have access to his conscience if she is a fair and loving parent. In the long run this is a lot more important than whether the boy agrees with her or obeys her at the moment.

When it comes to the relationship between a husbandless mother and her daughter it will be similar to her relationship to her son in some respects, different in others. The mother is less apt to feel apprehensive about her ability to raise a daughter because she has learned about all there is to know about rearing a girl by having been one. This is an advantage in itself, because a confident parent can bring up a child with greater ease than an anxious parent. And the girl will have her mother as an ever present model throughout childhood to pattern herself after.

There is every evidence that a girl needs a father as much as a boy does. In infancy and very early childhood she needs to become familiar with how different men are from women — but still enjoyable — so that they won't seem too strange to her later. Between three and six years of age she will need a flesh-and-blood father or an image of a father, to make a romantic attachment to. If she has little recollection to go on she, like a boy, will create one from what she hears, from the men she sees, from her yearnings. The image of this man and the image of her mother's relationship to this man will probably have a strong influence on the ideals she will set for her eventual marriage as an adult. This is why it is important that her mother help her to think the best of her father. Just as important is how the mother feels and how she acts toward other men who come in contact with the family — in a business or social way. If she shows that she thinks most men are selfish or unreliable or brutal, because of her experiences with one, her daughter may pick up this attitude and be looking for the worst instead of the best when she grows up. It's surely wise for the mother to keep what contact she can with other families among the relatives and neighbors that have fathers, so that the girl can experience them at close hand, in casual gatherings. Otherwise the image of males may become unreal, either frightening or overidealized. Since widowed or divorced mothers fairly often go to live with their own parents or see them often I want to add specifically that a girl or boy can use a fond grandfather very effectively in creating a good father image and in establishing a child-father type of relationship.

There is the question of how a child will be affected if his widowed or divorced mother accepts dates with another man and considers marriage. Some widows in earlier times automatically ruled out any further romance, insisting loyally that it could never come up to their first love and would desecrate it. There are few who take this position arbitrarily today. Psychiatrists believe, like most people, that what made a woman a wonderful wife to one man should make her equally successful with another if, after her sorrow has diminished, just the right man turns up. A problem that occurs fairly often, when a woman has felt spurned as a result of a marital breakup, is that she's too anxious — consciously or unconsciously — to prove to herself and the world and her ex-husband that she's still highly desirable. If she's conscious of this motive she's less likely to get into further trouble than if she has no awareness of it. For in the latter case it may seem to her that she is being pursued by several attractive men who'd make great husbands. But her critical acquaintances might say that in her desperation she is throwing herself at men and not being too particular. Anyone who's gone through a divorce needs time and professional help to get over the hurts and, more importantly, to try to learn something about his or her own participation in the failure. Otherwise there may be a greater chance of a quicker tragedy in the next marriage.

The child, too, needs a period of adjustment after the departure of a father from the home, a chance to see that he still has his mother as much as before, that he has not lost his father altogether. If his mother becomes immediately and obviously involved in numerous dates with one man or with several, it will seem to the child (who still feels of course that his mother and father belong together) that her love is shallow, unreliable, and promiscuous. So she has to show discretion, especially at first. Most young children will help the mother sooner or later by asking why she doesn't provide another father. (The idea may be more appealing to the child than the actuality.) She can say that she might, someday, if a man that she and the child could love appears, or that there is a nice man at the office who would like to be invited to dinner. From then on the song has to be played by ear. In one case mother and child and man will become increasingly sure of their mutual love, in spite of the fact that there may be temporary episodes of jealousy at first, on the part of one or the other. On the other hand if the suitor remains critical of the child, or if a child's jealousy of the man continues to stir up chain reactions of resentment in the man and quarrels between him and the mother, there's every reason to go slow and to seek advice from a family social agency or marriage counseling service. It might be that the marriage in question would still be good all around but that the child needs psychiatric treatment first to help him outgrow a possessive dependence on his mother. In any case antagonisms that can't be solved before marriage would only be accentuated after it occurs.

Most husbandless mothers find that they can raise their sons and daughters as successfully as other parents do. In some cases it seems as though the added responsibility and considerateness which the children feel (and which it is quite appropriate that the mother let them feel, as long as she doesn't try to do this by making them feel sorry for her) builds unusual maturity and character into them.

THE STEPCHILD

*The tensions are easily explained but they require
unusual cooperation between the parents.*

HERE IS a letter that's remarkably honest and graphic in describing the problem of stepparents and stepchildren:

Your hair would stand up on end if you knew the difficulties my husband and I have been through with our respective stepchildren, his daughter of fifteen, my own son of nine. And we are both reasonable, logical, affectionate people who try to thrash out our problems honestly when they come. And yet all this has hardly counted at all where *our own* feelings for the children were concerned. In the beginning, when my stepdaughter was twelve, I tried to do "as the book says" and treat her in the same way as I treat my own son, same punishments, same affection. This didn't work at all, though she has never been the slightest bit resentful of my taking her mother's place — in fact she liked me very much. But she would not stand for the discipline part of it (the ordinary variety and not at all severe), nor would she stand it from her father. Every gentle admonishment like "Please don't put the milk there, it'll leave a mark" ended in a full-blown row with tears, tantrums and worst of all, lies. Believe me, we tried everything to make her look normally at things — made sure she wasn't frightened of me and lying because of that; gave her lots of affection and security. But it didn't help one hoot — at the first sign of trouble she'd blow her top and rush off in tears to complain bitterly to her mother — and yet, she doesn't live with her mother *from choice*. She wants to be with us — or with her father, I suppose. And the mother unfortunately sympathizes with her and sets her against us. Since it couldn't go on the way it was, I forced myself to stop worrying (that was hard) and I stopped trying to control her. If there is any scolding to do now, I ask my husband to do it, but only rarely, as it doesn't have any effect otherwise. The result is manyfold: the child is completely happy, and though she *is* utterly selfish still, she behaves herself as well as can be expected of a fifteen-year-old. As far as I am concerned I somehow lost all affection and interest for her when I stopped worrying about her, and I just can't get it back. Our relationship is a complete farce — we joke together and have chats on this and that; *she* likes *me* — and I can hardly stand the sight of her. But this is something she will never know. Yet it makes me feel very sad because, goodness, if a woman can't feel affection for her husband's child what good is she then?

This also affects my own boy, as I frequently find myself taking out my frustration on him for all those things she's done — ruined clothes, ruined through sheer indifference, furniture spoiled with ink stains just left to dry, mud all over the house because she can't be bothered to dry her feet. These things just add fuel to my dislike of her.

I've kept my ears open and noticed the different comments passed by various stepchildren and stepparents about each other. It's patently obvious that they all have the same problem: a basic dislike for each other — probably that nasty old primitive instinct of "getting rid of the outsider." God knows that it's a terribly strong one.

My husband has problems, too, though not quite the same ones. We turned out to be extremely fortunate in that we *both* were in that situation; if we hadn't been — if just one of us had been the stepparent — our marriage would probably have broken up, because *no one* can understand the problem — at least not enough to be sufficiently tolerant. Instead of ending up being against each other, we have been able to help each other. And we can be completely honest about ourselves to the other, though goodness knows it isn't a very kind or pretty picture we present of ourselves that way. All this has helped tremendously. Despite the impression you may have got from the above, our antipathy against "the other child" has lessened noticeably — through sheer will power. Which shows what *can* be done when you really pull your socks up and have a lot of help from the spouse.

There are lots of malicious stepparents in fairy stories and novels. They pop up in newspaper reports too. With all the divorces and remarriages in America there must be a great number of stepparents and stepchildren. Yet there is no excessive number of them coming to child-guidance clinics and other agencies that cope with family problems. So we must assume that the majority of them do a good job in solving a difficult situation. This is remarkable when you think of all the opportunities for antagonism and jealousy among the members of an ordinary, unseparated family. A marriage between people who already have children will obviously create new tensions between all the individuals who are abruptly thrown together in the intimacy of family life.

In the average unseparated family the most visible conflicts are usually between different children or between the parents. But the investigations of Freud and his followers have shown us that the rivalry a boy feels with his father or a girl with her mother is apt to be more far-reaching in its effects, though it may not be noticeable on the surface in a happy family. Most of the effects of this rivalry are constructive for a healthy child. They are conditioning him for his complex role in adulthood. In a strained family, however, they may cause neurotic symptoms, or break out into the open in crude antagonisms.

As I explained in the last chapter, the boy at about three or four is apt to declare that he plans to marry his mother, and the girl says the same about her beloved father. But this possessive attachment gradually creates a sense of antagonistic rivalry toward the father in a boy, toward the mother in a girl, just as the possessive love of a man for a woman makes him jealous if he thinks another man is trying to take his place. But in the normal child the sense of rivalry is being repressed into the unconscious mind — partly because he too is overawed by the size and authority of his parent, partly because he loves him very much and wants to be loved by him. The increasing uncomfortableness of the unconscious rivalry, plus the child's growing sense of reality as he reaches five and six years of age, forces him to deny the wish to have the parent of the opposite sex all to himself. But this repression of a boy's attachment to his mother and rivalry with father (and of the corresponding feelings in a girl) does not mean that these feelings have been extinguished. They stay under the surface and may show up again in adolescence in an intensified rivalry with the parent of the same sex, which causes at least mild difficulties in a majority of families.

It is in strained or unusual family situations that we see these romantic attachments and rivalries causing serious trouble. When fathers came home from World War II we saw the fierce jealousies of some little boys who had been having their mother's company all to themselves. Likewise, boys who are much too close to and dependent on their mothers, despite the fact that the fathers live at home, are apt to be exaggeratedly fearful of their fathers or antagonistic to them. Some little girls who are in a sense closer to their fathers than are their mothers, because of disharmony between the parents, may be surprisingly arrogant to their mothers.

I emphasize these romantic ties and rivalries once again because they can so easily cause trouble when a parent remarries. A son who has had his mother pretty much to himself for a while is apt to feel extraordinarily jealous, at least underneath, when a new man moves into the household and usurps much of his mother's attention. The hatred for a stepfather is well described in the novel, *David Copperfield*, and the play, *Hamlet*. Even though a boy has had a previous opportunity to get to know and love his future stepfather and has encouraged his mother to marry him, we believe there will be some rivalry underneath.

The same disturbances can take place between stepdaughter and stepmother, as the woman describes so vividly in the letter. But the stepdaughter-stepmother relationship does not so often upset family life because daughters of separated parents most often live with their own mothers. A girl will usually welcome a stepfather if he is an agreeable, fair person. In adolescence, however, when a girl is apt to feel rivalrous with her mother in any case, as well as slightly romantic toward attractive males of all ages, she may get very much under her mother's skin by playing up to a stepfather and making a great show of how well she understands him and takes care of him. She might have done the same thing with her own father and mother if they had not separated; but a mother is apt to feel more threatened by such provocation when it's not the girl's own father.

I've been calling attention to the exaggerated jealousy of the romantic type. But there can also be antagonism toward a stepparent of the opposite sex, though it is not as likely to be as bitter. Even in unseparated families one can sometimes see a similar resentment. A two-year-old girl who is intensely dependent on her mother may act hostile to her father when he comes home for supper because he usurps part of the mother's attention. Yet she may be quite trustful of her father when her mother is out of the house. In happy families this pattern usually fades out as the girl becomes more independent of her mother and begins to have romantic feelings for her father at about three. But it's not too hard to see why an older girl, who has had her mother all to herself for a few years (or, what is less common, a boy who has had his father), may resent a new stepparent even if he is of the opposite sex. The stepparent is still an interloper from the child's point of view.

What the mother points out so frankly in her letter is that the parent's own primitive feelings compound the trouble enormously. She still finds it hard to believe that as a mature adult she can react so hostilely to a child. But this isn't really too hard to explain. It isn't just that this fifteen-year-old girl is messing up her house and refusing to be controlled. If the woman is human she has some possessive and rivalrous feelings of her own which will be stirred up by having to share her new husband's love with a grown girl to whom he is deeply attached and who may be making quite a show of her affection for him. The mother does not specify what her clashes with her husband are about but I presume that if he shows any inclination to side with his daughter against her during a family dispute, it makes her furious. And he no doubt will be hypersensitive to any unfairness she shows toward his daughter. He may appear overly critical of his stepson or of his wife's handling of him.

A stepfather may feel considerable rivalry, at least unconsciously, toward his stepson who has been loved by his new wife longer than he has been, especially if he thinks the boy has been spoiled by her or is still claiming too much of her attention or is acting rudely resentful of him. If the stepfather becomes even slightly mean to him, the mother is apt to take sides instinctively with her son. This will further accentuate the stepfather's resentment. It may make the boy cling ostentatiously to his mother for protection. But if the mother appears to side with her husband, the boy's resentment toward him will become fiercer. Each individual excuses his own jealous feelings by magnifying the unfairness of the other.

When I list these multiple opportunities for jealousy my admiration goes up for the couples who make a go of these relationships. How do they do it? There are a few factors in their favor. The child who lacks a father or mother just naturally wants a replacement, partly because he senses the quite different needs he has for mother *and* father, partly because he just wants his family to be like others. Furthermore the newly married husband and wife have needed each other — for love, for company, for sharing of responsibilities — so they should be happier people when remarried and therefore more enjoyable as parents. But how do they get around the pitfalls? I'm sure that there is no one approach. In every successful family it must work out differently because the personalities are all different. One stepmother will claim that she succeeds because she loves and treats her stepchildren exactly like her own. I've always argued that no parent can even treat two of his own children alike, since they are such different characters. I'd explain, instead, that the good parent keeps all the children feeling secure and relatively un-rivalrous by intuitively sensing each one's individual needs and responding to them. In this sense he would realize the special insecurities of a stepchild and do his best to meet them. (By contrast, an immature stepparent would be too threatened and angered by a stepchild's hostility toward him to be able to think of the child's needs.)

Another successful stepparent may say that the answer is to leave the disciplining of the stepchild to his own parent. I imagine that in many such relationships this is a helpful rule, especially in regard to matters that seem particularly important to the child. And especially, too, in the early stages of the relationship, before the child has really accepted the stepparent at all. Yet this cannot be a solution for all situations. A mother is forced to make a hundred quick decisions every day while the father is away. If she is able to make these in a manner that leaves no great resentment in a stepchild it would indicate to me that it is her general tactfulness toward the child — the rule about serious discipline is only one example — which is keeping the atmosphere happy. What reassures the stepchild, even when the stepmother sometimes has to impose a penalty that hurts, is that she is generally a fair person and is not taking advantage of the father's absence to be mean to the child.

I've been talking here as if there were the mature, tactful stepparents, and the others who lack these qualities. This is obviously an oversimplification. Most stepparents — like most parents — are in between. We realize that we can handle one of our own children with ease and judgment, while another frequently gets under our skin. When we invite a neighbor's child into the family for a week's visit, we are apt to find that, unless he is a very polite person, he irritates us for a while because of some characteristic we hadn't noticed before or because in an open or subtle way he challenges our authority. Later we get used to him or we get him under control. Even the most effective of stepparents must have plenty of grim moments at first. The maturity and lovingness that enables him eventually to respond more understandingly to a stepchild's touchiness has to be learned gradually. It's like the case of the beginning resident in child psychiatry training who imagines he can get along with all children. But he finds himself becoming surprisingly angry with the first difficult patient who openly defies him or abuses him. After more experience he learns what it was in the child's past or present family situation that makes him suddenly turn hostile, and then he doesn't take it so personally. He also learns how to manage the child better so that he doesn't lose control of him. Feeling less threatened, he can act more friendly and thus gain the child's trust.

When I say that a stepparent can learn to respond with increasing understanding, I certainly don't mean that he will solve his problems by patiently ignoring misbehavior or submitting to abuse. This doesn't work any better than becoming openly antagonistic or harsh with him. When a child gets away with murder it's apt to have two unfortunate effects. He feels guilty underneath and responds to this by worse behavior, hoping unconsciously to provoke the firmness of discipline he knows he needs. He senses also that the parent is guilty about something, to permit such abuse, and feels tempted to be ever meaner. (It's impossible for any of us not to take advantage of a guilty, submissive person.)

A conscientious man or woman is bound to feel at least slightly guilty as a stepparent if the situation is not working out perfectly, because he realizes that the marriage he has wanted for himself is posing something of a threat to his new spouse's children and his own. But we can be sure that if he lets himself be intimidated by his own guilty conscience he will only foster a vicious cycle. He should focus on the other side of the coin. He should recognize that if he plays his part well the marriage should be a boon to both sets of children and to his spouse as well as to himself. By showing his confident self-respect and by requiring respect from the children he makes it easier for them to like him and to adjust to the situation.

How far should a stepparent go in encouraging a stepchild to treat him, feel toward him, as if he were the real parent? My hunch is that almost every stepchild, even though he develops an excellent relationship with the stepparent, will want to continue to think of this as different from his relationships with his own father or mother. He may not want to call a stepfather "Father." This should not be felt as a reproach by the stepparent or as a sign of his failure even to a slight degree. The stepparent may in actuality be a much better parent than the absent mother or father. Nevertheless it is basic human nature for a child to want to feel loyal to his own parent and think well of him, whatever and wherever he is. This will help him to believe in himself, since he knows he is made of his parent. The wise stepparent should not feel hurt by this distinction but show that he understands and respects it.

On the other hand a stepchild who is young, or whose own parent is dead, or who is quite dependent or competitive by nature, may soon want to call a stepfather "Father" and be treated as if he were one of the stepparent's own children. He may start with this attitude and then change his mind as he grows older. I feel that the parents should, generally speaking, follow the child's preference as long as they do not deny the actual fact or encourage the child to forget it. It is a mistake for a child who doesn't remember his own parent to be told that his stepparent is in fact his real parent. The impulse to tell him this comes from the worthy motive of wanting to make him feel secure. But experience shows that in almost all cases the child eventually discovers the truth (just as in the situation of the adopted child) and that he may be seriously upset by discovering that his parents have deceived him in this vital matter.

This brings up the questions of whether a child should use the last name of his stepfather and whether he should be adopted by him. When a young child, who has been separated from his father and is yearning to have a substitute, acquires a likable stepfather whose last name is used by everyone else in the family, it is natural that he may want to use it too — to be regular, to belong to the household. This doesn't mean in most cases that he wants to deny his own father — the two matters are in separate compartments in his mind. The real father who is still attached to his child may object to this, feeling that it is an effort at alienation. If I were the father I'd let the child use the other name if that made him comfortable. I'd keep his attachment and trust in me by means of regular contacts and other expressions of love.

A stepfather may generously propose legal adoption of his stepchild as an expression of his love and generosity toward him and toward his wife. The true father may agree because of good or not-so-good motives. But even if a loving father permits this just for his child's presumed security, it may loosen the ties between them to at least a slight degree, may lessen the father's urgency to see the child as often. If adoption occurs at a young age, the child may later get a feeling that he was taken away from his father without his own consent. The factors to be considered will vary in different families, being financial and social as well as emotional, and I'm sure there is no one answer. My own inclination, as long as there was no great urgency, would be to wait until the child could participate in the decision, at least until he was eight or ten, preferably until he was sixteen or eighteen and out of the worst vacillations of adolescence. Meanwhile he could be given most of the sense of acceptance, which is his stepfather's intention, by being told that his stepfather would like to adopt him as his own son someday if the child should decide, when he is older, that he would prefer this. Meanwhile he could use his name informally if he wished.

In discussions with the child about such matters, it would be all wrong for the stepparent and parent to use as an argument that the absent parent is less devoted, less admirable than the stepparent. No matter how close the child is to a stepparent, he still needs, for his own good, to think well of the separated parent.

Now I want to get back to some of the good points which that honest stepmother made in her letter. She is certainly right that she and her husband have succeeded because of their love for each other and their ability to talk over their conflicts. I'm sure that another valuable quality is her sense of humor — not jokes directed at someone else but the good grace not to take herself too seriously.

I feel that she blames herself unjustifiably for the fact that she hasn't achieved complete harmony and that she often feels quite antagonistic to her stepdaughter. The girl's character was fairly crystallized by the time of the marriage — rather thought-less, explosive and not very honest. No one should expect a stepmother to be able to change a child greatly at this late age, nor expect that a very honest, well-organized woman could come to accept such a child completely. It's a triumph that the girl likes her so well and that they can pass the time of day so cheerfully. I've known lots of reasonably capable mothers whose own daughters were sulking or provoking them a great deal at this age. But when a woman has shaped her own daughter from conception she cannot so easily permit herself to frankly dislike the girl. Her dislike is muffled by her sense of responsibility and guilt. The fact that this stepmother can honestly admit her antagonism, to herself and to her husband, has probably helped her to get along with the girl.

As a wild guess I'll add that I suspect that this woman likes her stepdaughter, in most respects, more than she realizes. How else could they get along as amicably as they do? How else could the girl be so obviously fond of her stepmother?

I think that the woman's sharp feeling of antagonism, of which she is so ashamed, is only partly related to the girl's irritating faults, that it is more basically caused by the common rivalry between mother and daughter in adolescence, which can come closer to the surface in the case of a stepmother. It is probably also greatly accentuated by the fact that this mother, being a much more responsible person than her stepdaughter, has

made all the concessions — perhaps more than were necessary —
for the sake of her marriage. But if she hadn't made any, the
strains would be showing in the girl instead. She's done a wonderful job and should be proud of it.

VII

Critical Problems of
Today and Tomorrow

❰❬❬❭❬❬❭❬❬❭❬❬❭❬❬❭❬❬❭

TELEVISION, RADIO, COMICS
AND MOVIES

Parents should set the standards, keep
track, and stick to their guns.

FOR A LONG TIME there's been controversy about the effects on children of television and radio programs, comics and movies. The chief concern has been about the influence of so much violence, crime and sex. There have also been questions about the effect on schoolwork, homework and the reading of good books.

Let's tackle violence and crime first. A certain number of judges, prosecutors and psychiatrists have been impressed with the frequency with which a severe delinquent, asked in court where he ever got the idea for his crime, has promptly answered, "In a comic book," or, "On a television program." They have taken this as evidence that a child can be seriously corrupted by these means.

Most psychiatrists haven't been willing to go so far. They've admitted that much on the air and in the comics is unwholesome, especially for certain children. They've conceded that a cruel youth might pick up an ingenious or fiendish idea from something he'd seen. But they've denied that a child who was anywhere near normal to start with could be turned into a scoundrel or a thug by any number of hours of viewing or reading. Most parents have felt the same way, too. They know that their own children have been exposed to a good deal of storied villainy without changing character.

A child acquires his basic standards from his parents. If they are decent people and love him, he loves them deeply, too, and patterns himself after them. In this way he acquires a conscience which will not let him get into serious trouble later.

To be sure, a child's standards are affected to a lesser degree by a variety of other influences as he grows gradually away from his early dependence on parents: the attitudes of school and Sunday school teachers, of his classmates, his friends, and friends' parents. (I can still remember, as a strictly brought up child, being quite impressed at eight or ten by some of the things that parents of my friends permitted.) But even an adolescent's standards are not markedly changed by his contemporaries' (though his urge to conform to them is great at this age), because he instinctively limits his friends to those brought up much like himself.

It has often been pointed out, as a reason for not worrying too much about the effects of violence in television programs and comic books, that children of earlier generations listened to fairy tales that were every bit as cruel. I'm not sure, though, that a couple of hours of these fairy stories *every* night of the week would have been harmless for young children. Sensitive individuals certainly got nightmares from them. Most important, perhaps, is the fact that a story read by your mother had a different impact from that which comes from seeing live people apparently involved in brutality, night after night. During storytelling, the pictures you formed in your imagination were pretty well limited by your experiences. Your mother's voice and explanations were a constant reassurance that this was make-believe. Her comments reminded you that she and you abhorred the acts of the villains. On the television screen the prevalence of real-looking cruelty must give the child the impression that it is widespread, and that it is taken for granted in the outside world. A nursery-school teacher recently told me that since the advent of a popular program which is loaded with slapstick violence, the children have been casually bopping one another with great frequency. When she objects, they explain that this is the way it's done on the program. So, though I don't for a minute claim that good children are being turned into bad by such a diet, I think that it may lower their standards somewhat, and give them a poor impression of humanity.

The attitude the parents take in regard to various programs and comics will make some difference in the effect these will have on a child's own ideals. If the parents are keeping track of what is being viewed, and show their concern by ruling out certain programs and strips, the child will be reminded of what standards he is expected to have, even if he continues to peek at them. If the parents show no disapproval, he will feel none either.

It is true that psychologists and doctors (including myself) have been pointing out for years that even the best of children have aggressive feelings in them which can find healthy expression in playing games of mock violence, in hearing stories and seeing shows that involve a certain amount and kind of hostility. The question of what amount and what kind is important. A cartoon of a mouse punching a lion in the snoot makes children chuckle with satisfaction. A little fellow is getting back at a big bully. But a man's real face being battered by the fist of a snarling criminal is quite a different dose to swallow.

A lot of parents have been dissatisfied with some of the programs their children are viewing. But every time they've tried to rule out a certain one, or to put a limit on the total viewing time per day, their children have argued indignantly: It's the best program of all; all their friends are allowed to see it; the other kids can watch as much as they want to; why do their parents have to be the only mean ones? Strong-minded mothers and fathers are able to stand up to this kind of pressure and make their rules stick. Others have wilted under the heat of their children's reproaches. They've given in right away; or they've relaxed their vigilance after a couple of nights, half suspected that the forbidden program was being viewed again, but done nothing about it. They've had the same uncertainty about how strict to be about comic books and movie shows. I think all this illustrates the point that parents have relatively little trouble laying down in matters about which there were definite rules in their own childhoods: bedtime, table manners, lies, bad language. But when new activities for children develop — like television, or car driving in adolescence — parents have no traditions or convictions to guide them. They get conflicting reports about what other parents are doing. They have opinions, but they don't feel sure. They try to make reasonable rules. Then when their children protest violently, the parents vacillate. The children sense the parents' uncertainty and redouble their arguments.

Parents' confidence in their ability to make correct rules has been lowered by other developments of this century too. There has been the entrance into the child-rearing field of the psychologists, psychiatrists, educators, pediatricians, who have written and lectured about the needs and the problems of children. The unfortunate effect on some parents — especially the most conscientious ones — has been to make them conclude that parents are just as apt to do wrong as right.

Another unsettling factor has been the rapid rise in the standard of living of so many families, especially since the end of the war. We think of this as fortunate, and in most ways it is. On the other hand, the histories of many lands show that when the circumstances of life change suddenly it disturbs the stability of the family and weakens parental discipline. And, strangely enough, unusual prosperity is more upsetting than depression or even war. It's apt to produce increases, for instance, in delinquency, crime and suicide. When parents can provide their child with an environment quite different from that in which they themselves grew up, they have fewer reliable guideposts to go by. They have to grope for more of the answers.

Since the beginnings of children's movies, radio and television, doctors have heard from mothers about the problems of the unusually sensitive small boys and girls who are frightened by what they hear or see. They cry, or they're afraid to go to bed, or they have nightmares. A few of these children have enough sense to refuse to have anything more to do with such programs. Unfortunately, a majority of them, being as illogical as other human beings, keep going back for more of the stuff they can't stand. Clearly it's up to the parents to be more sensible than their small fry, and see to it that no more harm is done.

The fact should be faced that a good proportion of children under six years of age fall into the sensitive category. I say this from personal experience years ago in taking my own and other young children, on a very few occasions, to movie houses that were showing cartoons just for children. Adults and older children were laughing happily, but a lot of the young ones were cringing. We have to be reminded by such experiences that wild animals and cruel stepmothers in cartoons are as horrible to three- and four-year-olds as real ones would be.

So far I've been discussing the effects of violence and frightfulness. This leaves the problem of sex. It comes up more commonly nowadays in regard to movies because recent court decisions have put an end to advance censorship by government boards. I realized this recently when we went to a neighborhood theater to see one foreign picture and were given a bonus of a sneak preview of another. The first was excellent. But the second would never have passed a board of review and was so crude — by American taste — that there was a lot of embarrassed giggling in the audience, particularly by the teen-agers.

All children seek knowledge of the facts of life, not just on a few occasions but bit by bit at each succeeding stage of development. They come to their parents if the parents make this easy. In any case, they ask questions or pick up ideas from older brothers and sisters and from friends. They learn some aspects in school. As they get into the teens they begin to search privately for revealing books. They draw conclusions from movies, television and magazine articles. There is great variation in the rate of romantic and sexual maturity. Some children are much more precocious than average. Others are very shy; they don't want to know much for a long time and so they protect themselves if they can.

More significant than the facts that a child acquires is the emotional or spiritual atmosphere in which the learning takes place. A loving parent, in explaining the facts of life, adjusts the amount of information to the child's readiness and speaks in terms which are in harmony with the family's ideals. A schoolteacher starts with the biological facts and usually does not get so close as parents to the personal and emotional aspects, unless the children draw the discussion in this direction. By contrast, the knowledge (or misinformation) that a more worldly child insists on imparting to a shyer one may be shocking rather than enlightening. The same thing applies to a motion picture that is not appropriate for a child. It may confront him with aspects of sex which he is quite unready to accept comfortably. It is more apt than not to present these with characters and with a view of life which are disturbingly different from what he has known.

On the question of the effect of television on schoolwork, homework and reading habits, the studies made have been inconclusive in their results. In most American schools, homework in the elementary grades is omitted or held to a small amount, because educational research has shown that homework does not contribute to performance in school. So television viewing, at this age when it is most absorbing, does not usually interfere with schooling. In the high school years, when homework is assigned primarily to develop the habit of independent study, most pupils have enough self-discipline to put study first; besides, some of the infatuation with viewing has worn off. At any age — in childhood or adulthood — there are individuals who are always putting off unpleasant work by taking refuge in the television set, but it's not fair to blame the set for this.

One of the most hopeful aspects of television is that thoughtful educators believe that, despite its drawbacks, it has been beneficial. They are convinced that the programs which have told about something real have, over the years, broadened the horizons of children and kindled their enthusiasm to learn more.

The fear that comic books will debase a child's reading tastes has been strong among parents who themselves read and enjoyed good books in their own childhood. I know this from talking with many of them. But time has proved that *their* children, after fairly wallowing in comic books for years, outgrow them in adolescence and go on to books that are appropriate to the family's intellectual level. On the other hand, the reading matter that absorbed a majority of G.I.'s during the war was the comics. But I doubt if most of these would have been reading Dickens, even if there had never been a comic book. In other words, the main thing that determines the eventual level of a person's reading in adulthood is not the books he reads at nine, but the atmosphere in which he grows up.

When it appears that so little is known for sure about the subtle effects of broadcasting, movies and comics, what line are parents to take? Obviously different ones will take different courses, just as they have always done. That's why children turn out differently in different families and different neighborhoods. Some parents have always had high aspirations about the tastes and ideals they want their children to develop. Others have been quite willing to let nature take its course. I think the main way I can be helpful is to encourage those who are dissatisfied with some of the fare offered in broadcasting, movies and comics to stick by their guns, not let themselves be bullied by their children or by neighborhood opinion.

When children are planning to see a movie, I think it's the job of sensible parents to find out whether it's suitable, by checking reviews in the papers, or in parents' and religious publications, or by calling the theater manager — just as they keep an eye on their children's companions and haunts.

In the same way, they need to keep track of what their children are viewing on television and in comic books. They should feel no hesitation in forbidding programs or books which they consider definitely incompatible with the family's ideals.

One method for improving the quality of children's movies and television programs is for parents to communicate directly with the neighborhood theater manager, the local station manager, the network, the sponsor. This is a privilege of citizenship that's usually neglected by all but a few cranky souls. Yet the evidence is clear that a relatively small number of sincere letters or calls makes a strong impression on an official.

Parents should not only complain about existing programs which they consider offensive. They should demand worthwhile programs.

Television is potentially the greatest educational force that has appeared since schools were established and printing was invented. It can go anywhere in the world to find its subject matter. It can provide us with inspired performers, speakers, experts in all fields, and use every dramatic aid. It can deliver the production visually and audibly — and quite personally, too — to every corner of the land. Children can be fascinated by demonstrations of phenomena in electricity, chemistry, biology, geology. They can respond to inspiring stories from history and literature just as well as to meaningless tales of violence. This is too valuable a medium to be left entirely to the discretion of children and advertisers.

PREJUDICE AND CHILDREN

The prejudiced child loses trust in
people and in himself.

MOST OF US have some kind of prejudice. Though a prejudice
may be positive, we usually think of the negative kind: the objection to a whole class of people on the basis of experience with
a certain number, or simply on hearsay. Some prejudices, like
those against divorcees, artists, clergymen or Ivy Leaguers, cause
disadvantage only to the people who hold them, in the sense
that these individuals automatically cut themselves off from contacts which might be valuable in different ways. It's the prejudices shared by the members of a dominant group and carried
out into discrimination against others which really hurt.

I try to imagine, sometimes, how painful it must be for a
parent to have to tell his young son (and it has to be told by
the time he is five or six) that he will automatically be considered undesirable, no matter how good his character and behavior, that he will have to be prepared for slights and insults
beginning soon. If your child is being picked on by one bully,
it's not difficult to explain that this individual is rude or all
mixed up. But what do you say when it is the bulk of the community? It must be hard to reconcile this, for him, with the
religious and ethical ideals you are trying to teach — about
God's justice, the good intentions of most people, the obligation
to respect them. We know that children (and adults) are influenced to behave according to what the community expects of
them. I think it's a tribute to the good job done by the over-

whelming majority of parents of scorned groups that their children have grown up not too seriously impaired by the low opinion in which they are held in the community.

We are less apt to think about the effect of serious prejudices on those who hold them — and on their children. At first glance you might think that, being in the supposedly preferred position, they wouldn't really be harmed. But I think that from the psychological point of view there must always be at least some damage to personality. The young child who is being taught — by parents or playmates — to look down on or shun a group is usually being given the impression that they are somehow dangerous. Remarks such as "They aren't like us" . . . "They aren't nice" . . . "They're dirty" have a vaguely ominous sound. It's left to the anxious imagination of the preschooler to picture just what the danger consists of. This has the same effect on children as giving them fears about policemen or bogiemen or kidnapers, which most educated parents try to avoid nowadays. To the degree that the child takes the warnings seriously, he feels endangered by the group. This impairs his trust in people and — more seriously — his trust in his own ability to deal with people. It also gives him, as he grows older, an unwholesome method for bolstering his ego when he secretly feels inadequate. I think that most of us, when we hear a grown man making sneering remarks about a minority, immediately sense his lack of self-confidence, his readiness to seek solace through scorn, and we lose some of our respect for him. So it seems to me unhealthy, from the point of view of the child's own welfare, to start him out with ready-made fears, ready-made self-doubts, ready-made props.

I suppose that the readiness of human beings to believe ill of an entire group, or to swell their dislike of a few individuals into a wholesale prejudice, is a capacity which was built into humanity during the savage process of evolution, so that men who were threatened with a genuine plot or an enemy tribe would be suspicious enough to fit little pieces of evidence together and to take alarm. It is illuminating and disheartening to read, for instance, a description by an anthropologist of tribe A on a Pacific island who are nice people, but who believe that tribe B, a few miles away, are fiends. When the anthropologist moves over to live with tribe B, he finds that they, too, are agreeable people, but they feel terribly threatened by what they consider the bloodthirsty barbarians of tribe A. In a discouragingly similar way, in times of hot or cold war in the twentieth century, Russians, Germans, Britons, Japanese, Americans have been easily convinced that the enemy were hardly human.

But experience in the psychiatric clinic as well as in life shows us that there is enormous variation in the amount of suspiciousness and hostility in different individuals. One child grows up ready to hate almost everybody. Another, reared in an unusually loving and peaceful family, cannot be taught a deep distrust of anyone.

It may be helpful for our discussion if I point out some of the violently prejudiced distortions of thinking which are obvious in the mental-hospital patients whom we call paranoid. This should aid our understanding of some of the deeply hidden roots of ordinary prejudice in everyday people, since most of us have the capacity to think in a slightly paranoid way when we feel threatened. If insecurity drives the paranoid individual into delusions, he imagines that he is both a victim of persecution and at the same time a highly important personage — the head of the F.B.I., for instance, or the leader of a worldwide religious sect. He keeps enlarging his estimate of the plot against himself until it involves an entire fraternal order, or the hierarchy of another religion, or international communism. Though his reaction is insanely exaggerated, it reminds us of the ordinary person whose sense of inadequacy makes him feel threatened by a whole group and who tries to overcome it by talking about how superior he is to them.

Paranoid individuals are also haunted by sexual jealousy.

They frequently imagine, when sick, that many people are carrying on successful affairs with their spouses. Hitler, who was not insane by the usual definition but who was severely paranoid in personality, rose to power in part by selling his idea that the Jews were all plotting together to destroy Germany. And he and many of his henchmen kept themselves in a frenzy with the fantasy that the Jews were successfully seducing "Aryan" girls on a wholesale scale. In the end he nearly destroyed his nation.

This reminds us of the preoccupation of some race-prejudiced Americans (from all parts of the country) whose most impassioned argument for segregation is their assumption that if white girls should go to school with Negroes or work with them, they'd automatically prefer to marry them. These men repeat, with childish belief, fantastic tales about the superior virility of Negroes. (Doctors know that sexual success and doubt and failure are the monopoly of no race.) When the integrated use of children's public swimming pools has been discussed in certain cities, the agitated opponents have not objected so much to boys swimming with boys or girls with girls, but to white girls swimming with Negro boys. These examples from the hospital and from the outside world give us clues to the basic importance of insecurity — including sexual insecurity — in prejudice. (Fear of competition for jobs is another factor.)

But this is not to say that only the sick or the very insecure are prejudiced. If that were true, the solution would lie entirely within the field of preventive psychiatry. (It would be an enormous burden for psychiatry, but it would excuse the rest of the community.) Unfortunately, a degree of prejudice can be taught easily to all except those who are thoroughly trustful and loving. A tragic example is the apartheid movement in South Africa, in which political leaders have convinced a majority of the electorate (without valid evidence or provocation) that they are so threatened that they must enact harshly discriminatory laws against Negroes and Asians. This campaign of fear and hostility is creating, of course, the corresponding feelings in those who are attacked. Thus the political majority has made itself sick with suspicion and is inviting its own destruction.

Babies and small children may be temporarily frightened by someone who appears strange — in pigmentation or garb or manner or tone of voice. But they sooner or later come to trust anyone who is sympathetic and affectionate. By four and five they are interested in their parents' ideas about the world and sensitive to their parents' feelings about individual people. But they are not so ready for generalizations and rationalizations that they can be said to have fixed prejudices. What is more important in regard to their future is whether they have learned to trust their parents' consistent love and, through this, to trust other people generally, and themselves.

For the specific teaching of tolerance or intolerance I think that the early school years are particularly vital. At this age the child by his very nature is easily able to be pushed in either direction. He is seriously interested in what the outside world — of contemporaries and adults — considers right and wrong. He feels the obligation to channel his aggression within socially acceptable limits. He wants to be a member of the "right" group and to conform to its pattern. He's ready to disapprove of "wrong" individuals and groups. If he spends these years with friends and adults who have common prejudices, he takes these to be not only permissible but noble. He's proud to be included as a soldier on what he assumes is the righteous side. But if his parents and particularly his teacher (whom he now considers a higher authority than parents) take advantage of the occasions provided by books, the news, the neighborhood, the classroom itself, they can teach tolerance instead. They can agree with him that everyone has personal likes and dislikes, most of which he's entitled to. They can show him that every racial, religious and nationality group has produced benefactors, scoundrels and everything in between. They can point out that the very same groups which are looked down on in one country are well accepted in another. They should explain with regret that prejudices are held in all parts of the country and that much of the undesirable behavior of certain members of groups, for which the whole group is blamed, are fostered by the discrimination they suffer. They can demonstrate by all kinds of examples that acceptance brings out the best in everyone.

When children are taught tolerance they do not merely accept it grudgingly. They respond to it and practice it with enthusiasm because it appeals to their straightforward sense of justice. I know because I've seen it happen, in families and in good schools.

COLD WAR ANXIETY

Parents can help their children by clarifying
their own beliefs and acting on them.

WHAT CAN parents do to keep their children from becoming more and more anxious as the cold war persists? Here is part of a letter a mother wrote me which is unusually vivid because it shows how a young child visualizes world problems:

I wish that you would give mothers your thinking on this problem. It seems almost fantastic to relate how my little four-year-old is reacting with the same fears as her older sister. Some time ago she told us most matter-of-factly that "the bomb would kill Daddy, Mommy and everybody, and then God would have to make new people." Yesterday she told me, and I had to write it down to believe it, "God and President Kennedy takes care of the whole world. Especially God because He's up in the sky anyway. God shoots the bad bombs with his magic gun, and President Kennedy shoots the bad bombs with his real gun. So we won't have to have any bombs to make people die." Her five-year-old friend told her not to eat the snow "because there is a piece of the bomb in it."

I admire the spirit of this child. She has great concern about the possible destruction of everyone she loves — that's why she's talking about it — but she remains calm and she clings to what hope she can find for the future. Like other very young children she naturally puts her trust in certain important individuals she knows about, rather than in impersonal organizations which are hard for her to imagine. In a sense she's probably right, even though she doesn't yet understand the methods that God uses and the methods that a president uses. And there is an altruistic love of all mankind in her last sentence. Her friend's remark, by contrast, expresses only worry.

The question of how to keep children from becoming unduly anxious during wartime was debated frequently when the United States first entered World War II. The experiences of that war gave some of the answers. When it was a matter of actual bombing, as in London, the children who remained with their parents proved to be much less emotionally disturbed than those who were sent out of town. (There was the story of the small child who was playing happily and noisily near her family in a shelter and whose mother said crossly, "Sit still now and listen to the bombing!") The children in America who worried excessively about the war were, in general, those who had had other phobias before, and those who had unusually anxious parents. There have, of course, always been things in the news for fearful children to become obsessed with, like polio, kidnapers, killings. And all children, being dependent in every respect on their parents, have always mirrored their parents' moods to a greater or lesser degree. So a basic question is: how can parents cope with their own anxieties in times like these?

We are apt to assume that the normal state of affairs for the world and for people is to be free from anxiety. Or at least we have always been saying that it wasn't so bad before the Russians had the bomb, or before the war, or before the long depression. The more you think of it, especially when you consider the less fortunate parts of the world, the more you realize that a large part of the human race has regularly had to exist face to face with danger — either from enemies, epidemics, famine, occupational hazards, economic depression or natural disasters. Even in our own favored land a majority of children in colonial times were destined to die of disease before they grew up. In some regions there was the threat of Indians. Nowadays automobiles kill 30,000 of us yearly, an appalling slaughter. Yet relatively few people are chronically anxious about the everyday dangers.

This is partly because they grow accustomed to them, often without justification. More importantly, human beings are relieved of much of their worry if they feel they have taken what steps are possible to protect themselves — whether it's getting inoculations or installing seat belts or forming a volunteer fire department.

The mechanism of anxiety is given to us, as it is to all animals, to make us use our wits to analyze where the danger lies and then to overcome it. The body is charged with excess energy and determination. A young man chased by a bull can run faster than he ever could in a track meet. There was the mother, you may remember, who raised the automobile which was pinning her child down, though she crushed her own vertebrae in the effort. The timid boy cornered by bullies can fight like a wildcat. When anxiety leads to effective action, the emotions eventually return to normal. But when a person sees no way to flee or to fight or to take constructive action he stews in his own fear, or he finds an unrealistic method for denying the danger. What action can individuals take to meet the threat of nuclear extinction?

I've read articles recently about the knowledge and lack of knowledge concerning the worth of fallout shelters. It is evident that only a very limited proportion of the deaths would be prevented, and that the shelters will be too expensive for most families to build privately. There is a little more point to community shelters, but the building of these would compete for public funds which could be used for other purposes that would surely benefit children. The issue will probably be decided in each community, which is as it should be. The debate that has been stirred up will at least make people more aware of what they face and of the primary and overwhelming importance of striving for a secure world. The issue of shelters seems to me quite secondary and defeatist by comparison.

The real question about death is not whether it will occur but for what reason. All of us have to die in the end. To worry about death without coming to any positive action only turns living into an anticipation of death.

On the other hand, we scorn the individuals and the nations who are so stupid that they do not see danger coming, or who are so soft that they can't arouse themselves, or who surrender because they are afraid to fight. Man gains dignity — in his own eyes and in the eyes of mankind — when he lives his life according to principles. If he dies young in the cause of his ideal, his life and his death are both inspiring. Consider the life and death of Christ. Some causes, such as the founding of empires, seemed noble at the time but they proved curses in the end. So the highest destiny for man is to live or to die for principles that will be respected not only now but centuries hence. He need not doubt his own beliefs just because they are unpopular today. At times of fateful crisis we should only feel sorry for those who have no aspirations — aside from a concern for their own safety — or who are too timid to take any action to support them.

We see a variety of reactions to our nation's danger today. The right-wing groups have visualized the peril as primarily due to widespread collaboration among Americans and have recommended impeaching the highest government officials. Some legislators and citizens demand that we ignore the cautions of our allies and the opinions of the neutral nations and act as belligerently as is necessary to make our enemies back down. Others see this as the surest way to isolate ourselves from all our friends and to court disaster. There are the pacifists who sincerely believe that unilateral disarmament is the best way to reassure and to set the example for our enemies, and that if this fails it would still be better to be Red than dead. Between these groups there are many Americans who don't know what to believe and many others who manage not to think about these crucial problems at all.

What causes a sense of anxious helplessness in many people who do have a real concern and an opinion is the assumption that there is nothing effective they can do. What influence does one citizen among 180,000,000 have, they say — not as a question but as a gloomy answer. This attitude expresses a fundamental skepticism about democracy. Worse still it expresses a sickness of the spirit, a resignation to pessimism. Actually it's quite unrealistic, too. The course of action in any nation — even in a democracy — is influenced tremendously by the small minority of the population who have the gumption to express their convictions and to join in groups to arouse others with similar views. If only one in ten thousand citizens were to write a note to the President on any issue, it would add up to an overwhelming torrent of mail that could not fail to impress him and the country generally.

Some people who would like to register their opinions are stopped, I imagine, by bashfulness. Yet a letter to the President or to one's senators and representatives doesn't have to be formal or long. Informality and sincerity are what make it impressive. Organized groups have their full-time lobbies. Citizens have to speak for themselves. Parents have to speak for themselves and their children. A factor that should spur parents with moderate views to speak up is to remember that those with aggressive views have no hesitation in voicing them. The most important point to realize is that the crucial decisions in foreign and military policy have to be made initially by the President alone, though he must have the support of Congress. He has the advice of military and atomic and intelligence experts. But most of these specialists will be primarily and rightly concerned with how to achieve and maintain a superior strength, rather than with the larger question of whether that alone will secure peace in the long run. If a President wishes to steer a moderate course he needs the backing of a majority of the population and of Congress, since there will always be vigorous opponents of such a course who will call it appeasement.

As you have suspected, my own views are moderate. I would rather be dead than submit to a police state and I think that the stands we took in Korea and Berlin were necessary to convince the Communists that we were prepared to fight. On the other hand, I think it is extremely important — for our own good — to remember that part of the hostility of the Soviet and Chinese regimes is based on fear, as we have been almost continually hostile to both of them since their respective revolutions and now have them surrounded with our bomber and missile bases, military allies and nuclear submarines. If we forget this fear, we misinterpret some of their motives, overfrighten ourselves about their intentions (which are aggressive enough in any case) and fail to see opportunities for agreement that would be mutually advantageous.

The Russians have shown evidence of genuinely wanting disarmament and test agreements (quite apart from their propaganda proposals). But from our point of view they have always demanded too much and conceded too little. We have always demanded so much inspection that the Russians, with their suspiciousness, say we are only interested in spying. Several times in the past ten years we might have secured a test ban agreement that in retrospect would have been very favorable to us, but our fear that the Soviets might benefit made us pass up the opportunities. Our previous fear that they might be able to conceal nuclear tests unless there were many detection stations all over the Soviet Union was proved greatly exaggerated during their 1961 series of tests when we, from outside their country, detected them easily. So each side, in refusing to take the smaller risks, increases the great risk. If progress toward real security is to be made, one side at least has to show more self-assurance. Though we cannot let down our guard I do think that, since we are stronger in most respects and a little less suspicious, we should not be afraid to take the lead. Fortunately most Americans agree that we should continue to negotiate and to search for possible areas of agreement, no matter how often we're disappointed.

To many Americans, including myself, it seems self-defeating to resume nuclear testing while we are still ahead of the Russians.

For it will surely provoke more Soviet tests, further dishearten the world including our own people, make more certain the entrance of China and other nations (who will be even more difficult to deal with) into the nuclear race, increase the problem of finding the eventual way to control and decrease armaments. This is the kind of situation in which I think it is particularly appropriate for people with moderate views to write to the President, expressing their hope that, to show America's desire for peace and concern for all people, it will be possible for us to refrain from testing, as long as our power of deterrence is not impaired.

But it appears to me that there are further opportunities of a more positive kind that we could be taking to convince the Russian and Chinese people and governments that we are truly unaggressive in our intentions. Suspicions between nations as between individuals thrives on distance and threats, decreases on contact. Our partially open channels of communication with the Russian people, our cultural and scientific exchanges, have helped to keep them basically friendly toward us, admiring of our technical skills and material advantages, despite their government's efforts to instill fear of our intentions and scorn for our system. Our government appears cautious about visits between high level officials until agreements are in sight, presumably for fear of giving the impression — to the Soviet government, to some of our allies, to certain of our own citizens and politicians — of possible appeasement. To me it would seem there was every advantage to regular visits back and forth — even of the President and the Premier — not with any obligation to find a quick agreement but to become better acquainted with members of the opposing government and people, their views, fears, hopes. The good will and sincerity of our President would make a profound impression on the Russian people and he would find opportunities to say at least some things to them directly.

Premier Khrushchev himself has admitted, in so many words,

that his nation has inferiority feelings and wants to be treated as an equal. I think it would greatly impress all Russians if we could honor their astronauts, scientists, musicians, dancers who have made contributions we respect, with such recognition as official receptions, awards, even ticker tape parades. In ways like these, hearts are warmed, even in high officials.

You may think I have gone all around the lot in answer to a mother's question. I've been saying that parents can't reassure their children about the cold war as long as they themselves feel uncertain and helpless. They need to inform themselves on the issues, test alternative views against their own philosophy of life, come to their own conclusions. Then they should put their convictions into action in the ways available in a democracy — voting, writing to the President and their senators and representatives as often as they feel concern over any issue, joining groups to advance their cause. I've discussed some of my own convictions because that's the only way I can feel I'm doing my part, though I realize that many may disagree vigorously.

I'll add a few specific suggestions about how I think we can help our children to take the cold war in their stride, as we do with all the other dangers and worries they face. We can refrain from talking in a pessimistic or alarmist manner, and from exaggerating the ferociousness of our enemies. We can point out with cheerful confidence all that our government and the United Nations are doing to avoid war and what we as citizens are doing to influence the course of action. We can say with a grin, "We're all alive, aren't we?" And if our children press the question of what happens if attack comes, we should be able to show some of the serenity and courage that the early Christians, pioneers, good soldiers have always demonstrated when they were sure that their cause was right.

WILL OUR CHILDREN MEET
THE WORLD CHALLENGE?

Three perspectives on our problem.

⟨ OUR SOLDIERS CAPTURED IN KOREA

ARE AMERICAN youth underdisciplined, overcoddled? The question has been asked frequently in the last few years. People have been worried by such matters as the rising figures on delinquency, and the criticism that our schools are "soft," but nothing has shaken thoughtful citizens as much as the behavior of many of the American soldiers taken prisoner in the Korean war.

Recently, in one of the regular weekly meetings of the staff of our children's hospital, we listened to a tape recording of a talk by an Army psychiatrist about the demoralization of these prisoners of war. We were shocked, not so much at what the Communists did, but at how easily these Americans went to pieces. After hearing the tape we went on, as planned, to discuss among ourselves whether the kind of upbringing American children are getting these days played a part in the poor discipline.

The tape was a recording of a talk given before the American Psychiatric Association in 1958 by Dr. William Mayer, who had been on one of the Army teams of psychiatrists and intelligence officers who interviewed the returning prisoners in 1953 and analyzed the data. The same story can be read in detail in the book *In Every War But One*, by Eugene Kinkead.*

* New York: W. W. Norton and Co. (1959). $3.95.

One in seven of our men became an active collaborator with the Chinese Communists in one or more of the following ways: he worked, side by side with the captors, to indoctrinate fellow Americans about the superiority of Communism and the rightness of the Communist cause in the Korean war; or he made broadcasts on the enemy radio, or wrote articles for them defaming the American nation (declaring, for instance, that American capitalists instigated the war for profit); or he informed on fellow prisoners; or he agreed to become a Communist organizer or spy in America after the war.

Only 13 per cent of the Americans stood on their rights as prisoners of war and flatly refused to tell anything except their names, rank and serial numbers, refused to take part in Communist-indoctrination sessions. The captors soon segregated these men, whom they called "reactionaries," into separate areas and didn't bother them any more. All the rest responded to "reasonableness" or threats by cooperating — actively or passively — in the communists' indoctrination program.

Orders of American officers were defied. Vital rules of sanitation and health were often ignored. Some of the strong prisoners stole food and possessions from the weak. The injured and diseased were often neglected. No American soldier managed to escape from a permanent enemy prison camp to the safety of our lines, in marked contrast to every other war.

The death rate among the prisoners reached the shocking figure of 38 per cent. Our military authorities consider this only partly explainable on the basis of the severe climate, the inadequate food, the poor medical facilities provided by the Communists. Some Americans, especially at first, said they couldn't or wouldn't eat the basic prisoner diet of boiled corn and millet, as if they expected that American food would then be provided instead. An Army doctor described how some men died from "give-up-itis." They would become despondent, lie all day curled up under a blanket, cut down their diet to water alone, and be dead within three weeks.

What did the Communists do to bring about this demoralization? There have been vague references in America to "brainwashing," which has led many to assume that some mysterious serum or hypnotic method was used. There was no such thing. In fact, even brutality and torture were used relatively little, and these almost entirely with Air Force prisoners, from whom the Communists tried to extract false confessions of germ warfare.

The Communists threw our prisoners off guard at the start by welcoming them with smiles, handshakes, cigarettes. They congratulated them on having escaped from the bondage of an imperialist army, into a country devoted to peace. "Aren't you for peace?" they asked. "Won't you sign a peace appeal?"

In five hours of indoctrination class a day Chinese instructors, who were well educated, presented a Marxist picture of the exploitation of American workers by their bosses, of the militaristic ambitions of American capitalist leaders, of the noble aims of the Communist nations. Few prisoners apparently knew enough history to refute these statements. American collaborators assisted in the lectures. Marxist books had to be read, memorized, recited. The prisoners were required to write their life histories. Excerpts from these were used to prove the lecturers' points and to get some of the men talking against their country and criticizing fellow prisoners.

Those who lagged in their cooperation were ordered to headquarters for repeated lectures, scoldings and threats. Individuals who argued in class were humiliated by teachers or fellow prisoners. In increasing numbers the prisoners came around to confessing their own previous "wrong thinking" and condemning those who were less compliant. Informing was rewarded. These methods led to a breakdown of any sense of cohesion and mutual loyalty among the Americans. In the end, no one trusted anyone else. Each was for himself. Each withdrew into himself.

In striking contrast to the behavior of many American prisoners was the high morale maintained by the Turkish soldiers who were captured. (The Turks were also part of the U.N. forces in Korea.) They stuck together, obeyed their officers, refused to criticize their country or to inform on one another, laughed at Communist efforts to indoctrinate them, adhered to health regulations, cooperated in the care of their sick.

What possible explanations can be given for this collapse of morale and discipline? Eugene Kinkead in his book quotes an Army officer who blamed primarily the Army's revision of disciplinary procedures following World War II, which, he felt, decreased the authority of company commanders and noncommissioned officers, made privates less respectful and obedient. This officer spoke critically of the poor discipline in many units from the time they landed in Korea.

It has certainly been shown in other situations that the change from an authoritarian sort of discipline to a more democratic type is extremely difficult to bring about, for adults or children. I remember well what happened years ago in an institution I knew about for handicapped children. The superintendent believed that children had to be regimented strictly if they were to be kept under control. They were given no free time but were scheduled from one prescribed activity to another. They had to march from place to place and were not allowed to talk to each other at meals. The better toys were kept unused in glass cases "because the children would spoil them." Mail from home was distributed only once a week. The individual had no private place to keep his own possessions. The superintendent had, of course, selected and trained a staff who agreed with his philosophy. And the place ran efficiently though not happily. Eventually the board of trustees insisted on a humanization of the program, and as a first step recruited a couple of imaginative group workers who genuinely enjoyed children. These two people were greeted with suspicion by the rest of the staff, blocked at every turn, and they soon resigned. Next the board took the bull by the horns and secured the resignation of the superintendent. His replacement was a warmhearted man trained in the understanding of children's needs and in a more trusting, democratic type of leadership. He instituted new rules across the board, for staff and children.

But the staff people, who had little skill in democratic leadership, felt helpless under the new regulations. They acted grumpy. The children released their pent-up resentment against the old regime by becoming — to varying degrees — uncooperative. As things got out of hand, the staff people took considerable satisfaction in saying "I told you so." It was apparent that they didn't have their hearts in making the new system work. The only solution in the end was to send all the children home, dismiss the entire staff, and start slowly and painfully to recruit a new staff in sympathy with the new philosophy. Eventually the institution functioned smoothly again, and in a friendly, cooperative spirit.

Similarly, experiments at the University of Iowa comparing how groups of children respond to authoritative, democratic and laissez-faire disciplines showed, among other things, that the transition from authoritative to democratic discipline resulted in much more trouble, temporarily, than the reverse shift.

So I can well imagine a major disturbance of morale at the time when, by decree, noncommissioned officers and company commanders were deprived of some of the arbitrary power they were accustomed to use in maintaining discipline.

I suspect that another extremely potent factor in the lowered morale in the Korean war was the natural letdown, after World War II, in the American people's spirit of devotion to the common cause and their readiness to sacrifice for it. For the time being they wanted to be let alone to follow their individual pursuits. When the North Korean Communists suddenly invaded South Korea it was impossible for many Americans to see that this was their fight. In fact, our participation in the war became a partisan political issue. It must have been particularly disheartening for a young man to be exposed to death on the other side of the world if his family or some of his friends and leaders at home doubted the necessity for his being there at all.

But what about the influence of the way in which the soldier was reared, before he put on a uniform? Dr. Mayer in his talk to the psychiatrists specifically suggested that a basic remedy for this poor military discipline might lie in a stricter discipline in civilian life — in the factory and in the home, "at the parent's knee and over the parent's knee." It's a reasonable-sounding assumption. But if lack of discipline in childhood was the *main* source of poor morale in the Korean war, why did it not have a similar effect in World War II? The discipline and morale of the great majority of men in our armed forces during World War II were considered satisfactory, when they had proper leadership and training, and when the country was united behind them. Yet there were only five years between the two wars. I know of no sudden shift in child-rearing practices that would have affected differently these two groups.

Certainly there can be a low military morale which has no connection at all with indulgence in childhood. The French Army collapsed when the Germans broke through the Maginot Line in 1940. Yet France could never be accused of having anything to do with so-called "permissiveness," in the family or in the school.

It's always difficult to come to conclusions about whether one generation of children is being brought up with less discipline than earlier generations. At any period you can find young people with good character and high motivation, if you are looking for them and look in the right places. At the same time you can see — or at least read regularly in the papers about — deplorable specimens. What conclusions you come to depend in part on whether your own attitude is basically optimistic or pessimistic. There's always a tendency among quite a few adults as they grow older to see widespread evidence that the younger generation is being pampered outrageously and is turning out soft and worthless.

It is true there has been a disturbing rise in the amount of juvenile delinquency in America in the last twenty years. But a great majority of delinquent acts are not serious offenses. And most of these minor offenses do not spring from serious character defects in youth but from unfortunate social conditions caused by migration, slum housing, discrimination, inadequate schools, contrasts of poverty and prosperity. It is true that young men who have real personality disturbances or criminal tendencies will make unreliable soldiers. But such types constitute only a small percentage of the population and are generally weeded out before induction. They do not explain the large-scale demoralization in Korea. The Army reports confirm this point. In fact the psychological tests and psychiatric interviews that were given to the prisoners as they were returned to this country did not reveal any significant differences in personality or family background between the men who behaved well and the "cooperators" who easily gave in and the active collaborators.

Since a large majority of the prisoners went to pieces and since there were no basic psychological differences between them and the ones who stood firm, we next must logically ask whether it could be that most of our young people are weak in character. Obviously they are not. The college and medical students I teach and the majority of the high school students I hear about conform to discipline and show self-discipline at least as well as any recent generation. They are studying harder and going farther in their education. Compared to my fellow students of forty years ago, they are certainly more conscientious and a lot more thoughtful. The best of them are asking for more depth and speed in their studies, which would have been considered madness in my day. Our college students are helping to remove discriminatory barriers against minority groups which their parents and grandparents clung to without question.

The young adults in today's work force are generally doing their jobs well, taking responsibility, contributing their share to advances in technology, science, the arts. The commonest criticism of our youth today is that they are somewhat more conforming than the previous generation. Many of them admit that they prefer security to bold ventures. But they are still not as conforming as the youth of the 1920's. The thoughtful ones are also groping for the deeper meaning of life. The visiting lecturers who fill the auditorium in my university community are philosophers from the fields of theology, science and psychology.

To return to the demoralization of the Americans in Korea: I believe that it cannot be ascribed to a fundamental lack in the character of our youth. I think it was probably due to a combination of a disorganized system of discipline, an admittedly insufficient training, an inadequate indoctrination in the meaning of the war. But the greater responsibility, to my mind, lay with the millions of civilians who, like the soldiers, were unprepared to see beyond the horizon of their private pursuits, to understand the relationship of their lives to the fateful issues confronting their country and their world. I will be coming back to this in the last section of this chapter.

Meanwhile I want to discuss another aspect of childhood in America — permissiveness in child rearing. This uncertainty about what to ask of children in behavior sheds further light, I think, on the lack of a sense of direction in many of our people today.

❰ OVERPERMISSIVENESS, AN AMERICAN PHENOMENON

A woman I know who runs a children's clothes shop recently told me about a situation which comes up fairly often in her business. A mother will bring in a three- or four-year-old boy who needs new blue jeans. She looks at the style that is available and approves of it. Then she proceeds to ask her son, with some hesitancy, "Charlie, don't you think you need some new blue jeans?" If he chooses to say no, she has to set to work to persuade him that he really does. If and when he agrees that he needs them, she asks him, "Do you like these?" If he says he doesn't, she has to try to convince him that he does, or that he's got to accept them because this is the only kind there is. My friend the shopkeeper said that she doesn't think this is a sensible approach. It bothers her. She quickly explained that she was all in favor of letting a child have a choice when a real choice was appropriate — if, for instance, two styles or colors of shirts were available, both of which seemed attractive and practical to the mother. She also added that of course an older child, who desperately wants to dress just like his friends, should be given more choice. I agreed with her on all scores.

In the first place, a mother has enough to do carrying out all the essentials of child care and housekeeping without having to spend hours a day in unnecessary argument. Even if there were all the time in the world, it's bewildering to a small child to present him with a lot of choices which serve no useful purpose. Certainly it rubs him the wrong way to encourage him to make choices if half of them then have to be denied him. But I don't think that a mother who leaves many decisions to a small child is doing so mainly because she really believes that this is educational. On the surface it's an absent-minded habit she has fallen into. But behind the habit in many cases is a mother's vague fear that she may impose her will on him too strongly. If questioned, she might say that she doesn't want to squelch his individuality or that she doesn't want to make him resent her authority. I think of this hesitancy in guiding children, this anxious deference to their wishes, as one aspect of what is commonly referred to as overpermissiveness. It often goes along with the tendency to let children be somewhat rude and disobedient to parents, or whiny, or continually quarrelsome with each other, or careless with property, or very noisy, excitable and aggressive in their play.

Overpermissiveness seems to be *much* commoner in America

than in any other country. Of course no one claims that all our children show these traits. One observer might put the figure at 10 per cent, another at 25 per cent, another still at 50 per cent. It depends on where you want to draw the line. I regularly receive letters from sensible-sounding grandmothers who are distressed by the rudeness and wildness of their grandchildren, and by the failure of the young parents to make any effort to exert control. I have talked with dozens of professional people from other countries, visiting the United States for the first time, who have had trouble concealing their surprise and irritation at the behavior of certain children they have seen here.

I should quickly add that though all the visitors I've talked with have seen at least a few badly spoiled American boys and girls, the more tolerant foreigners have been frankly charmed by the middle range of our children. They've admired their friendliness and trustfulness toward adults, their spontaneity in making interesting conversation. The visitors contrast this behavior favorably with the more subdued, less approachable manner of many children brought up conventionally in certain European countries, where adults are treated with a certain awe.

I myself am all for a considerable degree of friendliness between the generations. It makes for the lack of stuffiness that I like in Americans. I suspect that it plays a part in the spontaneity with which they tackle any new situation. (The fact that friendliness toward adults does not necessarily lead to the slightest disrespect toward them is shown in descriptions of Russian children given by American visitors, which I will discuss later in this chapter. These observers make the particular point that almost all the Russian children they saw were noticeably friendly and trusting with adults and yet they were also remarkably well mannered toward them.)

If you agree with me that permissiveness is carried too far by some parents, we should try to analyze where it comes from. During the Victorian period the tendency in America was toward traditionalism and strictness in many respects. Parents and teachers and employers were inclined to be authoritarian. Manners were proper. There was general prudishness and repression in regard to sex. It was widely believed that the child was a barbarian to start with and could be civilized only by continual pressure. When children turned out badly it was assumed that this was because they had not been disciplined enough or were just unappreciative.

Then in the twentieth century the reaction began to set in, gradually at first but with increasing momentum. Many different sociological factors were at work. Among them were the growing respect for science and its tendency, for a while, to lessen the authority of religion, the "emancipation" of women, the increasing acceptance of divorce, the spread of education, the acceleration of productivity and prosperity, the shift of the population from farms to cities and the tendency of young adults to move away from home towns and relatives for better jobs, the disillusioning effect of two world wars. Such changes as these tended to weaken traditions generally and to put people in a mood to accept new ideas. Young parents no longer were as much influenced by relatives, but made their own decisions about raising their children.

At the same time there came a flood of new concepts about child development, from researches in education, psychology, psychiatry and pediatrics: Children raised in loving families want to learn, want to conform, want to grow up. If the relationships are good they don't have to be forced to eat, forced to learn to use the toilet. Interest in sex to a limited degree is normal and wholesome. A certain amount of jealousy between brothers and sisters, a certain amount of resentment against parents are inevitable. Excessive hostility between children and parents may be harmful. Severe repression of hostility or sex may lead to neurosis or distortion of personality.

These ideas were startling and unsettling at first. But why did they unsettle some parents much more than others? There were a number of factors, more or less overlapping, but I think three were particularly important. The parents with a lot of inner security took these new pronouncements in their stride. In a sense they had known these things intuitively all along. They were not made uneasy or guilty by them. So they brought up their children with the same old-fashioned combination of affection and firm leadership with which they themselves had been reared. But parents who themselves had been raised in a somewhat overpermissive manner did not have either this self-assurance or the clearcut expectations of just how they wanted their own children to behave. So this pattern of insufficient control was passed on to the new generation. Another group of parents, those who had been raised with more than average crossness or severity, had grown up with insufficient confidence in themselves, a bit too much irritability in their make-up, a lingering resentment against some of their own parents' attitudes. When they heard some of the new theories — that children's behavior problems can often be traced to incorrect handling, that excessive parental severity may be harmful — they worried in advance, consciously or unconsciously, that they might take out some of their own cross feelings on their children and make them dislike them. So they leaned over backward to avoid antagonizing them.

Of course the main trouble when parents try too hard to be tolerant and patient is that children miss the guidance they need, and they also sense the underlying impatience in their parents. So they are apt to provoke their parents with worse and worse behavior in order to force them to assume control — and to get the air cleared.

There is a third factor which can also lead to overpermissiveness. I am thinking of certain parents who themselves are unusually considerate of the feelings of other people, yet have children who are known in the neighborhood for their rudeness, demandingness, minor destructiveness. These traits in children are not too surprising when the parents have similar attitudes. They are hard to understand when the parents are quite the opposite. What particularly irritates the neighbors with such a family is that the polite parent will sometimes be looking right at his child with a proud, beaming expression at the very moment when he is being obnoxious, as if the parent didn't see the behavior at all. Such parents often quote theories about the importance of self-expression and individuality, the unwholesome effects of repression. When such cases get completely out of hand and are referred to a child-guidance clinic, it often turns out that the parents were so properly brought up that they never dared act, speak or even think aggressively. When they come to have a child of their own they unconsciously enjoy letting him express the impoliteness, selfishness and aggressiveness which they had to suppress so completely in themselves. This blinds them to the fact that the behavior is offensive to others and disturbing to the child. In fact, they manage to express pride in their own progressiveness and in its good results.

I've been talking as if all parents could be divided into a few neat types. Actually there are many overlapping patterns and none of them is simple. Some parents, as you know (the ones without guilt or submissiveness), can be remarkably uncontrolling without spoiling their children at all. Other parents (the ones without much harshness or irritability) can be stricter than average without cramping the style of their children or making them resentful. None of us as a parent follows one pattern. Each of us has a mixture of feelings and attitudes about discipline, and we react to one child in one way, to another somewhat differently.

My fear in discussing overpermissiveness is that a few readers may get the idea that I'm saying, "Stop indulging your children; get rough with them," as if there were only the two alternatives. Perhaps I can clarify the point that neither is necessary by mentioning a few situations in early childhood about which there has been a lot of controversy in this century, and at least three different attitudes.

Until the mid-1940's it was usually taught by doctors that,

to avoid spoiling and indigestion, it was necessary to be absolutely rigid about the amounts and timing of a baby's feedings, even if this made him miserable. When this theory was discarded, some parents jumped to the conclusion that regularity itself was the bad thing (rather than the too hasty enforcement of regularity), and boasted of how long it took their babies to get on any kind of schedule. The sensible approach, I think, is to make allowances for the baby's unstable digestion the first few days or weeks of life and then to guide him toward a regularity which will be helpful to him and his parents.

Up to twenty years ago it was often recommended that a baby be trained to the toilet at an early age, with vigorous methods if necessary. When this was shown to be harmful in certain cases, some parents came to the anxious assumption that it was dangerous to make the slightest mention of the toilet or any move toward training, whatever the child's age, and that the only safe system was to wait indefinitely for the child to get the idea entirely by himself. (I think I helped to intimidate these parents by stressing too heavily the risks of severe training, in the earlier edition of *Baby and Child Care.*) Comfortable parents have almost always succeeded by tactfully watching for the child's readiness and by regularly encouraging him to be grown up in the use of the potty or toilet.

For many years parents were told exactly how many hours a baby of a certain age should sleep and were warned against picking him up during the hours assigned for rest, for fear of spoiling him. Then when the emphasis was placed on individual differences and the need for security, a few overconscientious mothers became fearful of letting their babies cry for a minute. Some of them eventually found themselves pacing the floor with thoroughly tyrannical infants until ten or eleven o'clock every night. Parents blessed with self-assurance realize that sleep needs and patterns vary somewhat in different children, but they generally have no difficulty setting sensible bedtimes and teaching their children to conform to them.

When parents are overbearing or irritable, they can make any household duty they assign to a child seem unpleasant and unfair. On the other hand, those who are afraid of imposing on their children or of becoming disliked by them may ask no help from them at all, and this contributes to a selfish, demanding attitude. Mothers and fathers who have no inner doubts about their children's affection and who think of cooperativeness as an essential part of preparation for life don't hesitate to ask for appropriate assistance from their children. Yet they can do it, most of the time, in a manner which makes the children proud of their contribution.

My aim in discussing overpermissiveness is not to try to solve the serious problems of the parents who have a great deal of trouble exerting any kind of discipline. They need the help of a child-guidance clinic or family social agency in getting at the deeper causes and the solution. My aim is only to be helpful to the larger number of parents who are not concerned about any particular difficulty but who nevertheless are wasting valuable patience and energy every day in an excessive deference to their children's whims and moods and minor misbehavior. It's no favor to a child to let him get tangled up in a succession of decisions that are not really his, or to let him go on nagging his mother or churning up commotions in the household.

I'm hoping to make it clear that a mild, unthinking overpermissiveness is a uniquely American phenomcnon — an American style — of the twentieth century; and that it is partly due to the fact that many parents who are not completely self-assured have taken too guiltily the ncwer concepts of child development. I am hoping that if I can show them that this was a mistake — in more than one sense — they will be able to throw off their hesitancy, to the benefit of themselves as well as their children.

More to the point, I've included this particular topic in this chapter because it brings out sharply what I consider a basic quandary of so many of our most conscientious parents: We are uncertain about how we want our children to behave because we are vague about our ultimate aims for them. This in turn is a reflection of the haziness of our own philosophy of life. The situation is very different in most other parts of the world. A farmer in India sees his responsibility as primarily to teach his son how to be a good farmer too. The devout Moslem will be sure that his son is spiritually sound if the youth carries out the five specific duties of a true believer, and particularly if he learns the Koran by heart. A French boy's excellence is judged mainly by how closely he conforms to the particular traditions of his own family and to the wishes of its elder members. The goal is very concrete in each case. Furthermore the entire family and often the entire community is in complete agreement with the parents about the correctness of these goals.

By contrast, we Americans believe that we should not even try to influence our children's occupational choice. Young couples must decide for themselves, quite independently of the relatives, what qualities they desire in their children and how they will try to achieve them. Many parents are not sure enough of their own religious and spiritual beliefs to be able to make them have much meaning for their children.

The worst problem of all is that, unlike the rest of the world — which assumes that if a child does not benefit from his upbringing it's due to his own perversity — Americans have accepted all too completely and guiltily the popular psychological saying that any maladjustment in the child is probably due to the mistakes of his parents.

When asked what we want for our children we are apt to fall back on such general aims as happiness or good adjustment or success. These sound all right as far as they go, but they are quite intangible. There's little in them that suggests how they are to be accomplished. The trouble with happiness is that it can't be sought directly. It is only a precious by-product of other worthwhile activities. Good adjustment and success are certainly elusive ambitions, becoming greater or less without the parent being able to exert direct control. And the questions always remain: Adjustment to what? For what ultimate purpose? Success by what standards? Then if the child is not doing very well, the American parent has to grope for the answers to the next questions: Just what am I doing wrong? How do I change my methods and my attitude? Often the exceedingly conscientious parent then decides to try being still more understanding, more patient, more giving.

In summary, I am making the point that the popular American philosophy of child rearing can be very hard on parents and confusing to children unless the parents themselves happen to have had an unusually stable and purposeful upbringing to rely on. It is based too largely on the negative fear of maladjusting the child. Its positive aims are vague and do not closely gear the parent or the child to the positive aims of the family, country, religion. It leaves parents too much on their own. In order to have more assurance in the raising of our children, I think we will need to be more clear about what we are bringing them up to be — and to believe.

A discussion of the rearing of Russian children may give us some ideas.

(CAN WE LEARN ANYTHING FROM RUSSIA'S CHILDREN?

It helps me to gain a perspective on American children and their upbringing to read about child rearing in other countries. Nothing I've read in recent years has given me more to think about than two reports on Russian children. One was a book by Herschel and Edith Alt called *Russia's Children.** The other was an article by Dr. Milton Senn, *How Russians Bring Up Their Children.†*

* Bookman Associates, 1959. $3.75.
† *McCall's Magazine,* October 1958.

Edith Alt has had a distinguished career in medical social work. Herschel Alt has for years been head of a social agency in New York, the Jewish Board of Guardians, which provides a variety of expert services for normal children as well as those with problems, through child-guidance clinics, nurseries, and special-treatment schools and special-treatment homes for disturbed and delinquent children. So the Alts know about all kinds and ages of American children and what we try to provide for them. They were particularly interested in learning how the Russians treat their delinquents, and with what success, since their ideas about psychiatry and psychology are amazingly different from ours. (They won't even use intelligence tests because they think it would imply that they believe children are born with different capabilities and cannot be changed by environment.) But the Russian officials blocked the efforts of the Alts to see an institution for delinquents, with dozens of excuses.

However, the Alts did visit all-day nurseries for children up through three years of age and all-day kindergartens for those from four to seven. What struck them most was the conforming, cooperative behavior of these children:

What was startling was that, as we went from room to room, children of two years and two and a half, in groups of at least twenty in each room, were awakening without sound. Some in each room were still sleeping, but those whom we observed had their eyes open; they looked up at us but remained impassive. At no point did we see any of the awakening children jump up, cry out, demand attention or do anything that was mischievous, demanding or spirited. It was the lack of any impulsive behavior and the degree of control in the way they were awakening that startled and troubled us. Never had we seen a group of healthy children awaken after afternoon naps in this fashion.

The Alts describe an outdoor scene in an all-day kindergarten:

Despite earlier rain, the day had turned out beautiful, the sun was shining, and the children were working, studying and playing in small groups in the spacious grounds. Fine fruit trees and delightful walks were interspersed with elaborate flower beds arranged in great precision. Again we were told the children themselves had planted and tended these flowers, and again it was hard to believe. The boys and girls were playing, laughing and listening to teachers tell stories, and seem unrestrained, free and enjoying themselves.

At five o'clock these youngsters who had been in the kindergarten since eight o'clock in the morning prepared to go home. We followed them to the locker rooms. As they moved about, changing their clothes, sitting on the benches, putting on their shoes, we were struck by the absence of any of the jostling and horseplay seen at home under similar circumstances. Only occasionally did a child give another a poke, and when he did it was a very gentle poke.

We commented to the director on this perfect conformity of behavior. "But some children must misbehave," we said. "What do you do with them?"

She pointed out one little boy who was meticulously folding his uniform and putting it in his locker.

"At the beginning of the term," she said, "Boris was rebellious, disobedient and destructive. We gave him jobs we knew would interest him and brought up his status and prestige in the eyes of the other children."

Again and again we met with an overrational common-sense attitude. There was no probing into possible causes, as to how a child might be feeling; there were just matter-of-fact "sensible" methods based on social approval.

When American parents and professional people see a child behaving in such a docile, polite manner, their first thought is that he is perhaps being treated too harshly, or at least too strictly and coldly. This question must have occurred to the Alts. Yet they keep reminding themselves and the reader that they saw no such signs. Quite the contrary:

In our visit to this nursery we were favorably impressed, as in other institutions, with the quality of serious dedication we observed in the women caring for the children. The staff are serious-looking people, involved in their responsibilities toward the children; they give the impression of warmth and kindness. The cleanliness, orderliness and general quiet set these places off as markedly different from similar institutions in the United States.

An even more favorable impression was made on Dr. Milton Senn. He is professor of pediatrics and child psychiatry at Yale, where they study normal children in nursery school and well-child clinics as well as sick ones. Dr. Senn did not say he was impressed but troubled by the behavior of Russian children. Though he is a scientist not given to easy enthusiasm, he was moved to admiration and delight by them. He watched them not only in nurseries, kindergartens and schools, but also on the street with parents, and in playgrounds near their homes:

They are good-humored, easygoing, carefree and friendly. Yet they are remarkably well behaved. They are not given to yelling, fighting or breaking things. They play together in notable harmony, even when there is a remarkable disparity in their ages. They never seem to whine; they cry only when they hurt themselves, and then only briefly. They are warm, spontaneous, polite and generous; and it is impossible, from one's hiding place on the park bench, to keep from falling in love with them.

Dr. Senn, too, emphasized that the nurses and teachers were models of kindness and patience. They obviously enjoyed caring for children.

One late evening in Moscow, just at the end of my visit to Russia, I saw a boy of four or five years walking down the street between his mother and father. He was dawdling a little and looking cranky. The mother stepped back and made a little motion to slap him on the backside. She did not actually hit him — just threatened. I watched with great curiosity, not realizing at first why I found the scene so startling. Then it came to me. During the weeks of day-and-night observing I had done in Russia, I had never before seen a hand raised against a child.

Well, it all sounds like the millennium, doesn't it? Such descriptions make some of our American children seem rather disagreeable by comparison.

Do the Russians have some magic secrets of child rearing which we lack? Or at least could we learn a few pointers from them?

It takes a wise sociologist months or years of living in a nation to gain an understanding of the roots of the character of the people. I'm not a sociologist and I've never been in Russia. But I do have guesses about some of the factors that might help to explain this stable behavior of Russian children, based on familiarity with different kinds of American families, and on various descriptions of life in Soviet Russia.

In America we recognize that children raised in stable homogeneous communities are better behaved on the average than those growing up in changing, mixed neighborhoods. Parents who have little self-control are not usually able to control their offspring. Families with strong religious convictions are less likely to have difficult children than families with no such beliefs. Studies of certain religious sects whose people live in isolated communities show this difference even more strikingly.

When we discuss Russian people it's important for us not to be thinking of those Soviet leaders of the past forty years who have been belligerent and ruthless. Travelers from America and England stress the friendliness, the sincerity of most of the people they talk with. Despite all that the Russians have been told about the aggressive militarism of America, they remain eager to be friends with us as human beings. They are only troubled as to why we allow ourselves to be governed by leaders who they believe are warmongers and oppressors. They have no idea that their nation appears threatening to us.

As a result of the intensive indoctrination they have received from their leaders for two generations now, and the pressure to conform which is exerted on them by committees of their fellows at their places of work and residence (even in the early school years a great part of the guidance and correction of uncooperative individuals is carried out by committees of earnest fellow pupils), the great majority of the Russian people have a very strong sense of common purpose. They are convinced that they are creating a nobler political and economic system than has ever existed before and that the other peoples on the earth will want to join with them as soon as they can be free of their present leaders. They are proud to be playing their individual roles in such a mighty effort. They don't feel any of the indignation or oppression that we Americans would at the idea that a citizen's only important purpose is to serve the state. They have never in their history been familiar with our Western credo, derived from democratic and Judeo-Christian traditions, that the welfare and salvation of the individual are the ultimate good and that the state is only the servant of the people in this quest.

About 85 per cent of women of working age are employed by the state. Of the young children, somewhere between 10 and 20 per cent spend the day in nurseries and kindergartens; many of the rest of them are being cared for by grandmothers, either their own or someone else's.

There is tremendous striving on the part of a large proportion of the people for more education. Adults who work a full day then take technical courses or cultural courses. Visitors sometimes get the impression that almost everyone in public is reading a book. Citizens pack lectures and concerts and theaters and exhibitions. All this is not only for their own advancement and enrichment. They are encouraged to feel — and do feel — that it is a service to their country.

What influence would this earnest, dedicated way of life have on the raising of children? Herschel and Edith Alt quote from the writings of Anton Makarenko, the educator who had more to do than anyone else with establishing the principles of child rearing and education in Russia. "In the struggle for Communism . . . our moral code should march in the van of both our economic structure and our laws. Only if we do this shall we maintain that high moral sense which now distinguishes our society so strongly from any other." And the decisive factor in successful child rearing lies "in the constant, active and conscious fulfillment by parents of their civic duty toward Soviet society . . . where this duty is really felt . . . no failure or catastrophes are possible."

Mr. Alt had a conversation with the director of research in the children's division of a psychiatric hospital: " 'In America,' I said to her, 'we are very much concerned with the feelings of the individual. We observe them, we record them, you might say we virtually put them under the microscope.'

" 'Our workers,' she said earnestly, 'are interested in feelings, too, but feelings, Mr. Alt, must be directed to a useful purpose.' "

When the Alts asked a kindergarten director to explain the conformity of the children, she said, "The good behavior you see is the result of the clarity and agreement on the part of all teachers as to their expectations from their children."

If you have been able to keep from feeling angered by the tone of moral superiority, or suffocated by the picture of unprotesting conformity, you can see the point I am raising. I am inclined to agree with these Russian spokesmen that one reason — perhaps the most important reason — why most Russian children are so well behaved is that there are clarity and agreement everywhere. The parents and child-care professionals are all devoted to a common cause that inspires them. They understand the social importance of their jobs. They are proud of their contributions. They are unanimous about the qualities and ideals that are to be inculcated in children — industriousness, love of education, cooperativeness, dedication to country. The children sense the consistency that surrounds them, in both the adults and the other children. They accept this uniform guidance with relative ease. They show no signs of having been intimidated or made resentful, as they would if they had been trained too severely.

You can see that the aspects of the Soviet philosophies of life and child rearing that I've selected sound quite opposite from our own. In America the ideals of different families vary considerably. An ambition that a lot of us share — getting ahead in the world — does not bind us together but puts us in competition with one another. We have a great belief in progress, but this makes for changes in our attitudes rather than stability. Education is not widely thought of by Americans as primarily a means of making a greater contribution to society or as enrichment of the soul, but as simply the road to a better job (or matrimony). None of these common American attitudes is unworthy. It is only that they do not serve to unite and inspire us. Religious beliefs which, back in colonial days, provided the main reason and guide for man's existence seem to have lost much of their intensity for many of our people, especially in the twentieth century.

America in earlier generations was excited, and unified to a degree, by the drives to push back the frontier, found a new nation, welcome pioneers and freedom seekers from all over Europe, create plenty for everyone by industrialization. In two world wars there were prodigious feats of total mobilization in the cause of saving our country and of preparing the way for a better world. But after each war the sense of high purpose gave way to preoccupation with individual and material concerns.

Probably the fact that our population has been built up of a mixture from many national backgrounds, all impatiently seeking a new life, has been a potent factor in delaying the emergence of a common philosophy.

Our diverse and individualistic aims, our lack of old traditions, would have made it difficult for us in any case to settle on a philosophy of life which would give us all a firm sense of direction in rearing our children. But the problem has been enormously complicated by the flood of unsettling new concepts which came from the professions concerned with child development. (It is significant that European parents have been *much* slower to accept these ideas.)

Eager to bring up well-adjusted children according to the new theories but anxious about all the pitfalls, many of us have been hesitant and overpermissive. Our children have felt the lack of firm guidance and have acted up. We have been irritated by their misbehavior, of course. But instead of giving them more direction we have felt guilty about our shortcomings and tried harder to be patient. These tangled feelings of ours are just the ones which will provoke children to rudeness, whining, squabbling, abuse of toys and furnishings.

How do Russian parents manage to avoid these exasperating faults? Part of the answer, I think, is that they don't have to worry about different theories of rearing or whether they will know how to bring up their child. They don't have to wonder what particular attitudes they will want him to develop or whether they are entitled to ask him to conform to their wishes. They take it for granted that they only need to pass on to him the straightforward ideals to which the entire nation is devoted and that these will guide him to a productive, satisfying life. This serene trust combined with a very genuine love of children seems to work.

Can we learn anything from this contrast? I think it should encourage us to set high enough standards for our children so that they are respectful of us, of one another, of their homes and possessions, of themselves. We should be clear about what we expect, and this does not imply parental severity. We can see not only in Russian children but in plenty of our own that the children who are guided firmly are not only pleasanter to live with but much happier themselves.

We Americans certainly won't ever want to let our leaders set the goals and impose them on us. But this does not mean that the only alternative is aimlessness. Many countries with democratic governments have developed a strong sense of national purpose which gave meaning and direction to every aspect of life. The most dramatic modern example is Israel: A band of idealists established a new nation, provided refuge and opportunity for hundreds of thousands of the oppressed from all over the world, made the desert bloom, created industries, founded universities, all with free discussion and democratic leadership. I have never spoken to a traveler returned from Israel who was not moved by the fervor of the people.

There are plenty of causes crying for America's concern. We urgently need more and better schools and universities, new housing, more adequate provisions for medical care, a solution for our racial discrimination. The poor, underdeveloped countries of the world are begging for our technical, educational, medical and financial assistance. The Communist nations which are out to beat us in every field of competition are gaining in productivity, giving more assistance to backward peoples, winning allies and friends faster than we.

We only need to rouse ourselves, with the inspiration of bold leaders, and we'll have enough crusades to absorb us for decades. Then we might simultaneously find ourselves, save the world from destruction and give our children a new sense of dedication and worth.

INDEX